CultureShock!
A Survival Guide to Customs and Etiquette

Taiwan

Chris Bates
Ling-Li Bates

Marshall Cavendish
Editions

This edition published in 2008 by:
Marshall Cavendish Corporation
99 White Plains Road
Tarrytown, NY 10591-9001
www.marshallcavendish.us

Other Marshall Cavendish Offices:
Marshall Cavendish International (Asia) Private Limited. 1 New Industrial Road,
Singapore 536196 ■ Marshall Cavendish Ltd. 5th Floor, 32–38 Saffron Hill,
London EC1N 8FH, UK ■ Marshall Cavendish International (Thailand) Co Ltd.
253 Asoke, 12th Flr, Sukhumvit 21 Road, Klongtoey Nua, Wattana, Bangkok
10110, Thailand ■ Marshall Cavendish (Malaysia) Sdn Bhd, Times Subang,
Lot 46, Subang Hi-Tech Industrial Park, Batu Tiga, 40000 Shah Alam, Selangor
Darul Ehsan, Malaysia

Marshall Cavendish is a trademark of Times Publishing Limited

ISBN 10: 0-7614-5497-7
ISBN 13: 978-0-7614-5497-7

Please contact the publisher for the Library of Congress catalog number

Printed in China by Everbest Printing Co Ltd

Photo Credits:
All black and white photos from the author.
All colour photos from Photolibrary ■ Cover photo: Photolibrary

All illustrations by TRIGG

ABOUT THE SERIES

Culture shock is a state of disorientation that can come over anyone who has been thrust into unknown surroundings, away from one's comfort zone. *CultureShock!* is a series of trusted and reputed guides which has, for decades, been helping expatriates and long-term visitors to cushion the impact of culture shock whenever they move to a new country.

Written by people who have lived in the country and experienced culture shock themselves, the authors share all the information necessary for anyone to cope with these feelings of disorientation more effectively. The guides are written in a style that is easy to read and covers a range of topics that will arm readers with enough advice, hints and tips to make their lives as normal as possible again.

Each book is structured in the same manner. It begins with the first impressions that visitors will have of that city or country. To understand a culture, one must first understand the people—where they came from, who they are, the values and traditions they live by, as well as their customs and etiquette. This is covered in the first half of the book.

Then on with the practical aspects—how to settle in with the greatest of ease. Authors walk readers through how to find accommodation, get the utilities and telecommunications up and running, enrol the children in school and keep in the pink of health. But that's not all. Once the essentials are out of the way, venture out and try the food, enjoy more of the culture and travel to other areas. Then be immersed in the language of the country before discovering more about the business side of things.

To round off, snippets of basic information are offered before readers are 'tested' on customs and etiquette of the country. Useful words and phrases, a comprehensive resource guide and list of books for further research are also included for easy reference.

CONTENTS

INTRODUCTION

Taiwan is a place of contradictions begging to be explored, enjoyed, and contemplated. Few locations so small can boast snow-peaked mountains, bountiful plains and tropical beaches, all within a few hours' drive of each other. Culturally, it is just as diverse. You will find yourself surrounded by the ancient traditions of the Chinese as you visit temples and festivals, or watch the *tai chi* practitioners commune with the *Tao* in the park; you will also be caught up in the bustle of Taiwan's state-of-the-art department stores and trendy boutiques, selling goods and designer products from all over the world.

Taiwan is home to a Chinese-speaking population of hard-working, hard-playing people. The more you know about them and their country, the more you will enjoy your stay. In trying to introduce Taiwan and the Taiwanese to you, we have emphasised interpersonal communication, usually a major source of frustration to any foreigner. Besides coping with a foreign language, one must remember that Taiwan is a 'high context' culture; much is communicated beyond the spoken. Vocal and facial expression, hand and eye action, body contact and ritual are part of dialogue. Communication may be difficult between a low context culture and a high context culture when the unstated meanings of body language differ between the parties. In Taiwan, *how* you communicate is as important as *what* you are actually saying. This book will help you make your message clear.

FOREIGNERS IN TAIWAN

Most foreigners you will meet in Taiwan are there for work. Many will be teaching English in cram schools, which is a huge industry. Some will have been sent by overseas headquarters to perform management jobs. Others will have come in search of a more meaningful job than they could have gotten at home, in the IT industry for example. All will have stories about culture shock or the strangeness they found when settling in. But many, you will find, have stayed for years. Teaching English, managing a factory, studying Chinese, Chinese medicine or martial arts, whatever the reason, Taiwan is seductive. Once one has settled in and become accustomed to the pace and the people, Taiwan starts to work its charms and a temporary affair becomes a permanent love.

CultureShock! Taiwan also discusses things important to the Taiwanese and why they are so. The 'alienness' of the foreign culture is a major component of culture shock. We hope this book will help you understand and cope with your new environment. Situations you are likely to face during your stay are fleshed out in the following chapters. Hopefully, these experiences will be less shocking when you yourself encounter them.

This book distils the experiences an American and a Taiwanese have garnered through 27 years of close contact with the other's culture. We were often at the interface of the Taiwan/Western communities. Where we felt our experience was uncharacteristic, we have sought the advice of other Westerners and Taiwanese. We thus present a broad perspective. Do note however that much of the information about arrivals and settling in pertains to Taipei, which seems to be the jumping-off point for most residents as well as short-term explorers of the island.

We hope you will enjoy your stay in Taiwan and that this book can increase your pleasure, decrease anxiety and misunderstanding, and make your visit a growing experience. Happy trails to you!

Chris, Ling-li and Diana Bates

ACKNOWELDGEMENTS

Many thanks to our friends who discussed their experiences and shared their perceptions of Taiwan with us, especially Dini and Dr Mark. Kudos to Robyn and Diane for their insights on cross-cultural relations, Confucianism and the spirit of independence. We are indebted to Tan Chin for help in organising the resource guide.

NOTE

A WORD ON ROMANISATION

As you will learn in more detail in Chapter Eight, there are many ways of writing Chinese using a Western Alphabet. In this book, we will present phrases and vocabulary using the Pinyin system originated in Mainland China. This system is not universally used in Taiwan. In fact, under martial law in years past its use was formally discouraged. However, it is slowly becoming accepted in Taiwan. It is also the medium of transmission for most Mandarin instruction worldwide, so it is likely that if you have studied some Chinese, it will have been in Pinyin. When romanising Taiwanese place names or Chinese terms widely known in the West under a different spelling, we employ the spelling method common in Taiwan plus the Pinyin in italics and parentheses so you will know how to say it. Taipei, for instance, is romanised and pronounced *Taibei* in the Pinyin system. Terms and phrases not commonly known in the West will be romanised directly in the Pinyin system, with the translation in parentheses. For example, *Ni Hao Ma?* (how are you?)

DEDICATION

We dedicate this book to
Richard and Ethan, sons and brothers—
The best of both worlds

MAP OF TAIWAN

EAST
CHINA
SEA

CHINA

TAIWAN STRAIT

TAIPEI

TAIWAN

PACIFIC
OCEAN

SOUTH
CHINA
SEA

PHILIPPINE
SEA

Taiwan boasts magnificient mountains and gorges.

FIRST IMPRESSIONS

CHAPTER 1

'A journey of 10,000 miles begins with one step.'
—Ancient Chinese proverb

WHEN CHRIS FIRST ARRIVED IN TAIWAN in July 1976 for a year of university, it was a very different place from what it is today. International flights landed in the downtown area of Taipei at the Songshan airport. The air was so polluted by industrial, automotive and motorcycle emissions that it was several weeks before he realised that mountains he finally espied on a clear day surrounded Taipei. There were no Western fast food restaurants, few international hotels, only one large department store and society lived under martial law and Kuomintang Nationalist Party rule. The American military still had a significant presence in Taipei and Taichung and US State Department language training for Mandarin was conducted in Taiwan. It was a hot, humid, unairconditioned and odorous place. High grey walls topped with shards of broken glass to prevent intruders surrounded many houses. In the countryside, children riding on the backs of water buffalo in the rice paddies were a frequent sight, but fine automobiles were not. A major north-south expressway was planned, but not yet built. Few people spoke English and Chris was disappointed to find that seemingly his several years of Mandarin training in the USA were for naught, he was incapable of communicating effectively.

His very first lunch in Taiwan, though, gave him reason enough to play down the hardship. He dined with classmates in the Hsimenting (*Xi Men Ding*) district of Taipei in a famous old, al fresco eatery, now closed, called *Dian xin shi jie* (Dim Sum World). The specialty of the house was hand made *Guo tie* (Pot Stickers) better than any pretenders made in restaurants in the West or Japan. Crispy brown on the bottom, steamed tender on top, these quintessentially Chinese dumplings filled with pork and chives and dipped in sauce were and are a dream to eat. A plate of ten only cost US$ 0.12 (present price about $1.50). This was served with a fragrant bowl of hot and sour soup. On the side, was a plate of chili and garlic pickled cucumber. Dessert was obtained at a nearby fruit stall where ice was shaved on fresh halves of Taiwanese ruby mangoes. For one US dollar, one could eat very well.

Chris first roomed with a Chinese family, the parents were from Zhejiang and Jiangsu Provinces but the children were born in Taiwan. He shared a closed room with the son and on many nights felt the sweat trickle down his face as he fell to sleep under the warm breath of the electric fan that ground back and forth. It was several months before he realised that one of the reasons he did not understand what they were saying was not only that his Mandarin was insufficient, but they were not speaking Mandarin, they were speaking Jiangsu dialect. The father would wake every morning and conduct a long, loud, ritual expectoration in the bathroom. An old China hand Chris met guessed correctly the man was from Zhejiang ("They are great expectorators," he said confidently) and noted that people from that province had a higher incidence of throat cancer.

Chris was scolded by his foster family for underestimating the power of an approaching typhoon and wanting to go out on the streets during its blow through the city. Because of local custom and small wall mounted water heaters, he had to learn to take baths standing on the wet bathroom floor, not in a tub, with several scuppers of water, rather than have long luxurious showers. Dinner during his first Ghost Festival *Bai Bai* (ritual obeisance to spirits) was a boiled whole chicken, its head hanging grotesquely over the side of the pot on the dining room table staring squarely at Chris. This with other cooked dishes was served first to the hungry ghosts while the family burned incense and bowed to the four cardinal directions. When the ghosts had eaten their fill, the family and Chris sat down to eat the 'leftovers'.

Although he had studied Chinese language, history and culture, he was surprised to find how deeply ingrained and personal the expression of Chinese culture was to the many Taiwanese he met. The local people were acutely, consciously aware of their cultural traditions and identity, an awareness he had not found among Americans when he grew up in the USA. Their cultural identity influenced how they dressed, what they ate, how they arranged their homes, how they interacted with each other and with their government, how they prayed and raised their children, basically every aspect of their lives. They were openly curious about Westerners, Western culture and habits, but not with any intent of slavishly imitating or adopting what they learned.

FIRST IMPRESSIONS TODAY

Today's first time visitor will travel on a highway from Taoyuan Airport to Taipei, and possibly stay at one of the luxurious international hotels like the Grand Hyatt near the World Trade Center and impressive Taipei 101, the world's tallest building and shopping complex. Taipei 101 is filled with trendy boutiques and local shops and has a large food court selling local and regional eats. Nearby is Warner Village, a modern cineplex where one will no longer have to fight with ticket scalpers to get a good ticket to a blockbuster movie.

The air in Taipei is much less polluted than in decades past after several effective mayors pushed through and maintained momentum on Taipei's urban redevelopment agenda. The city now has several elevated highways running North-South and East-West through it, plus a modern monorail and rapid transit system coupled with a modernised bus system. The astute visitor will also note the emergence of some major Taiwanese brands, like Acer, BenQ, Chimei Optoelectronics, Giant, TSMC and Evergreen Lines shipping. 'Made in Taiwan' now denotes some of the highest quality, highest technology products on the planet.

Down island, the transformation has been just as dramatic. Whereas a trip to Taiwan's 'ricebowl' of Ping Tung county in 1976 revealed comfortable, hardworking farmers riding motorcycles, the recent visitor will note the number of BWM, Mercedes Benz and Volvo dealerships. The wealth has been spread around. Unemployment is still low by Western or African standards, destitution and homelessness are rare exceptions. Martial law was lifted decades ago and with it several political parties contend for seats in the legislature and the presidency. The government has instituted a national healthcare plan that provides affordable healthcare and medication to all. The government has strengthened management of the environment and the national parks now boast wonderful natural scenic areas not to be missed, like Taroko Gorge and Kenting.

Perhaps the greatest visible change that will strike the first time visitor is the transformation of the retail economy. In the 1970's there were few chainstores, a role filled by thousands of 'mom and pop' shops catering to specific needs. Many of these have been replaced, or converted to, chainstores: 7-Eleven, Nikko Mart, McDonalds, Cosmed, Watsons, Starbucks and others. There are also many world class department stores, like Mitsukoshi, and specialty shops, like Eslite bookstore, HOLA home furnishings and accessories, B&Q do-it-yourself megamarts, Carrefour hypermarts and more.. At the same time, the Taiwanese entrepreneurial spirit pushes back with great fads that sweep even the region outside of Taiwan, like bubble-tea stands. Especially when it comes to restaurants and eateries, the entrepreneurs prevail. Everyone eats out all the time, breakfast, lunch and dinner. And if you are willing to eat in local food stalls and small restaurants, one can still eat really good food, nutritious, delicious and filling, for a fraction of what you would pay in Tokyo or the USA. Noodles, fried rice, roast meats, cold plates, stir fried vegetables, dumplings, steamed buns, fresh fruits and fish are all available at shop after stall after cart after bakery all representing great value.

Some things don't change, though. Taiwanese are still hard working, hard playing people. Children continue to go to cram schools to prepare for testing in to good high schools and colleges. Men and women work long hours to advance their

The bounty of Taiwan's orchards and fields on display in the Shihlin night market.

careers. Despite the hustle and bustle, Taiwanese maintain their spiritual traditions. You will frequently see red metal bins along the street with locals burning 'spirit money' in them as offerings. Many buildings still have a raw, grimy, unfinished look to the outside, but the apartments within will be cool havens of comfort and modernity. Taiwanese still stare at foreigners, still ask questions the foreigner might find intrusive and still talk in Chinese about the foreigner as if she is not there. Take advantage of their gregarious curiosity about you and hang out where they do: local restaurants, beer halls, teashops, KTV, pool halls, bowling alleys and parks in the morning. Taiwanese are avid golfers so if you are a well-heeled duffer, hit the links. Taiwanese will warmly embrace you.

And remember, the best weapons in your arsenal against culture shock are patience, tolerance and an easy smile.

THE HISTORY OF THE FIRST 'LITTLE TIGER'

'Not until the mid-seventeenth century, under pressure from Europeans' arrival in coastal Asia and from Manchu efforts to quell the resistance of Ming loyalists in South China, did a Chinese imperial administration manifest a greater political interest in Taiwan.'
—Gary Marvin Davison,
A Short History of Taiwan: The Case for Independence

THE GEOGRAPHY OF TAIWAN could be said to have created its history. Surrounded by different cultures, the island of Taiwan was often a pawn in the geopolitical games of nations. The modern economic miracle we see now owes much to this fact.

Taiwan's geopolitical status at various stages throughout history laid the foundations for its evolution into the first of the 'Little Asian Tiger' economies, later to be joined by Singapore, South Korea and Hong Kong.

Taiwan is a leaf-shaped island running north to south, approximately 450 km (280 miles) by 97 km (60 miles) wide. It is sandwiched between the South China Sea and the Pacific Ocean. One hundred and sixty kilometres (100 miles) to its west is the Chinese province of *Fujian*. To the north-east lies the Ryukyu chain of islands that comprise present-day Okinawa, while beyond these, roughly 1,930 km (1,200 miles) away, is mainland Japan. On Taiwan's southernmost horizon is the first northern island of the Philippine chain.

Taiwan belongs to the Pacific Rim of Fire. It is volcanic in origin and experiences frequent earthquakes. A ridge of glorious mountains runs north-south down the centre of the island. This range has over 100 peaks and exceeds 3,017 m (9,900 feet) in height. Bisecting the island east-west is the Tropic of Cancer. The eastern face of Taiwan rises precipitously from the blue Pacific, while the lush western plains drop gradually into the silty China Sea. The island lies right in the corridor most frequented by typhoons (a word that comes from the Mandarin *taifeng*) and the east coast is regularly battered by these winds during the typhoon season. In Taipei, it is true that, apart from several hot and humid months in the summer, the weather is generally miserable, resulting in the popular saying, 'Taipei weather is like a stepmother's temper'.

EARLY SETTLERS

The first settlers in Taiwan migrated from Luzon and Malaysia. There were eight distinct language groups, which suggests that the settlers arrived in waves and from different places. These settlers populated the coastal regions and engaged in hunting and rudimentary farming. They also engaged in intertribal warfare and headhunting. They were primitive peoples without a written language, but with a tradition of storytelling and ritual. Today, about a quarter million of these original settlers remain in Taiwan, where their interests have been protected since 1945 by the Nationalist government.

THE CHINESE

The first political power to take notice of Taiwan was China. For centuries China has been called *Zhongguo*, the 'Middle Kingdom'. It placed itself at the centre of all nations. Emperors expected tribute from bordering nations, payment of which they felt constituted the subservience of these nations. Mongolia, Tibet, Burma, Thailand, Vietnam, Japan and Korea all paid tribute from time to time. Nations that refused were sometimes attacked, though another ploy was to try to marry a Chinese princess to the ruler to bring them in line. China felt that it was the focal point of the political and cultural universe. Thousands of years of political sophistication, urban mercantilism and exquisite arts added to this image the Chinese had of themselves. Even being taken over by Mongols and Manchus at different periods in time did not decrease this sense of superiority. The Chinese acculturated the new emperors and harmony returned.

But when we speak of 'Chinese', what is actually meant? Modern China lays claim to many ethnic minorities, including Tibetans. It is the Han Chinese, originating in the valleys and flood plains of the Yangtze (*Chang Jiang*) and Yellow (*Huang He*) rivers, who have always emphasised their 'Chinese-ness' and who have created many of the traditions associated with Chinese culture. The Han Chinese spread north, south, east and west into the many present-day provinces of China, developing their own dialects and cuisines. They now constitute 96 per cent of the population.

In the 7th and 14th centuries, imperial expeditions were sent to explore the island of Taiwan and later to repulse Japanese and Okinawan pirates who were using the natural harbours as bases from which to prey on Chinese trading vessels. A migration of farmers and traders began in the 15th century. Most of the immigrants came from two principal groups: the Han Chinese from Fujian province and the Hakkas. Hakka (in Mandarin *Kejia*) refers to a homeless group within China. Much like the Jews in their unsettled history, the Hakkas have wandered throughout China and Southeast Asia in search of a place for themselves. Their name literally means 'guest of the house'. Perhaps they thought they could find a permanent haven for themselves in Taiwan.

THE EUROPEANS ARRIVE

The 16th and 17th centuries saw increased activity in the development of Taiwan. In 1517, the Portuguese Admiral Andrade sailed to Taiwan and became so enchanted by the place he named it *Ilha Formosa* (Beautiful Island). The Portuguese established a small but important trading presence there.

The Dutch were already established in Indonesia when they sailed north in 1622 and visited the Pescadores (Penghu Islands), a group of small islands between Taiwan and the Chinese mainland. One year later, they returned and twisted the Fujian governor's arm to allow them to establish several forts on the island of Taiwan. Forts Zeelandia and Providentia were built as a result of these agreements and the Dutch immediately began to scheme with the aborigines to prepare for greater control. During that period of growing European imperialism, it was inevitable that wherever the Protestant Dutch sailed, the Catholic Spanish would not be far behind. In 1626, the Spanish set up forts in Tansui (*Danshui*) and Keelung (*Jilong*).

Taiwan was becoming an important entrepôt. It was located right in the middle of what was expected to become a major trading route to Japan. Trade with the Chinese mainland was still conducted offshore, so Taiwan was a door to that market and was a major source for certain valuable commodities like camphor. In 1628 though, the Japanese pulled up their trading outposts and returned to Japan. This may have been ordered by the new Shogunate as part of policies that closed Japan's borders and battened down the hatches for 250 years of isolation.

In 1642, the Dutch, assisted by aborigine warriors, kicked the Spanish off the island. However, major events in China were brewing that would result in the expulsion of the Dutch too. The year 1644 marked the end of the Ming Dynasty, the last of the Han Chinese dynasties. China was taken over by Manchurian horsemen invading from the north, who then created the Qing (Manchu) Dynasty. However, it was not an overnight coup d'état. Countless books, novels, operas and movies tell how the Ming Loyalists retreated to the south and tried to recapture the empire for their emperor. (The custom of moon cakes is tied up with them, as was the formation of Chinese secret societies.)

One ally of the Loyalists was a rich and influential man known as Koxinga (Zheng Cheng Gong). Koxinga was born to a wealthy Fujian trader and his Japanese wife in 1624. It was said that Koxinga's father commanded a fleet of 3,000 sailing vessels and had a business empire that extended into Japan. When Koxinga sided with the Ming Loyalists, he had the power to sail to Taiwan and engage the Dutch in battle. After negotiating their departure in 1662, he established his own state. The resistance to Qing control continued throughout Koxinga's life. His son and grandson eventually took over the reins of power, but in 1683 the resistance was crushed.

For 200 years, the Qing authorities paid little heed to Taiwan other than installing a governor and taxing trade in certain commodities. Their political control of Taiwan actually came to be a burden in the gamesmanship played with the European powers, who used any excuse they could find to try to claim damages from the emperor's government. Repayment for damages usually meant forced trading concessions and other shamelessly unequal treaties, which can be read about in more detail in histories of the Opium Wars.

Taiwan was also a burden on China in another way. Its east coast, with its treacherous shores and frequent typhoons, meant that Western traders often lost their ships when navigating this route. The traders could hardly complain to their governments about Taiwan's rugged geography, but when the aborigines began to hunt down and behead the shipwrecked sailors, they had an excuse for action. The British demanded punishment of the aborigines. However, at the time, Taiwan was far from the emperor's mind. He had never been there and could do very little about these non-Chinese mountain people. He demurred. The British would not relent, so he had some aborigines punished. It was not enough and sailors continued to disappear. Finally, a British punitive expedition was sent.

JAPANESE COLONIALISATION

Considering the history of political hassles surrounding Taiwan, it is not surprising that when China was punished by Japan at the end of the First Sino-Japanese War (under the Treaty of Shimonoseki, 1895), the Qing emperor ceded the island to its northern neighbour in perpetuity. There was no discussion with the Taiwanese. The Japanese trumpeted, in a bit of overblown propaganda, that they were finally in possession of the favourite island of their own native son, Koxinga!

A Taiwanese delegation, perhaps at the instigation of the emperor, immediately proclaimed an independent republic. It was doomed to failure. The Japanese landed in Keelung, systematically and quickly fighting their way south. The Japanese were not kind colonial administrators, but they were efficient. Everything the emperor's government should have been doing but had not was now done by the new masters. It has been commented by historians that

Japan had just emerged from its own isolation, was striving to emulate and, as we now know, exceed the West, and wanted to make Taiwan its showcase colony. Roads were built, schools erected, quarantine checkpoints maintained, a railroad line put in and industries developed. Planned forestry, coal mining and steel production, not to mention agriculture, all became major industries.

It was the Taiwanese who paid the price for this. Japanese became the medium of instruction in schools; all business with the government had to be conducted in Japanese, even if the clerk was Taiwanese; secret police continued to quash any attempts at Taiwanese independence; Taiwanese conscripts were forced to labour abroad for the Imperial Army; and Taiwanese women were sent to 'comfort' Japanese soldiers. During World War II, Taiwanese conscripts served as far away from home as Manchuria and Indonesia. It was said that when a Taiwanese died during the occupation, he wanted his casket to be taken to the grave under a black umbrella so he would not have to be buried under a Japanese sun.

Meanwhile, events in Mainland China continued to heat up. In 1911, Dr. Sun Yat Sen (*Sun Zhong Shan*) overthrew the Manchu Qing Dynasty and in 1912 proclaimed the Republic of China. This led to 38 years of revolution, weakness, strife, massive corruption, cronyism and untold misery for the Chinese people, until the consolidation of power in 1949 under the Communist leader Mao Tse Tung (*Mao Ze Dong*). In between, there were constant battles between the Nationalists (the Kuomintang, KMT or *Guomindang*), the warlords, the Communists and eventually the Japanese during World War II.

A major figure to emerge in China at this time was the leader of the KMT, Generalissimo Chiang Kai Shek (*Jiang Jie Shi*). This practiced opportunist married into one of the most powerful families in China. His sister-in-law was Dr. Sun's wife, while his other in-laws were the Soongs and the Kungs, among the richest people on the face of the earth. His cultivated connections, assumption of Western airs and staunchly anti-Communist position won him almost undying support from the United States

Congress who, through the years, gave billions of dollars to support his cause. As the KMT army retreated across China, leaving the Chinese people to face horrors at the hands of the Japanese, the United States continued to support Chiang. The famous Flying Tigers, an American squadron based in Southwest China, were formed in order to harry Japanese forces with strafing and bombing runs. An air supply route from India to China, 'over the hump' of the Himalayas, was also created.

As the war drew to a close, the United States developed a plan to island-hop to Japan by capturing Taiwan. It was problematic because Taiwan had only three serviceable ports. However, its strategic location and the ability to efficiently supply Chiang while cutting off Japanese supply lines made solid sense. As there were many in the State Department who were leery of Generalissimo Chiang (not so affectionately labelled 'The Gismo' or just 'Peanut' due to his closely shaven head), the island would have been administered as an American trust territory until it could be turned over to a free and organised China. However, the plan was trashed by General MacArthur who, with his vow, "I will return", had promised the Philippines that the country would be first on his agenda. So, instead, Taiwan was bombed up and down.

UNCLE SAM'S TURN

With the surrender of the Japanese on the battleship *Missouri* in August 1945, Taiwan was returned to Chinese sovereignty. The Taiwanese, freed from the yoke of colonial servitude, looked forward to the prospect of membership in a free China. But China was in shambles! After World War II, Chiang immediately went on the offensive against the Communists, who in turn got support from Stalin. The Chinese people became victims in Chiang's mass scramble to accumulate wealth and Mao's scramble to defeat him.

At the same time, it seems that the Kuomintang's view of Taiwan was not very strategic; they believed it was populated by Japanese sympathisers who should be punished by appropriating their property. Chiang sent in one of his less diplomatic generals to do this. Officials from the United States and the United Nations watched in bewildered horror as the new Nationalist governor systematically alienated the local population of Taiwan. Criticism of Chiang by state department officials was silenced by congressional anti-Communist forces. The situation worsened.

The festering resentment of the local Taiwanese erupted on 28 February 1947, a day for decades whispered about in Taiwan as *Er Er Ba* (2/28, the date the massacre began). Two of Chiang's tobacco and wine monopoly tax agents approached an old woman street hawker who had some cigarettes and her change before her on a small wooden board. They confiscated her goods and her money and roughed her up. An angry Taiwanese crowd gathered, shots were fired by the taxmen, and six weeks of bloodshed began. All told, it is estimated that 20,000 Taiwanese were killed during this incident. The Governor was recalled, but, following a report discounting the number of deaths, the matter was ordered to be forgotten.

In 1948, however, Taiwan suddenly became more important to the Kuomintang as it dawned on Chiang that it might be his only retreat from China. In another example of his opportunistic genius, he withdrew from the Chinese presidency (with an option to reclaim it at his choice), retired to Taiwan and diverted US military aid to the island and away from the general he had left in China to fight the Communists. When China fell to the Communists, he could say it was not on his 'watch', reclaim the presidency and plot his return.

With the victory of Mao's Red Army in Mainland China, two million Mainland Chinese, mainly soldiers and their families, poured across the Straits and into Taiwan. Many of these men were war-weary, 'grunts' who had nothing and had known nothing but revolution and the corrupt ways of the old regime. They came from far-flung provinces of China, each with its own customs, traditions, and cuisines, and together they spoke a dozen different dialects. The Taiwanese Chinese considered these people interlopers and they resented the uncouth brusqueness they represented, as well as their burden on the island's resources. They were referred to as *wai sheng ren* (people of foreign provinces).

Chiang realised several things. His benefactor, the United States, would no longer support him if he continued to ride roughshod over the local population, allow cronies to stuff their pockets and not develop the local economy. Without US support, his cause was as good as dead. The United Kingdom had already given diplomatic recognition to the People's Republic of China and his faction was losing support in the United Nations. The several hundred thousand soldiers who had retreated from the mainland were unoccupied and unwilling to sit forever without taking action—against him if he was not careful. Moreover, the local population would certainly not put up with the dramatic deterioration in their lifestyle since the defeat of the Japanese without also taking action. Taiwanese politicians who opposed the KMT and were exiled to Japan and the United States began to fight for *Tai Du* (Taiwan independence), activities that were viciously suppressed by the Kuomintang in Taiwan.

Masterfully, Chiang began to orchestrate the development of Taiwan in moves that were to result in the modern economic miracle people talk about today. Under martial law, Taiwanese business was allowed to flourish and farmlands were redistributed to farmers. Agricultural output increased. Government corporations were created to absorb the excess military personnel. These companies focused on big projects and industries (where it was easier for Chiang and his family cronies to profit), like construction (RSEA), steel (China Steel), shipbuilding (China Shipbuilding), power (Taipower), brewing (Tobacco and Wine Monopoly), sugar (Taisugar), and tourism and travel (China Airlines). These companies became known as *gong jia ji guan* (public corporations).

Tens of thousands of men were thrown into the difficult construction of an east-west scenic highway that served no strategic purpose. Thousands died in landslides and tunnel collapses during its construction. Public schools were built wherein the local population could be indoctrinated in Chinese history and geography, national language, thought and loyalty, in preparation for recovery of 'the Mainland'. The message was basically: 'We can build our prosperity, but dissent from the Kuomintang line will not be tolerated.' A political prison was set up on Green Island (*lvdao*) where conditions were tough and escape inconceivable. The island is now open to tourists and a memorial plaque says simply, 'For the mothers who wept long nights for their children imprisoned on the island.'

It should be noted here that until little more than a decade ago, it was the official line of the Kuomintang government in Taiwan that it was the sole legitimate elected government for the whole of China. Until recently, citizens were not allowed to publicly or privately question the reality of this stand or to have an election for the national legislature which threatened those aging officials originally elected in the 1940s. Stories were told of such officials attending the sessions in the 1980s in wheelchairs or lying on portable hospital beds with intravenous tubes in their arms!

The Korean War, and more importantly the Vietnam War, were other tremendous supports to Chiang Kai Shek's government. With the US embroiled in anti-Communist battles in Asia, how could they let their old Nationalist friend sink? Massive military, economic, and developmental aid was invested in Taiwan in the 1950s and 1960s. Taiwan's economy also benefited from the dollars that came in from US servicemen sent there for duty or rest and relaxation. B-52 bombing runs on North Vietnam were flown out of Chiang Ching Kuo Airbase in Taichung. There was rapid and balanced economic growth for several decades.

TAIWAN ON ITS OWN

Then came several diplomatic blows. First was the 'ping-pong' diplomacy of Henry Kissinger and Richard Nixon when they opened the door to Mainland China, resulting in the Shanghai Communiqué of 1972. The Communiqué was brief, but its intent still influences the relations of China, Taiwan and the US. Taiwan was a part of China and therefore an internal problem of China. This buried the hopes of *Tai Du* advocates that the US might some day support a free Taiwan. The writing was also on the wall for the Kuomintang. The US recognised the problem as China's and this suggested that US intervention was not to be expected if China attacked Taiwan in an effort to recapture the island.

The second blow was US President Jimmy Carter's breaking of diplomatic relations with the Republic of China (Taiwan) and establishment of relations with the People's Republic of China (Mainland China) in December 1978. Already diplomatically isolated, Taiwan embarked on a path of 'dollar diplomacy'. Ten major infrastructure projects were already nearing completion and more were planned. These improved Taiwan's appearance as an investment site and delivered large contracts to companies in friendly countries. Taiwan was already a major manufacturing powerhouse for cheap products and the government encouraged investment in factories and industrial upgrading. The New Taiwan Dollar (NT$) was kept at a low value to encourage exports and discourage imports. As a consequence of this, double digit GNP growth was maintained.

The 1980s was an important period of economic, social and political reform. It began with the maintenance of martial law and Chiang's son, Chiang Ching Kuo (*Jiang Jing Guo*), in power, much as Koxinga family had done centuries before. There was no effective democratic opposition. Contacts with Mainland China were forbidden under penalty of imprisonment. The currency exchange rate stood at approximately NT$ 40 to US$ 1.

However, the decade ended with a Taiwanese-born Kuomintang legislator, Lee Teng Hui (*Li Deng Hui*), in power as president. Martial law was lifted. History books painting a negative picture of the Kuomintang appeared on the black market and then gradually as tacitly approved publications. These included translations of Sterling Seagraves' Chiang Kai Shek roast, *The Soong Dynasty*. Opposition members of the National Assembly from various grassroots parties could regularly be seen coming to blows (real fists!) with other members of the Legislative Council (*Yuan*). Open discussion of the *Er Er Ba* incident took place and the government apologised for its role. Legal contacts with Mainland China began, just in time to allow many of the ageing *wai sheng ren* (who had come to Taiwan so many decades ago) to see once more their homeland and the families they had left behind. In addition, the New Taiwan Dollar stood at NT$ 25 to US$ 1, a dramatic 60 per cent increase.

In the 1990s, Taiwan began to come to grips with the challenge of reconciling its past with its future. During the 35 years under martial law, all kinds of things were allowed or ignored by the government, so long as the population was politically quiet. The urban environment grew without enforced civic planning. Pollution, both from transportation and industry, rendered much of the landscape an eyesore and the atmosphere a lung-burner. Though corruption was perhaps less rampant than in decades past, it was still widespread.

However, change accelerated in the mid-1990s with the election of the opposition candidate Chen Shui Bian, aka 'Ah-Bian' by his supporters, as mayor of Taipei. This native-born politician opposed the Kuomintang, cleaned up the city and set Taipei on the path to becoming a more habitable, even enjoyable, place. This improvement has continued under the Kuomintang mayor, Ma Ying Jeou (*Ma Ying Jiu*) while Chen went on to run for president. Chen eventually booted the Kuomintang out of the presidency. Unfortunately for him, the opposition mandate did not extend to the legislature, which remains dominated by the Kuomintang and the splinter New Party. The combination of several blunders on the part of President Chen, a downturn in the economy, and the machinations of the opposition has made his tenure uncertain.

President Chen's stated views on the matter of Taiwan's relations with China have moved the country (or province, depending on one's perspective) closer to independence, pumping up the invective hurled at him and his associates from across the straits. Even the music of Taiwanese pop star Chang Hui Mei (*Zhang Hui Mei* aka Ah-Mei), who had a lucrative contract with Coca-Cola to perform in Sprite commercials in China, was banned from the Mainland for nine months after she sang the national anthem at President Chen's first inauguration (never mind that the anthem speaks of reunification!).

Emotionally, the Taiwanese are much more supportive of independence and are free to express their views as never before. They discuss the future in all conceivable forums, from talk shows to coffee shop chats. There are frequent rallies by the Green (Democratic Progressive Party, DPP) and Blue (Kuomintang, KMT) and the streets are plastered with posters by wannabe legislators. President Chen's re-election in 2004 after an assassination attempt, which the opposition accused him of staging, and his failure to win a majority in the assembly point to a split in public opinion. Taiwanese are definitely of two minds on this issue.

On 26 March 2005, a 'million man march' was called in Taipei to protest against the anti-secession law passed in Mainland China by the undemocratically elected People's Congress. The law makes it 'illegal' for Taiwan to secede, making the use of military force 'legal' in that event.

President Chen's Green DPP was heavily represented calling on all Taiwan people to 'resist invasion and protect Taiwan', but the other two major parties abstained. In a slap in the face, the chairman of Chimei Group, a world famous Taiwan based polymer producer with major investments in China, who was formerly strongly pro-Taiwan made a statement in favour of the anti-secession law and reunification. Pundits declared he had his arm twisted by Mainland authorities and had jumped 'from green to red parties'.

This is due to the increasing dependence of Taiwan on China for its economic future. Since the late 1980s, trade resumed between the two countries but only through third party ports, especially Hong Kong and Macau. Baby steps were also taken to open direct trade. In 1997, shipments between the Fujian province ports of Fuzhou and Xiamen and the offshore islands held by Taiwan—Jinmen and Matsu (*Ma Zu*)—were legalised. Under a 2001 agreement, more direct shipments between Kaohsiung and the two Fujian province ports have taken place, albeit on a limited basis. President Chen and his opposition rivals both favour a lifting of the restrictions, so we should expect liberalisation on this front.

Direct dial phone service now connects China and Taiwan, but there are still no regularly scheduled direct flights. This is an inconvenience to the reported 500,000 Taiwanese who now live and conduct business on the Mainland. Mainland Chinese workers being illegally smuggled into Taiwan and who work for low wages are also a growing problem. Many Taiwanese feel these people have contributed to the deterioration of law and order.

Opinions about the relations between Mainland China and Taiwan vary. Before expressing your views, understand the situation completely and the politics of the person you are talking to. Even an educated opinion from a long-term foreign resident can be misconstrued as imperialistically patronising or unsympathetic. In discussions of politics, foreigners would do best to just listen and ask questions.

In conclusion, Taiwan is still a part of China that is not a part of China. It is still a freewheeling and exciting place in which to live and do business. It still makes for a culturally rich experience. And in many places and in many ways, it is still the *Ilha Formosa*!

THE WEIGHT OF TRADITION

The long history of the Chinese people is a major source of cultural pride. It is the traditions that have sprung from this history that give the Chinese their identity. During the degradation of China, from the mid-19th to the mid-20th centuries, it was only China's traditions that sustained the self-respect of its people. Defeated both diplomatically and on the battlefield, robbed and torn asunder by corrupt and ruthless warlords, and exploited by empire-hungry nations from East and West, the Chinese people could only look to their past with satisfaction. By comparison, the present and future looked grim.

The same history, though, with its millennia of accumulated tradition, weighs heavily in the heart of all Chinese. It defines their social, familial, commercial, and political relations, as well as their relations with the spirit world and the physical universe. To deviate from expected behaviour is to be labelled, stigmatised, harangued and ridiculed. Taiwanese relate thoroughly and almost exclusively to their Chinese heritage, to the extent that when there is talk of *Tai Du* (Taiwan Independence), it is strictly political, not a break with cultural heritage.

American-born Chinese, for example, may either rebel against this tradition, or truly feel they carry it in their hearts. But, in any case, they will be seen as something less than full Chinese due to their upbringing—a source of frequent frustration for them when they wish to integrate into Chinese society. Taiwanese traditionally, and especially after the educational indoctrination of the Kuomintang, see themselves first and foremost as culturally Chinese (*Tai Du* sentiments notwithstanding).

One can become an enlightened barbarian by studying Chinese traditions, but never be accepted as a true equal. Some Chinese have asked foreigners, "Why do you want to be equal? Don't you feel superior anyway?" Because of inconsistencies in the Chinese heritage, a foreigner can always be told that he *bu ming bai*, in other words, he is not clear on or does not understand the nuance of a cultural problem. This is a source of frustration that can be minimised if the foreigner studies with sufficient breadth and depth the Taiwanese cultural heritage. What is fascinating is that the three major traditions influencing the Taiwanese were all born concurrently, five centuries before Christ. One came from India and the other two from China.

CONFUCIANISM

Confucius was a scholar and philosopher born in the year 551 BC in Shandong, southeast of Beijing. In Mandarin his name is *Kong Fu Zi*. He served kings and princes and is credited with the importance placed on education and bureaucracy by the Chinese. His school of thought was transmitted through several books known today as the *Analects* and are very conservative. He taught the importance of relations and of the conscious effort required to maintain them. All people, all things, have a purpose and a station in life. If they all understand that purpose and station, and perform their duties well, there will be harmony. He softened this by stating that benevolence was the key to leadership, that in order to be treated well as a subordinate, one had to treat one's subordinates well. During the Song Dynasty (960–1279), a branch developed called Neo-Confucianism, which adopted the meditative and alchemic aspects of Taoism.

Confucian harmony, forced through the conscious exercise of 'proper behaviour' (defined by someone else!), is the beneficial result sought by the philosopher and the king. If you do not understand your station and behave improperly, you have not been taught correctly. If you wilfully neglect your duties, you have been tainted by bad elements. For example, a wife who does not act 'wifely' or a prince who does not act 'princely' can severely disrupt harmony. The proper relation is one of subservient attention to the needs and edicts of one's superior (heaven, in the case of the emperor). This selfless *xiao shun* (devotion) can be compared to what the West calls 'filial piety', though, technically, this term is limited to familial relations.

The units of social focus adopted in Japan, Taiwan, and post-revolutionary China are different and the contrast is worth noting. In Japan, heavily influenced by Confucianism, the unit of focus has traditionally been one's superior and the group to which one belongs (shogunate, village lord, army, or now, a company). In Taiwan, the unit of focus is the family. The family is self-regulating and self-controlled. Problems are usually settled within the family, and the individual who has his or her own ideas should create consensus within the family before embarking on them.

Consequently, the Taiwanese exhibit little civic-mindedness, the focus being on benefiting the family. To the saying, 'Charity begins at home' must be added '… and ends there'.

These units of social focus, group and family, are not all bad. Japanese corporations have a unity of purpose that is rare in the West, while Taiwan is a nation of family-owned enterprises. In contrast, the communists in China tried to make society itself, under the cloak of the Communist Party (or, at the very least, the socialist work unit), the focus of society. Many are the perverse stories telling of children

On Confucius' birthday, traditional rites include the waving of peacock feathers—symbols of respect and honour. The Chinese name for peacock (*kungchywe*) also includes the name of Confucius (Kung).

ratting on their parents during that era. Still today in China, when one calls for a person on the phone at his place of work, one will be asked "*Shenma danwei*?" (What unit?) It is possible that part of the disillusionment the young generation in Mainland China now feels is because their social unit is so ill defined. Their tempestuous upbringing has neither prepared them to be individuals nor parts of clusters, especially during the Cultural Revolution, which tried to destroy the family as a unit of society

Even today, proper relations manifest themselves in the hierarchy of society and the respect that must be properly extended within the hierarchy: husband/wife, parent/child, teacher/student, boss/secretary, government/opulation, old/young, dead/living, etc. Attached to these relations are expectations of behaviour, rituals, gift-giving and 'face-giving'. There are young Chinese (perhaps in every generation since Confucius) who have chafed at the yoke of this tradition. They are labelled as 'unfilial' (*bu xiao shun*). Severe punishment has been used through the ages to bring children back in line so they will be 'educated' and not 'tainted'.

Another cultural result of Confucian tradition is the focus away from the self as the unit of society. In Western 'liberal' tradition, society is made up of individuals. Our solitary mythical heroes challenge nature and the gods (who themselves exhibit human foibles) and occasionally win. Not so in China. Sun Wu Kung, the Monkey King who accompanied Tripitaka on his trip to India to bring back the Buddhist scrolls, challenged the gods and as a result was punished by the Buddha, who put a gold band around his head. This band crippled him with pain if he became too cheeky. In Confucian society, you are a part of another unit, and don't you forget it!

Confucianism is not a religion. There are, however, many Confucian temples in Taiwan and China, and there are various rituals and rites associated with Confucian obeisance. Many of these pay respect to him as the Master Teacher. Scholarship was as much the key to success in ancient China as it is in modern Taiwan and the success of one's children is frequently prayed for. Think of Confucius as the patron saint of scholars, bureaucracy and regimentation, and you will not be far wrong.

BUDDHISM

The Buddha, a contemporary of Confucius, was born a prince in northern India near the border with Nepal. In his youth, he enjoyed princely activities such as archery, horsemanship and statecraft. Still, he was not satisfied with life and sought a deeper understanding of the unhappiness he felt plagued mankind. This took him on a path that was to lead him through all manner of hardship, involving physical and spiritual testing. Eventually, having walked this bitter path, he achieved enlightenment. He told the world, through his disciples, that desire is the root of suffering and that man should compassionately tread an eightfold path in the pursuit of enlightenment. The path never ends until, after millions of years and rebirths, one finally gets it right and achieves enlightenment.

Buddhism spread from India to Sri Lanka and the Indonesian archipelago, north to Tibet, east to Burma and beyond. It grew into several schools, arriving in China in the first century AD Its popularity increased after the arrival of Tamo (*Damo*) who founded the Chan sect at the Shaolin Temple around AD 500. His discipline included meditation, exercise, and introspection. In Japan, and around the world, this school is more popularly known as Zen. The Shaolin Temple also was the source of one of China's most famous schools of the martial arts.

Buddhism is to China what Catholicism is to Europe, minus the Crusades and Inquisition. It fell in and out of favour with the emperors, controlled vast tracks of land and granaries of rice, and occasionally became a power unto itself, complete with intrigues and armies. It also made lots of money. In China, the Buddhist Pantheon expanded to include many helpers and hangers-on of the Buddha.

Whatever conception you have of Buddhism, you are almost certainly going to be surprised by what you will observe in Taiwan. Most Westerners' ideas about Buddhist discipline and serenity come from Zen austerity or Thai piety. For the Taiwanese, Buddhism is a relief from misery and uncertainty. They will pray for mercy from Kuan Yin (*Guan Yin*), the Goddess of Mercy, and then mercilessly pursue whatever end it was that created the conflict or unhappiness in their life. They will pray for a boy child, for a rich husband, for a good entrance examination, for a gentler mother-in-law,

The seated Buddha and stone lions on Bagwa Mountain show the extent to which Chinese traditions have influenced Buddhism in Taiwan.

not ever stopping to think that it is, according to the Buddha, their desire for these things that creates their uncertainty and unhappiness. The temples indulge this type of prayer, as will be covered in detail later in this chapter.

There are formal Buddhist monasteries and nunneries in Taiwan. Priests normally work out of formal temples that are supported by donations and benefactors. Most hotels in Taiwan will have a copy of *The Meaning of Buddhism* in the bedside drawer, atop the Gideon's *Bible*. It is a good place to read about the general tenets of this popular religion.

TAOISM

Born several decades before Confucius was a cantankerous ruminator named Lao-tzu (*Laozi*). A philosopher and librarian scholar at the imperial archives, his views were at odds with his king and he exiled himself. Legend has it that at the last mountain pass before leaving the realm, the border guard struck up a conversation with him and begged to be allowed to record his teachings. His words are passed down to us today in the *Dao De Jing* (also known as the *Tao Teh Ching*) and his philosophy is known as *Dao* (popularly spelled *Tao*), meaning 'the Way'.

The Western conception of Taoism is that it is based on quiet cultivation and respect for nature. As with Buddhism, however, the casual observer will find that the reality of its practice in Taiwan greatly diverges from this conception. This is because, in Taiwan, there is both Taoism the religion (*Dao Jiao*) and Taoism the philosophy (*Dao Jia*). The distinction is important, though many Taoists in Taiwan might not admit it. The philosophers have traditionally shunned the priests who tried to create a religious expression of *Tao* to compete with Buddhism. Similarly, they shunned organised Confucian society. The philosophers, even today, spend their lives cultivating themselves privately and at higher levels in the seclusion of mountain hermitages.

On the other hand, the priests of the religion are itinerant and lead normal family lives, save when they have to don their red and gold robes, perform special rituals, exorcisms, séances and the like. They do not lead celibate lives in monasteries. To the Taoist philosophical structure they have added numerous deities, spirits and rituals that Lao Tzu had no time for. Though the religion has a cultural impact, its roots are in the philosophy.

Taoism the philosophy deals with change. It accepts that all things are in a state of flux and change is ceaseless. That is the 'Way of Nature'. The person who understands this, who can observe nature without distraction, can thus move in harmony with nature. To move in harmony with nature is to tap its limitless resource. In their search to understand the Way of Nature, Taoists became perhaps the first empirical scientists. Through trial and error and recorded experimentation over hundreds of years and across various disciplines, they formulated basic scientific theories and practical applications.

Taoism is a practical philosophy developed by practical people who, in their search for health, longevity and self-cultivation, became many of China's most revered physicians, scientists, poets, artists and inventors. In fact, *The Stone Monkey*, by Yale anthropologist Bruce Holbrook, posits that Taoist scientific theory is superior to Western science in its holistic scope, humanity and ability to anticipate as yet not understood processes at work in the universe. It was only a Confucian geopolitical sense of superiority, coupled with the disdain for business and the self-seclusion of the Taoists, that prevented China from exploiting these inventions for greater global gain (the compass, gunpowder, crossbow and porcelain are just a few of their achievements). Taoist concepts permeate the everyday life of Taiwanese and it is worthwhile spending some time understanding them.

ANIMISM AND OTHER SPIRITS

Besides the well-known and formal religions and philosophies introduced above, there are countless other forms of spirit-worship, some loosely connected to one or another school, which are said to influence the world of the living. Perhaps as an offshoot of Taoist religion, or because the Taiwanese were traditionally farmers and fishermen, spiritual powers

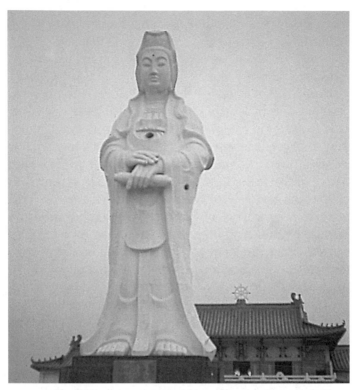

Kuan Yin, the Goddess of Mercy, ranks high in the celestial hierachy. Statues and figures of her abound in Taiwan.

are attributed to the earth in the person of Tu Di Gung, the Chinese god of the earth. By rice fields, tombs, and temples one will frequently see a small stone altar-chimney for use in burning spirit money in his honour.

Another important deity is Gwan Gung, the god of war. Befitting a world of military and industrial complexes, he is also the patron saint of businessmen. Beneath Buddha, Kuan Yin, Guan Gong and Ma Tsu (who is a protectress of fishermen and pregnant women) is a complete celestial bureaucracy. Every small town will have its own temple (or several), within which resides one of these 'divine ambassadors' who helps to communicate to the 'Big Boss' (usually one of the four mentioned above). This ambassador helps to keep tabs on the welfare of the pious.

Another group of spirits said to have a direct influence over the fortune and health of the living are the disembodied spirits. Man is said to have two types of souls. *Pwo* is the *yin* component of your soul that resides in the earth (in the shadow) after burial. *Ling hun* is the spirit that can go to Buddhist hell or be forced to walk the earth without a body after death. A neglected *ling hun* can become a *gui* (ghost or demon), or worse, an *e gui* (hungry ghost).

Ghosts can wreak havoc on the well-being of the living. But what causes them to be neglected? In an application of Confucian thought to the afterlife, it is said to be a lack of attention to one's dead forebears, in the form of proper obeisance, feeding, clothing and remuneration, that causes these astral beings to run amok. Family descendants are supposed to keep an ancestor tablet (with the deceased's name on it) and sometimes a photo of ancestors on the family altar. As a minimum they should burn incense and make offerings.

Trance Mediums

Taiwan has its own class of trance mediums, called *dangki* in the Taiwanese dialect. These men and women are usually chosen by the spirit of the locally honoured divine

A trance medium, or *dangki*, performs Chinese martial arts whilst in a trance during Matsu's birthday.

ambassador, mentioned above, to serve as a mouthpiece to the world of the living. They have no choice in the matter, sometimes trying to escape the responsibility by leaving town, but frequently surrendering to duty. Most small towns will not admit to having them, though they still exist.

When a person has a chronic and recurring problem and they have exhausted all other remedies, a *dangki* might be called in. Once in trance the problem is described and the spirit reveals the remedy. Perhaps a hungry ghost is settling into their lives until he or she is properly pampered. It might be the ghost of a girl who died in youth and never had a chance to get married who is causing trouble in her spinsterly remorse. Though rare now, spirit marriages do take place in which 'forced' fate introduces a living suitor to the dead girl. Man and doll become wed in a formal ceremony. This has no legal effect, but the groom must now put the girl's ancestral tablet on his prayer table.

In the Temple

As you may have surmised by now, many temples do not serve only one deity or faith. There are dedicated temples to be sure, but it is also safe to say that most temples are heavily influenced by at least two of the schools introduced in the beginning of this chapter. So, what does a temple look like?

Unlike Western cathedrals, in which one can enter the great doors in the front and walk straight down the aisle to the altar, Taiwanese temples must be approached and entered through the side gates. This leads directly to a large open stone courtyard. From here you can clearly see the roof-line of the main wall and portals. Note that the roof is wave shaped. It was believed that if malevolent spirits perceived that the temple was under water (the wave shaped roof) they would not attempt to burn it down. The columns and roof-line will frequently have a dragon or dragons adorning it.

Across the courtyard and up perhaps six steps, you will reach the threshold of the main portals, again not in the centre facing the main altar further inside, but to the left and right. Painted on the massive doors will usually be fierce guardian spirits depicted in bright and realistic detail. You will have to step as much as one foot off the floor to cross over the threshold and enter the main temple courtyard area.

Think of all the architectural and ornamental detail you have seen so far as being 'security measures', just like a bank would install to prevent thieves from breaking in. Legend has it that ghosts cannot lift their feet over barriers,

Dragons are auspicious symbols. This one in the form of a column helps protect the temple from evil spirits.

are not capable of making 90-degree turns, and must walk with both feet always touching the ground. Moreover, ghosts are afraid of fierce demons, or even seeing themselves in a mirror. No temple wants to be troubled by inauspicious spirits hence the security measures.

Entering the main courtyard area from the right portal, you may see a window through which is sold incense, red candles and spirit money. To your left is the main courtyard area. Taiwanese young and old (actually, mostly middle-aged or old women) are making obeisance and praying. It is a colourful, fragrant and spiritually moving scene. Grandmothers are teaching children to pray and bow, one or two people might be crying, some are meditating. There is a solemnity not found in the street scene outside.

Prayer in the Temple

Depending on how serious the problem or how big the request, one might perform a simple or a complex obeisance. Let's walk through a full course. An old woman in front of you buys incense, a candle and spirit money. She is carrying a metal plate with *lian wu* (custard apples) on it, which she washed at a basin in the courtyard. She walks to a long table running parallel to the main portal wall. She puts the plate of food on the table as an offering. Other people have put down plates of various fruit, cooked chicken and other food. She goes to the candle-holders at each end of the table and lights one large fat red candle with gilt Chinese writing on its body, sticking the candle on an empty holder. She lights three sticks of incense in the flame of the candle and walks back to the centre of the offering table, standing just behind a knee-pad on the floor. She stands in prayer, with the three incense sticks held in two hands up at her forehead. She bows from the waist three times. She kneels, prays, and bows from the waist again three times. She rises and puts the incense in a brass censer about the size of a charcoal grill.

Walking to the side of the offering table again, she picks up two pieces of wood, the approximate size and shape of a wedge of apple. They are painted red; one side of each is flat and one side is rounded. (These are divining blocks. They are the primary method the Taiwanese use to communicate with the spirits and gods.) After silently asking the question on her mind, she drops the blocks. If they both land flat the answer is a 'no' (a flat refusal, if you like); if one is rolling around and one is down flat, the answer is 'yes'; and if both are on the rounded side, jiggling about, the spirit is laughing at the question—please rephrase it.

She walks down the steps to the centre of the courtyard at the front of which is a huge brass tripod censer, well over a metre in circumference. Sweet plumes of smoke are drifting forth from its lid. Here she lights three more sticks of incense, prays, bows and deposits the sticks into the censer. She goes up the steps into the main altar building which houses a gilt statue of the principal deity, bathed in red light with spiritual attendants to its left and right. She repeats the process with the incense. She walks to a chimney to the far left of the main altar area outside the building. Inside it, a raging fire instantly consumes the stacks of

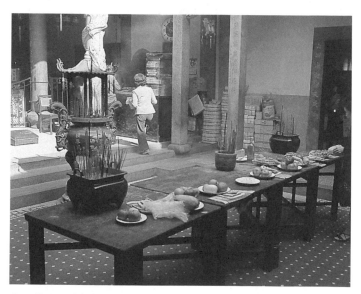

The offering of fruit and the burning of incense are a typical part of prayer in the temple. You will also see such offerings in the streets and in Taiwanese homes.

spirit money she deposits into her spirit's 'cosmic savings account'. Her prayers over, she goes to check on her son whom she put in the study hall dedicated to Confucius in the row of rooms adjacent to the main altar area.

You notice several college-age girls enter the main courtyard area. They each burn three sticks of incense, pray, bow and deposit the incense in the censer. Then they go to what looks like a large brass umbrella stand, filled with long, thin sections of bamboo that are dark brown with constant handling. One by one, they gather the mass of sticks, lift, shake, and release them into the stand again until one stick stands out. This is removed from the bunch and the number on it remembered. When they have all had a turn, they go to a wall of small wooden drawers which are numbered and contain coloured slips of paper which have their fortunes written on them.

The temple is a community centre facilitating communication with spirits. Communion is not normally sought, but rather help in solving some problem in the world of man. In this regard, people around the world are probably not so much different from the Taiwanese. We will explore in the next chapter how the weight of Chinese tradition affects the daily lives of your Taiwanese friends.

THE TAIWANESE

CHAPTER 3

'*Taike* (formerly perjorative expression for local
Taiwanese) as a term is not anti-Taiwanese, but
instead can be embraced as an integral part of local
culture and another aspect of *bentuhua*, or localisation.'
—*Taipei Times*, 28 July 2005

FACE: GIVE AND YOU SHALL RECEIVE

Much has been written about face and the weight Chinese and Japanese put on it. The term comes from two ways in Mandarin of referring to the physical face. A person can throw away or *diu lian* (lose face), or an action can be *mei mian zi* (without face). Curiously, one rarely refers to gaining face (especially for oneself). It is almost always referred to in terms of loss.

Face is the inexpressible pride one feels in oneself for one's station, education, employment, ancestry, family and accomplishments; in short, pride in one's 'self-concept'. It is a subjective store of value. Inexpressible because modesty forbids crowing about it; inexpressible because pride, conceit and defeat are closely related to the Chinese. The Mandarin equivalent of 'pride before a fall' is *ao zhe bi bai* (the proud one will be vanquished). One's face must be referred to indirectly and is best expressed in deeds, not words. A person who says he has great face is insecure and would be scorned by others. A person who, through actions, expresses greatness (at whatever is being done) has face.

Shame

Chinese culture is based on shame. This means that proper action is pursued lest it result in scorn being brought on oneself and one's family from others, who may be either family members or one's social group. This is inculcated from birth in the way the mother and father treat the child. It is the fear of losing face (feeling shame) that keeps people in line when they deal with others from their orbit. It also means that if they are around people from outside their orbit (i.e. foreigners and outsiders), they are relieved from caring about losing face. Hence, many actions considered rude or low-class elsewhere (cutting in line, dumping garbage anywhere, etc.) are done with abandon when not near people known personally to the perpetrator.

The Hierarchy of Face

Another person's face can be referred to directly and generously eulogised. Take note, though; the Confucian hierarchies play an important role here. If you are in the superior role (boss, teacher, father, customer, etc.) it gives face for you to praise your subordinates. If you are in the inferior role (employee, student, salesman) your attempt to give face by praising your superior may label you a 'poseur' (not aware of your own level), or as someone currying favour. The Chinese have two colourful expressions describing this. A *gen pi chong* is a fart-following insect ('brown noser' in the West) who likes to *pai ma pi* or 'stroke the horse's ass'. Face can be given to superiors by letting them instruct you or give you face in front of others. They gain face by giving face, you gain face by retreating.

Confucian hierarchies of face are no more evident than in the definition of family structure through language. Every familial relationship extending out in several branches carries a distinct term. For example, *gege* (older brother) and *didi* (younger brother) are separate terms. *Zu mu* (paternal grandmother) and *wai zu mu* (maternal grandmother-literally 'outside grandmother') carry a distinct difference in tone and apparent class. The term for 'Mister' is most telling: *xiansheng* means 'first born' (or 'first-born male heir'), a person with whom the hope and future of the family resides. In contrast, the term for 'Miss' is *xiao jie*, which means 'little big sister'. If you are speaking English to your Taiwanese counterparts, you will not need to memorise all the different relations. However, you will need to remember how you fit into the hierarchy of face in each particular conversation.

One gains face by understanding the role one is in and what actions are appropriate to that role (in the Confucian sense) to maintain harmony (see chapter four). Much of the content of this chapter is devoted to giving you a feel for understanding in which role you might be perceived and what action would be appropriate.

Always Asking Questions

Taiwanese are very curious and ask many questions about their acquaintances, friends, and guests. Short answers may seem perfunctory. If asked how your flight was, rather than just saying, "Fine, thank you" it is better to throw in some spicy details: "I think it was the best flight I have had. I was served some very good Sichuan-style shrimp. It was on time and the take-off and landing were as smooth as ice".

You may be asked some questions that you find intrusive: "How much did you pay for that?", "What is your salary?", "How old are you?". On the one hand, do not believe the questions are for the sake of just making conversation. They want to know as much about you as possible. It prepares them for the bargaining process. On the other hand, do not believe that a "None of your business!" type of answer will leave them satisfied or feeling good about you. It is best to say things like, "I got a very good price on it, but the merchant made me promise not to tell anyone", or "My salary is only adequate to begin to enjoy some of the wonders of Taiwan".

Equally important is how you ask your questions. Because of face, it is better to ask 'what', 'who' and 'how' questions rather than 'why' questions. For example, the question, "Can you tell me about the table in the parlour with the Buddhist statues on it?" allows them to explain their religious beliefs to you without bringing them into question. "How can I get a bus to Tienmu?" sounds better than "Why can't I get a bus to Tienmu?"

Almost Is Good Enough

Taiwanese will frequently settle for less than the ideal, perhaps because too much face would be lost if everyone went around asking to get exactly what they expected.

This is best described as a Chinese boxing master told it to Chris. Chris had learned a complex series of manoeuvres from the old man which were supposed to begin and end standing in the same place. Somehow, after doing the moves, he always ended up one or two steps to the right. Chris asked the teacher to correct his moves so he could do it right. The teacher replied, "*Mei guan xi—zhongguo mei you jue dui.*" (It doesn't matter; China has no absolutes). He went on to point out that before contact with the West, Chinese shoes had no left/right distinction; they could be worn on either foot. He cited another example of the Emperor who, unlike in Japan, was not considered an absolute ruler. His power was based on the Mandate of Heaven and if he lost it (if the empire began to decay) he could be overthrown. Hence, from the emperor on down, nothing in China was absolute.

There are two other words used frequently to denote this easy-going attitude. *Sui bian* (at one's ease or convenience) is used as an answer to a question about structure or restriction, for example, "What do you want to eat?", "What should I wear to the afternoon tea?". However, do not take the answer *sui bian* at face value and expect only peanuts and beer, or cut-offs and slippers. It is a way the Taiwanese have of saying they are easy about something and have no expectations. Your host may still go to great lengths to make a delicious meal or dress up to the nines. If entertained by Taiwanese, especially in their homes, the host/hostess may frequently be heard to say *daiman* (the food was brought out too slowly) or *zhe xie cai chao de bu hao* (these dishes are not cooked well). As a guest, it is not your place to agree, but rather to exuberantly negate what she has said.

Secondly, *cha bu duo* (not short by very much) means that the situation is almost what was expected. If a merchant or subordinate is saying this, he or she means 'it should be accepted as what was expected'. On the other hand, if you are asked if the item in question is what you want and you reply *cha bu duo*, it means 'no, it is not entirely what I wanted, so I expect room in the price'. Depending on the gravity of the task that was almost completed by a subordinate, together with your tone of voice to him and the words you surround it with, a *cha bu duo* can give or take away face. It means either 'in the face of a very difficult task, you still managed to do it almost to absolute expectation', or 'the task was not difficult and you still managed to provide the work incomplete'.

As far as your own performance is concerned, 'almost is good enough' has its own manifestations. When Chris was studying intensive Mandarin in the United States 30 years ago, his Chinese professor told him, "No matter how long you study, no matter how good your Mandarin gets, when a Chinese says to you, "My, you speak Chinese so well!", do not believe them." Indeed, even now, Chris might be conversing at a rapid clip with a group of Chinese strangers, when he senses that he has made a mistake. Invariably, they will choose that very moment to chime in Chinese or English, "My, you speak Chinese so well!"

This applies to all facets of Chinese culture that a foreigner is supposed to find difficult. When you drop your dumpling square in your lap, you will hear, "You really do know how to use chopsticks well!", sometimes followed by the telling, "Would you like a fork and spoon?" When you have ordered sweet and sour chicken, sweet and sour shrimp, and sweet and sour meatballs, no soup and no vegetables, you may hear, "You really do know how to order Chinese food!"

The point to this artifice is that they want to prevent you from feeling a loss of face. It is always inappropriate, however, to agree with their praise or make a statement to confirm it, such as, "Well, thank you. We use chopsticks all the time at home!" Conversely, if a Taiwanese host orders a meal for you which you find disagreeable, it is the height of ingratitude to say anything that implies he or she has not ordered well for you. Find something nice to say about the meal, even if it's only to comment that you have never sampled so many new and unusual dishes at one meal before in your life.

REN QING WEI—THE KEY TO YOUR HAPPINESS

Ren qing wei is as important as face in getting along well within Taiwanese society, but little is written or said about it. That may be because it is not easy to pin down. It means 'the flavour of human emotions' and is best described as an attitude of sincerity appropriate to the role one plays, or else a charisma consistent with Confucian modesty. Those who have it are considered to be civilised and people are willing to do things for them. It is the positive feeling left with those you encounter because your message has been delivered effectively and in a 'high context' way.

A component of *ren qing wei* is clearly sincerity. When you had a visitor, did you offer them tea and pour them a cup anyway, even after they had said they did not want any? If you did not, your first invitation to drink tea was not really sincere. When you invite someone out, do you sound like you are really interested in going out with them and insist again that this is something they should do with you? If you don't, they may be left with the impression

that you consider their company a necessary nuisance you would rather avoid.

A Chinese person will frequently turn down your first offer. It does not mean they do not want to participate. Confucian modesty dictates that they should not appear greedy or over eager. You must sincerely ask about three times to elicit the final response. Of course, if after your third consecutive invitation, the person still says they have a reason not to participate, it is best to let off and insist they do this with you 'next time'.

"Please, Dance with Me"

When Chris was a college student in Taiwan, he attended a dance party at a friend's house. He made two fatal errors in inviting the girls to dance, a task in which he did not ultimately succeed. Firstly, his question did not carry the proper role relationship, i.e. that of supplicant to the girl. He asked, "Do you want to dance with me?" "No" was the consistent reply. Better to have implored, "Please, dance with me." Secondly, he did not repeat the question, giving up after each refusal he received. Better to have added a bit of emotion to a second and third request to the same girl.

Gift-giving

The way of giving and receiving gifts is an important part of both face and *ren qing wei*, and it should be taken seriously. Different occasions call for different gifts to be given.

Gifts should be wrapped. The paper should be appropriate to the occasion. Red or gold are auspicious colours, but never just white, unless you are going to a funeral and giving towels away. The ritual of presentation and receipt is important. The gift should be held in two hands, palms up if possible, and formally presented to the receiver. She or he should in turn use two hands to accept the gift, taking the time to look at and admire the beautiful wrapping, commenting on it all the time to the giver and the bystanders.

The person receiving the gift will usually not open it when it is presented. Urging them to do so will cause embarrassment. This is to preserve the face of all parties: if they are disappointed with the gift and it shows, you lose face; if the gift is better than those presented by other guests, the others lose face. Though not opening the gift, they will chime with a chorus of 'you shouldn't haves'. This does not mean you shouldn't have. You should have! Giving a gift gives both of you face. The more generous the gift, the more face for you and the receiver. Do not skimp. An inappropriately cheap gift will label you as either a 'foreign devil' who does not know better, or even worse a 'niggardly devil' (*xiao qi gui*).

The Taiwanese are very practical people and gifts for rites of passage are frequently not purchased items, but cash. Except at funerals, money is always presented in even denominations in the ubiquitous *hong bao*, the auspicious red envelopes which often have gold characters on them. If a purchased gift is called for, then name brand or designer items are preferred because of the face they confer. Below we have listed some events that might call for gift-giving, along with the type and possible value of the gift to be

Unsuitable Gifts

- Knives or scissors. Sharp objects are not auspicious in Chinese culture. Giving any gift which is sharp or used for cutting suggests you want to cut off your relationship with the receiver.
- Clocks and watches. They are inauspicious; to 'send a clock' is synonymous with deliverance to one's final end. (However, one of Chris's business associates once gave him a beautiful cuckoo clock, so this custom may be dying out. On the other hand, he could have received the clock from a foreign friend and wanted to be rid of it, hence returning it to another foreigner.)
- Handkerchiefs. These are associated with crying and funerals.
- Towels. These are a common gift to funeral attendees, so they have a bad association.

presented. More information about ideal gifts can be found later in the book, under the individual sections on celebrations and rites of passage.

Gifts for Every Occasion

Occasion	Gift
House visit	Gift worth between NT$ 500–1,000
Graduation	*Hong bao* of NT$ 1,000, or an engraved pen
Engagement	Cakes
Wedding *Hong bao*	Usually NT$ 1,000–2,000 from each person attending the banquet
New house/business	Paintings of propitious scenes (rice fields, fish, oranges, the god of wealth)
Man yue	Gold
Man swei	Gold
Infirmity	Fresh fruits
Death	Wreath, canned goods display, or white envelope of at least NT$ 1,001.

THE TAOIST WORLDVIEW AND ITS INFLUENCE ON TAIWANESE

Though he is credited with the first succinct, if mysterious, statement of Tao, Lao Tzu was merely communicating principles that had been contemplated since the time of the legendary Yellow Emperor (c. 2700 BC) These were developed through an observation of nature. From this, Taoists surmised the beginnings of the universe in terms consonant with modern quantum physics. Three basic concepts to explain change relationships emerged.

In the beginning there was 'One'. One energy, one essence. This essence, the Prime Mover, is called *qi*. In humans, our breath is transformed into *qi* and we remain alive. A Taoist friend once described *qi* as the 'currency that maintains the economy of existence'. This essence then divided into two, which became all things. The two are *yin* and *yang*. *Yin* represents yielding, declining, shadow, pulling, femaleness, emptiness, the hole rather than the doughnut. *Yang* represents aggression, expanding, light, pushing, maleness, fullness, the donut rather than the hole. Everything in the universe contains elements of both *yin* and *yang*. For example, a coin has two sides and if it is illuminated from one side, the other side will be in shadow. Water is yielding, yet over millennia even the face of the earth yields to it.

It was from the *yin-yang* theory that binary numbers were devised, thus setting the stage for all modern computer language. The interaction of *yin* and *yang* sets the stage for all the natural change we see around us: tides, wind and clouds, the rise and fall of empires, natural selection, $E = mc2$.

The Taoists further divided elements of change into five archetypes. These elements could be placed in a Cycle of Birth and a Cycle of Destruction, rather like a 'paper, scissors, rock' sort of sequence. Everything in the universe can be assigned an archetypal element to symbolise its change relation to other similar things. There are, for instance, five types of seasons, emotions, flavours, colours and senses. Even body organs are classified according to elements.

Finally, lost in the mists of prehistory, early Taoist sages, using the binary *yin-yang* theory, created a system of divination to try to explain and anticipate change. They devised a series of symbols to represent the system. Using one of several methods (such as drawing straws or flipping coins) to generate a random chance event, the diviners would classify the outcome as *yin* or *yang* and symbolise it with a solid or broken line. Three repetitions of the event created one of eight possible three-lined forms. These were called *gua*. When repeated once again the combination of two three-lined *gua* would produce one of 64 unique six-lined forms. Each six-lined form, known in English as a hexagram, corresponded to a phase of change and had an explanation attached to it. This system of divination was brought to the West in translations of the Taoist classic, *I Ching* (pronounced *Yi Jing*).

For example, consider the hexagram *Kui* (Opposition) randomly selected above. 'Opposition' here can mean conflicting view points. However, it can also mean polarity or functional opposition, without which an entity loses definition. This can lead to new perspectives on the question one may have posed before going through the selection process and, hence, on a future direction to take.

MEDICINE AND HEALTH

Chinese medical theory, diagnosis, treatment and prescription are based completely on the above ideas. In a healthy body, balance and harmony of the *yin-yang*, five elements and the *qi* are maintained through proper nutrition (including nutritional breathing), activity and quiescence.

- Pulse diagnosis classifies various pulses corresponding to several organs in a state of health, excitement, or decline. The Chinese physician will place three fingers on your wrist, feeling for three separate waves. He may look at your tongue and eyeballs, smell your breath or look at your fingernails. This, coupled with questions about your regular activities, will give him the basis for a diagnosis and prescription.

- *Zhenjiu* (acupuncture) recognises meridians throughout the body in which *qi* flows. In a completely healthy body, the *qi* flows smoothly to all areas. If, because of fatigue, stress, chill or other pernicious influences, there is an interruption or diversion in the flow of *qi*, areas of the body may be affected. The acupuncturist, having made a diagnosis, will work to directly re-channel the flow of *qi* by inserting needles into the body. This will stimulate the affected point or divert energy to the required area.

- *Tui na* (literally, 'push-pinch') is called acupressure in the West and works on the same theory as acupuncture, without intrusion into the body. It can nevertheless be mildly painful.

- *Baguanzi* (cup therapy) is interesting and rarely reported in the West. After an examination, the doctor will place glass cups with hoses and one-way valves on the patient's body. A vacuum will be drawn which sucks the skin in the chosen area and draws the blood to the surface. After perhaps five minutes, the cups will be cloudy with mist and drops of liquid will be forming on the surface. This is the negative *qi* being drawn out of the affected area. The cups are then rapidly removed (pop!), the skin is massaged and liniment applied. Finally, the doctor might apply *moxa* (a bundle of burning herbs). These are gently stroked close to, but not touching, the skin. The patient will then be told to quickly put his or her shirt back on.

- Herbal medicines are frequently prescribed. Each herb has its own properties, according to the table of the five elements. Different herbs will be prescribed, depending on whether you have, for example, a deficiency or excess of heat or wind. You might receive prepared powders to be taken with warm water, or you may be given raw herbs to be boiled down in a clay pot to form a strong-tasting decoction.

Traditional medical theory is understood on a folksy level by the average Taiwanese. You may be warned not to take cold drinks, to wear a T-shirt under your clothes, to get out of a draft, not to eat spicy things, to eat spicy things, etc. This advice will be proffered with the best intentions and is based on the common understanding of health promotion. It is best to thank the person for their advice, ask them for more information about the reasoning behind the thought, and reply that you will definitely take it into consideration. But note that, although thoroughly understood by physicians, not all people remember the reasoning behind their advice. It has become for them a kind of folklore of prevention and remedy.

MARTIAL ARTS AND LONGEVITY EXERCISE
The popular martial arts of China have all been directly influenced by the traditional concepts described above and have, in turn, greatly influenced modern culture. You can

observe Taiwanese, young and old, partake in these arts if you are willing to rise early and go to the public parks at about 6:00 am. Taoists believe that in the very early hours (4:00–5:00 am), trees give off *yuan qi* or 'original energy'. This is the best time of day to do exercises and breathing that will absorb this energy. The bigger, healthier, taller and older the tree, the better the breathing.

Shaolin boxing came from the Buddhist Shaolin Temple. It is an energetic, comparatively acrobatic method, popular with the young. *xingyi chuan* (*hsing i chuan*, or 'form and intent boxing') is based on the interaction of the five elements and is a focused, largely linear art. *Ba gua zhang* (*Pakua Chang*, or the 'Eight Trigram Palm') is based on changes exemplified in the eight trigrams and 64 hexagrams of the *I Ching*. The student of this art is trained to repulse an attack by using the power of circles and vortices. *Tai ji chuan* (tai chi chuan, or 'grand ultimate boxing') is based on the principle of perfectly matching one's motion to the opponent's *yin* and *yang* in motion. It is usually practiced very slowly and with deep concentration.

You are never too young to start learning *Tai ji chuan.*

GEOMANCY

As of late, Chinese geomancy has begun to get a lot of press in the West. In Mandarin, the proper term is *feng shui*, which literally means 'wind and water'. It is the subtle art of crafting one's personal space to match one's mystic constitution. Properly choosing the direction one's bed faces, the elevation and position of one's house (relative to the natural surrounding elements), or adding the correct natural elements into an unnatural urban or office setting can motivate the flow of beneficial *qi* and discourage the entrance of pernicious influences. Health, wealth, and happiness may soon follow.

A Taoist geomancer can be employed (much as a diviner is in the West when searching for the location of a well) to help determine the best possible setting for your home or business, given the environment you have chosen. He will ask you some questions, walk the surroundings of your house or office, and frequently consult his *luopan*. This is a round or octagonal wooden plate, with a compass embedded in the centre. Radiating from the compass are lines (latitudes) intersected by circles (longitudes) which create boxes in which Chinese characters are written. At the periphery, there are 64 Chinese characters and hexagrams from the *I Ching*. By examining the direction of your setting, relative to surrounding elements and geography, he will determine whether good influences need to be brought in from one direction, or bad influences diverted from another. He may then prescribe modifications to the location of furniture (if you are lucky); the acquisition of some minor items, like a tree or aquarium (if things are not too bad); some structural modifications to the building, like changing the angle or hinge position of a door, putting a window where there is now a wall or vice versa (if the situation looks tough); or, at worst, recommend that you move or tear the whole building down (and it has happened!).

As a Westerner, your perceived lack of understanding of Taiwanese principles of life will be magnified. A Taiwanese boss who apparently lacks any knowledge of or belief in *feng shui*, would be accepted by his employees, at least until some bad luck befell one of them or the company. But, behind your back or in front of your ears (in language you do not understand), your employees will be sizing you up for your sensitivity and knowledge of what might be important to Taiwanese. If you are looking for an office site with your assistants, ask about the *feng shui* of the various options and seriously include it as a consideration in the final assessment.

The above concepts imbue many aspects of life in Taiwan and China with a flavour the Westerner might find superstitious. They are best not treated as such. For example, a modern university-educated Taiwanese might nonetheless describe your post-teen acne problem as a manifestation of 'excess heat or fire'. Were you to go to a Chinese doctor and receive treatment, you might even be pleasantly surprised by the results.

All of the above traditions weigh on the Taiwanese in a smorgasbord of spirituality. With some accuracy it can be observed that Confucianism dictates one's relationship with family (living and dead) and, to a lesser extent, with society; Buddhist beliefs dictate one's considerations of a personal afterlife and the need for compassion in this life; and Taoism indicates the path one follows in interacting with the world. There are other spiritual influences and manifestations and, in the temple, the smorgasbord is replete.

The Lunar Calendar

Based on astronomical observations, the Chinese developed a lunar calendar of 12 moons. The Chinese word for month is *yue* (moon). Because the traditional 'farmers' calendar' (*nongli*) is based on the lunar cycle, the dates of some holidays vary every year. The Lunar New Year is not on 1 January, but falls somewhere between 15 January and 15 March. Dates fixed by fortune-tellers as good or bad for certain activities are always expressed in *nongli* dates.

Chinese Zodiac

The Chinese zodiac is made up of 12 animals. Unlike the Western zodiac, which attributes one animal to one month, the Chinese zodiac attributes one animal to one year. The year begins and ends according to the *nongli*. The animals each have different strengths and weaknesses, different compatibilities with each other and varying fortunes in each year. The dragon is the most auspicious sign. Read about the Chinese zodiac, understand your sign, and enquire as to the signs of others you meet.

SOCIALISING WITH LOCALS

'The story of A-bian and A-chen (the popular nicknames of President Chen Shui-bian and First Lady Wu Shu-chen), their courtship, marriage and political career, has become a folktale in Taiwan. She hails from a rich and prominent family in Tainan, while he was a poor farmer's son, living in a mud-house. Her father wanted his daughter to marry a medical doctor to continue the family practice, but she married the young lawyer against the wishes of her family, and didn't get a dowry.'
—'A Profile in Courage'
Taiwan Communique No. 92, July 2000

HOW ARE TAIWANESE PERCEIVED?

There will be as many perceptions of the Taiwanese as there arc foreign individuals who come from different countries to perceive the locals. Invariably what we have heard, learned and been told from afar is going to be different from what we will perceive after we arrive in Taiwan, as long as we keep our minds open to change. The person who arrives thinking all Taiwanese are short will find that the current generation, raised on a higher protein diet, is considerably taller on average than in the past. The person who arrives thinking all Taiwan manufactures are cheap imitations, will find that Taiwan is home to some world class, high-tech industries, such as polymer production and semiconductor manufacturing. The person who arrives with the conception that all Chinese are inscrutable and conniving, may get this perception reinforced or be disabused of it depending on how willing she is to scrutinise her own culture and how it relates to the Taiwanese. Remember, you are the visitor, it is their country, you are there to learn about it, not change it.

The unimaginative expression 'All Chinese look alike', has been heard uttered by Westerners. While this is not true, it will be a long time before the average Westerner can discern the subtle differences that exist in the height, bone structure, complexion and attitude of Chinese from different parts of that large nation. Taiwanese society is made up of native aborigines, Taiwanese immigrants from

Fujian province and the *wai sheng ren* who came from all over China after WWII. There has been a considerable amount of inter-marriage plus a change of diet fertilising the growth of the young generation. As a result, it is difficult, but not impossible to discern differences. We are guided by how we have heard Taiwanese describe themselves and other Chinese, but there is no foolproof sieve through which to pass what you see and the following is merely an awkward guide. Compared to northern Chinese counterparts, Taiwanese are 'generally' shorter, with flatter noses, broader cheekbones and slightly darker skin. That said, it would be wrong to apply this test until you have met several thousand Taiwanese and Chinese, learned where their ancestry hails from and mentally compared them to others you have met.

HOW DO TAIWANESE PERCEIVE FOREIGNERS?

Pride in their Middle Kingdom heritage directly influences how Taiwanese perceive foreigners. Ignore the fact that most Taiwanese are the descendants of farmers from Fujian during one of its poorest times; and ignore the fact that the major achievements associated with Chinese culture were not accomplished by the people of Fujian. It matters not. The emphasis on family ties, together with the indoctrination of the populace by an educational system based on their 'Chinese-ness' (serving to strengthen the ties to Mainland China for eventual reunification), inculcates them with a sense of cultural superiority. This colours how they perceive all others from outside the Middle Kingdom.

Locals and Foreigners

'We had finished our warm-ups and basic drills when a little boy, about five years old, who had been looking at me, came over to stare at my arms. Without a word or a second thought, he pinched a mass of my arm hair and tore it out, then stared closely at the blond fuzz in his fingers. After completing his examination, he simply walked off.'

—Chris' diary, 15 October 1976, during a martial arts class in Taichung

Once your ear is trained and tuned to Mandarin, you may hear others call you various names. These epithets are used frequently and loosely. They do not denote bigotry in the sense of racial hatred, but they are used condescendingly, if unconsciously. All cultures create terms to demean or belittle that which they do not understand or are not comfortable with. The Chinese in Taiwan are no different.

Epithets—What They See Is What You Get!

Lao wai is the least offensive, perhaps most endearing, term. It merely means 'old foreigner'. Come to think of it, most Westerners do tend to comment that the Taiwanese look younger than their years, so perhaps the inverse is true of Westerners. Another less benign term, which is frequently translated into English as 'foreign devil', is *yang gui*. Westerners were very definitely a plague on the Qing emperor, during which time this appellation came into use.

Then there are also the physically descriptive terms. *Da bi zi* is common and means 'big nose'. This is given to Westerners who, by comparison with the Chinese, appear to have typically large proboscises. If you watch Mark Salzman's autobiographical movie, *Iron and Silk*, about his experience teaching English and training martial art in China, you will notice the large plaster cast nose he has attached to his dormitory room door. Touché! The final epithet is *ang mo*, as used in the Taiwanese dialect. It means 'red beards' and alludes to Westerners' relatively hirsute bodies.

These terms describe outward appearance. They tell us what Taiwanese find conspicuous about foreigners. "But I am blond/brown/black-haired, not redheaded!" you protest. It doesn't matter; you are still an *ang mo*. A foreigner's hairiness is a source of much condescension. They see it as being related to one's general level of evolution, body odour, neatness, and civility. Remaining clean-shaven and well groomed will improve their impression of you. This also applies to women's leg and underarm hair.

A Lack of Communication
A tall, mustachioed American, conversant in Chinese language and more, once attended a cocktail party. He entered into a conversation with the wife of a Taiwanese diplomat—a college-educated, internationally travelled woman. She began to discuss how much further evolved the Chinese races are, as evidenced in their relative lack of body hair and smaller, delicate features. He proceeded to inform her of several ethnic, historic and cultural facts in support of his premise that her view was utter garbage. Both people certainly left the encounter maintaining their original views.

Size

Although the younger generation of Taiwanese are often as big as their Western counterparts, size is still a major concern when relating to foreigners. Taiwanese think Westerners are BIG! Big noses, big beards, big torsos, big bellies (sometimes), big muscles, big bones and big limbs. In proper proportion, this might be attractive to the opposite sex (Taiwanese man to Western woman, or vice versa), but it is intimidating to members of the same sex.

In the West, studies have shown that the majority of the top 1,000 company chief executive officers are over 1.8 metres (approximately six feet) tall. Size can be used at sales meetings, cocktail parties or in the boardroom. And size and success usually have a correlation. Not so in Taiwan. The height of many chief executive officers falls around the 1.68 metre (five-foot six-inch) mark. The foreigner should be aware that their size may be making those around them uncomfortable. In keeping with the local preference for humility, this person should make an effort to physically bring himself or herself down to the level of the people he or she is addressing. Sitting with the person, rather than standing, or standing one step lower on the stairs to talk are some techniques you might use.

Smell

Taiwanese of the older generation are sensitive to the smell of foreigners, which is likened to rancid butter and is believed to result from the consumption of too much dairy products into adulthood. Bathe regularly as you are likely to sweat much on this tropical isle. Popular international brands of deodorants are available at most supermarkets.

Skin Colour

Many Taiwanese view black or darker-skinned people even more condescendingly than they do the Caucasian Westerner. This applies to the South and Southeast Asian as well as Africans. It is generally felt that dark skin indicates a life of manual labour out in the sun. To avoid the stigma, Taiwanese farmwomen traditionally cover themselves from head to toe, leaving only the eyes exposed to the sunlight, even though the summer in Taiwan is extremely hot and humid. Parasols are still popular as are skin-whitening products.

Unfortunately, it is commonly felt that African peoples have nothing to contribute to the Chinese, unlike the 'Western barbarians' who at least have technology, money and markets. Until recently, one of the most popular brands of toothpaste in Taiwan was called 'Darkie' and its tube featured a black man wearing a top hat and beaming a bright white smile. Under pressure from race relations groups, the English name of the product was changed to 'Darlie', and graphic designers utilised more negative space in the design to obscure whether the person on the tube was black or white. Yet, tellingly, the Mandarin name of the product remains *Hei Ren Ya Gao* (Black Man Toothpaste).

As difficult as it may be for a European to fit in, we have seen many occasions where it is even more difficult for a Chinese person born and raised in the West to assimilate. Though they physically blend in, the accent with which they speak will give them away as 'not from around here'. Under the circumstances, Taiwanese will usually be less forgiving, less gracious and less embracing than with a European.

A young third-generation Chinese-American lady of our acquaintance was descended from immigrants from the Taishan area of Guangdong province. She physically resembled women from that area, short, light skinned and had a round face but spoke Taishan dialect and Mandarin with an American accent. By the end of a bitter year, she was ready to go home. She had found it impossible to get Taiwanese to warm to her.

THE INVISIBLE MAN

As obvious and extreme as Westerners' features seem to Chinese, they nevertheless are able to treat you as if you do not exist at times. This becomes even more apparent once you develop some fluency in the language. You might be sitting down at a table in a crowded fast-food restaurant and some local youths may sit down to join you. If they are especially polite, they might have the gumption to ask you in English whether anyone else is sitting there. Otherwise, they may just sit down as if they haven't even seen you But as they converse, the conversation will probably include some comments in Chinese about you, "Look at this guy. Do you think he can speak Chinese?", "Are you kidding! I have never met a foreigner who could speak Chinese." And so on and so on. Alternatively, you may be walking down the steps in an office building and pass two secretaries who comment on the *ang mo*.

In other circumstances, you might find attention being drawn to yourself, as Chris did when he spoke Chinese at a trade show exhibition stand. Although you are not invisible, it appears that the Taiwanese do not recognise you as a sentient being. They will poke their nose right into whatever you are doing or saying, crowd right up behind you, and maybe even proclaim loudly, "Hey, he speaks Chinese." Or, if you are unlucky enough to be involved in a road accident or other altercation, you may hear such unsettling comments as, "Hey, this guy's guilty/responsible/gonna get the electric chair!" Such statements are made as if you are not there to hear them.

We believe this behaviour stems from several roots. Firstly, the Taiwanese truly do not expect you to be able to understand their language, even if they are commenting that you are speaking Chinese; and secondly, you are from outside their family, their neighbourhood, their country, their culture, their lives. You are from a place which is of no consequence to them, but, at the time, present some momentary fancy, like an animal in a zoo. Under such circumstances, it is best to keep your cool, remember the purpose at hand (selling, persuading, extracting oneself from a delicate situation, etc.), and ignore or try to befriend the 'peanut gallery'.

Taipei has an efficient public transportation system and it is easy to get around most parts of the city.

An evening view of Kaohsiung. Located in southern Taiwan, Kaohsiung is the most dense and the second largest city in Taiwan.

The night markets are *re nao* (busy) places and offer tasty snacks and cheap bargains. Popular throughout the country, they offer a taste of local life and should not be missed.

Taiwan features some excellent restaurants, with an increasing number of modern ones and some unique traditional ones, like this restaurant in Taichung.

Families come together as they await the start of a festival performance. The Taiwanese love celebrations and festivals are often lively and elaborate affairs.

The flip side of this situation is when you walk into an empty shop and face the owner. As you enter, a look of mild panic drains their face. They are speechless. They do not want to lose face by not being able to speak English, but they believe it is futile to speak Chinese to you. They cannot ignore you, so what can they do? A few words in Chinese, no matter how badly spoken by you, will immediately return the blood to their faces, which will then sprout a smile. You have demonstrated ability in their language, they know what they are dealing with and can cope with it without losing face.

RELATIONS WITH ANG MOS

Taiwanese preconceived ideas about dealing with foreigners should be noted. Because China has had an urban merchant class for several thousand years, they feel they are masters of the art of bargaining. The bargaining stance will constitute almost all relations that you have with Taiwanese, until you eventually become friends. Any informal relation has the capacity to include bargaining; with your workers, your landlord, anyone you buy products or service from. By comparison, Westerners are perceived as lacking. They are frequently taken to be overly honest, gullible, naive and 'straight'.

This translates into inflated prices being quoted at shops, which leads foreigners either to a lifetime of vigilance to prevent being 'ripped off', or the attitude that 'as long as the price is okay by my standards, I don't care if the shopkeeper made a healthy profit'. Regardless of the path you choose, congratulate the boss on his skill in defeating you after every transaction. She or he will respond by praising you.

'Overly honest' and 'open' means that foreigners express their true feelings too soon and too deeply. This sort of honesty will not be returned and can be embarrassing to the Taiwanese. It can lead to a loss of face (yours or theirs) and it can also be used against you by the gossipmonger. Reserve (but not cold stand-offishness) is seen as a virtue. 'Straightness' is another difficulty. This is related to the above. Making very direct comments, or even asking pointed questions and going right to the heart of the matter, implies impatience and a lack of civility. "Why didn't you finish the report yesterday?" might be better asked as, "Is there a problem getting the report finished?" If the answer is "Meiyou wenti!" (No problem!), then you can push for a commitment, "Good, I can have it within the hour, then." Now a problem may be revealed. Always probe deeper in a gentle manner, but don't take 'yes' for an answer.

If you show this book to a Taiwanese acquaintance and ask if the above perceptions of foreigners are accurate,

Tips on Socialising and Etiquette

- Compliment English when it is spoken to you.
- If you are staying as a long-term visitor with a Taiwanese family, keep the following in mind. They know you are a stranger in a strange land. Hope for your own sake that they feel some responsibility for you. Normally they will, so you should not unduly worry them by disappearing for a night, or leaving for the afternoon without letting them know where you are going and when to expect you back.
- Give and receive gifts and name cards with both hands.
- Stay calm, especially when the situation is not dire. Taiwanese are as likely to get emotional when things are difficult, like after a fender bender, and are not different from foreigners in this regard. However, a foreigner might get ticked off when being fawned on by locals, and this would not be appropriate. Smile and enjoy their hospitality even if it was not expected.
- Face is given and received. Make sure you are aware of the relation to you of the person you are dealing with (older/younger, superior/subordinate). When Taiwanese insist on treating you, concede with grace after initial resistance. Try to find some way to return the treat.
- Remember that age is venerated in Taiwan and pay proper respects to the senior person in the room.

they will consider the question too straight and will probably give you an emphatic 'no' to avoid making you lose face unnecessarily.

LOW AND HIGH CONTEXT COMMUNICATION

Cultures tend to be divided into 'low context' and 'high context' varieties. This describes how people within the culture communicate. A low context culture means basically that people accept what is heard as what they will get. They do

- Tipping is not expected at restaurants and a surcharge is added to the bill for service. Do not tip taxis. Bellboys can be tipped NT$ 20 per bag.
- Always take off your shoes when entering a home. In some offices this is practiced, too. Follow the lead of your local guide.
- If you find your way on the road blocked by an impromptu funeral gathering, do not try to power your way around it. Find another route.
- Don't write friendly messages in red ink, as that is the colour of criticism on exams and protest letters.
- Don't loan or give the gift of an umbrella to a friend. The word for umbrella sounds like 'depart' and will lead to the ending of your friendship.
- Western attire is perfectly acceptable in Taiwan.
- Be aware of face. When it comes to a loss of face, there is a limit to how forgiving a local will be of an 'ignorant foreigner'. Learn to word questions so that they are exploratory, not challenging. Be aware of your face, too.
- *Ren qing wei* is very important to make Taiwanese comfortable with you. It is a high touch sincerity that can be felt and returned by another party. Be sensitive to this in your Taiwanese friends and reflect it back.

not seek secondary visual cues to support what is heard. The United States is described as a low context culture. When an American boss tells an American sub-ordinate that his performance has improved and he is recommending him for a raise, the subordinate will accept the comment as a compliment and expect an increased paycheque in the near future.

In a high context culture, however, much is communicated beyond the words. Tone of voice, facial expression, physical proximity, body contact, hand action, eye action and ritual all become part of the dialogue. If both parties are from that culture, both will understand that this unstated form of communication is taking place and they will end up with the same message. A fundamental stumbling block in cross-cultural communications occurs when people from a low context culture and those from a high context culture try to communicate, or when the meanings of visual cues and body language differ significantly between parties in the communication. Taiwan is a high context culture. Much is communicated through body attitude, visual cues, symbols and ritual (in the sense of prescribed action appropriate to the occasion).

RITES OF PASSAGE

In the life of every Taiwanese are events which have profound significance and which call into play their most deep-seated feelings about their cultural traditions. They represent how your friends were raised and how they are raising their families. It is worth reviewing these one by one and understanding what they mean to your Taiwanese friends.

Childbirth

Pregnancy, childbirth and motherhood are all very important to the Taiwanese. The extension of one's family is the only way to ensure that one will be taken care of in old age and in the afterlife. For a man, the birth of a son ensures the continuation of the family line and name, vital in Confucian thought. Because families are smaller than in decades past, even more attention is lavished on the mother and child than ever before.

The parents want to make sure the child gets off to the best start. This manifests itself in obvious and practical ways, such as eating nutritional supplements and highly nutritious foods during the pregnancy. However, other ways are more esoteric. A fortune-teller will be consulted to try to ascertain the most propitious date and time for the birth. Providing they are full-term, mothers might request to be induced or give birth by caesarean section at the appointed time. They will also consult the fortune-teller on the selection of a name. The fortune-teller does not select the characters, but rather tells the parents the propitious number of strokes the characters of the name should contain. Since the surname is never changed and the first character of the given name is usually the same for all the male or female children in that generation of the family, it means that the second character of the given name must be chosen carefully.

Family planning measures by the government have been successful in controlling population growth, except during particularly auspicious years, such as the Year of the Dragon, when they explode. A Chinese friend once commented to Chris that he had hit the 'cosmic jackpot' by having twin sons born in the Year of the Dragon!

After being released from the hospital, the mother and baby will customarily go into one month of traditional confinement called *zuo yue zi* (literally to sit for a month). During this time, she will be physically inactive, except for feeding the baby. She is also not supposed to bathe or wash her hair (although now they surreptitiously do), and she will consume vast quantities of tonic foods prepared according to custom and Chinese medical theory. The most popular Taiwanese postpartum tonic is *ma you ji*, a whole free-range chicken cooked in a steamer in a combination of sesame oil and rice wine. All the cooking and tending were traditionally done by the baby's maternal grandmother, but *zuo yue zi* centres have now sprung up around the island to provide the service in a hospice environment.

Childhood: Man Yue and Man Sui

Childhood begins when the mother and the baby come out of confinement at the end of the month. A banquet for family and close friends is held. The mother gets to dress up and go out for the first time in a month, perhaps display some jewellery she received from her husband for giving him a child, and the baby gets initiated in Chinese banqueting. Infant and mother mortality rates used to be quite high in China and this banquet celebrates that the mother and the child have survived the first crucial month. It is called *man yue* (fulfilling a month).

If you are invited to a *man yue* banquet, it is appropriate to give the baby a gift of 24-carat gold. There are many traditional medallions and wrist or ankle chains made just for this. Depending on gold price, they cost around NT$ 2,000–3,000. If you and your spouse are invited, one gift is sufficient. It will come in a silken red and gold purse, so wrapping is unnecessary. If a friend has a baby but you are not invited to a *man yue* banquet, do not feel put off. Buy a gift set of baby clothes or accessories instead. To do so is very *ren qing wei*.

A similar banquet is held at the end of the first year on the date of birth according to the *nongli* farmers' calendar. This birthday is called *man sui* (fulfilling a year). By custom, a Chinese child is one year old at birth. At the beginning of the next Lunar New Year, the child is two. When you ask a parent their child's age, they may quote you the Chinese reckoning. If you ask an adult their own age, they will probably quote the Western reckoning.

When children are very young, they are almost commended for being naughty. It shows that they are lively and *jing* (sharp). They are doted upon, paraded around, dressed up and played with by siblings and cousins. They are scolded now and then, but it is only to begin to imbue them with a sense of their own shame, their obligation to the family and their responsibility not to bring shame. As they near school age, however, there is an end to innocence. Life takes a sharp right-hand turn into conservative and regimented activity.

Schooling

The education of children is the very top priority for parents. After a brief working career prior to marriage, most women will settle down to either help in their husband's business and/or oversee the education of the children. Raising a family is practically synonymous with educating them. Such a high priority is placed on education because of the Confucian tradition. Under the system instituted in Confucian China, a government of career bureaucrats could all be tested within the system and achieve higher rank through further testing. Anyone, even a farmer's son, could hope to scale the ladder so long as an education could be provided.

Education is seen as an investment in the future when the children will have to care for the parents in their old age. The medical professions or university-level teaching careers are the preferred end results, though high-level business qualifications (overseas MBA) and technological science degrees (doctoral level) are increasingly popular. Couple this with an extremely competitive and exam-driven modern educational system, and you have a situation where children are pushed to study at all hours.

Schooling begins at the age of three when children enter pre-schools and special study groups for dance, music, gymnastics and math. Parents will scheme to get their children admitted into elementary schools with better reputations. Most children enter first grade already able to add and subtract single digits in their heads, as well as write a handful of Chinese characters. Through *bu xi ban* (remedial study classes, or cram schools) parents may try to keep their children one year ahead of their actual study level. Nine years of free compulsory public education is provided. However, beginning with junior high school, the student must take a battery of tests to determine their aptitude and the school into which they will get placed. Competition is fierce for the best schools and students will cram all summer in preparation. Again, they will cram to get into a good high school and again for college. Those who do not get into university fall into other categories of schools, junior colleges and vocational-technical institutes.

Children are motivated to study hard through shame ("Aiya! Only 90 per cent average on your test. Stupid!"), fear ("There is no way you can get into Tai Da University with these scores. How will you find a good husband?") and physical punishment (Whap!). Teachers can strike students on the palms with rulers or make them *gui suan pan*, literally kneel on an abacus. Occasionally parents will use the carrot rather than the stick and promise a motorcycle or other inducement if the child tests into a certain level. Schooling is based on rote memorisation and is very strong in math, Chinese language and history, and the sciences. It is weak in creative thinking and problem solving.

Birthday parties for all but the first year of life are not customary, although with the advent of MacDonald's party rooms, the Western party is beginning to catch on. If you want to buy a gift for a friend's child, educational presents would be most appreciated. The parents' feelings about toys can be summed up: they have no time to play!

A festival celebration provides a welcome respite for these Taiwanese children who are very often pushed to study at all hours so that they can achieve top scores.

Bai Shi

During your time in Taiwan, you may wish to seek private tuition from an old master. This might be to learn any traditional art: calligraphy, painting, *feng shui*, martial art, *qi gong*, medicine, opera, etc. Teaching was one of the most venerated professions in ancient China and to gain tuition from a traditional teacher requires one to approach him or her properly in a process known as *bai shi* (to make obeisance to the master).

It is best for the first meeting to be arranged by a Taiwanese friend, preferably one who knows the teacher. Take a gift for the teacher, but do not expect to see them at the first appointment. You may be made to wait or come back another day. If so, bring another gift for the second meeting. When you do meet the teacher, compliment him or her profusely and sincerely on the art you observe. The more favourably intelligent your comments, the better the impression left with the teacher. Do not expect to be accepted as a pupil at the first meeting. You may be told that it is inconvenient, that the teacher does not have any pupils or no longer accepts them, or that the language barrier is too great. You are expected to persist to show your sincerity. You may be asked to train with a senior student instead. If you are already versed in the art and truly feel you can only benefit from the master's instruction, persist in your request. If not, ask the master to check on your work from time to time.

You may be told by other students about tuition fees. This is best given to the teacher in a red envelope. Eventually, if you are happy with your progress, if you like the teacher and she or he likes you, you may ask to formally *bai shi*. This means you are now a formal disciple of the master's lineage.

Courtship

The sexes are largely segregated throughout high school and mothers continue to preach the virtues of pre-marital chastity to their daughters. Pre-collegiate dating is more common than before, teen pregnancies do occur, and young men do rowdy things. But, in general, the problems that plague Western society, like promiscuity at a young age, drug abuse, teen gang violence and graduates leaving school with no marketable skills, are not as extensive in Taiwan.

College is a time when those who have passed into the system relax. Once you get in, you can coast. The women remain more mature than the men at this point. Indeed, it seems that Taiwanese men mature only during and after the compulsory military service, which takes place after tertiary education is completed.

Real dating and courtship begin after the priorities of education and career path are taken care of. Couples might have a first chance meeting at a social gathering, at a temple, during morning training in the park, or at the invitation of a friend. To *zuo mei ren* (be a matchmaker) for a successfully wedded couple is considered very lucky. Taiwanese women plan for securing a suitable husband like a military campaign. They have a specific objective, specific tactics, and classically employ the least expenditure of their 'military resource' to gain the objective. There is tremendous face and security in bagging a good husband for oneself. Romance is a secondary consideration.

A traditional concept, still much talked about (especially after one has met one's beau), is *yuan fen*, or predestined relationship. This is the idea that certain people, young lovers in particular, are fated to meet and fall in love. Their paths are inextricably entwined. Mothers might look hopefully for some sign that this relationship was destined for their daughters. In the authors' own case, the circumstance of our meeting in Taiwan leads us to conclude that *yuan fen* exists.

Do not mistake this to mean, though, that shotgun weddings are common. In Mandarin these are described in the phrase *xian shang che hou bu piao* (to get on the train first and then buy the ticket). To get one's husband in this way is a loss of face and shows no finesse.

Engagements

Engagements are increasingly elaborate affairs. Before they take place, the groom-to-be must approach the patriarch of the bride's family and seek her hand in marriage. Crossing this hurdle can be easy or hard, depending on how good a prospect the groom is. However, a token resistance will always be given to test his mettle and sincerity.

After this, an auspicious date is set, sometimes with the help of a fortune-teller, always according to the *nongli*. An engagement ring is normally given to the bride-to-be. Invitations to the wedding banquet, called *xi jiu* (joyful wine) are sent out, accompanied by a small gift, usually cakes.

Prior to the wedding day, the bride and groom will go to one of Taiwan's slick wedding centres. Taiwan is now a major exporter of fancy wedding gowns to the West and the local women take advantage of this. At a wedding centre they will be shampooed, trussed, made-up, filled out, dressed in many varieties of high-fashion outfits and photographed at each stage of the magic to preserve their beauty at that moment for posterity. It is truly amazing what these artists can do with the raw material that comes through their doors. Location photography is also part of the package. As much as US$ 2,000–3,000 might be invested in this extensive collection of portraits and framed poster-sized pictures.

Like weddings, engagements ceremonies (here before the family's prayer altar) are increasingly elaborate affairs, involving great finery and expense.

Weddings

The big day arrives. The wedding might be held in a church, at home or at Taipei's City Hall. Less time is spent in planning the exchange of vows than the banquet. The banquet is a very big event, very important, and much face is attached to it. It is paid for by the groom's family. The size of the banquet is measured by the number of tables required, each seating 12 guests at a cost of between NT$ 12,000 and the sky as the limit! This price is per table for a set banquet menu not including drinks. An average-size banquet might require 30 tables. Bookings for the best menu at the best restaurant that can be afforded must be made well in advance for auspicious days.

The Hai Ba Wang (Ocean Emperor), prominently located at the corner of Chungshan North Road and Mintsu East Road, is an example of a banquet hall that caters to weddings. Formerly the Roma Hotel, all 12 stories were converted into a restaurant with private function rooms. Business is booming and they have set up branches in many locations.

The grandparents and parents of the groom and the guest of honour normally sit with the bride and groom at the head table, always located furthest from the entrance, next to a wall. Behind the table on the wall is a red neon light or silk banner with *Shuang Shi*, the 'Double Happiness' character on it. At other tables will be seated friends and business associates of the groom's parents, relatives from both sides, and you perhaps. For a description of proper dining and banquet etiquette, see chapter six, which deals both with casual and banquet dining and drinking.

You will need to bring a cash gift in a *hong bao* for the newlyweds. The amount will vary depending on their relation to you. You should give more if one of them is a subordinate, a very special friend or the child of an important business contact; less if they are just casual friends. The *hong bao* should contain at least NT$ 1,000 for each person you bring with you. If you and your spouse attend, that means NT$ 2,000. At the entrance to the *xi jiu* will be a table, perhaps covered in a bright satin cloth, on which people are writing names. The people at this table are accepting, counting and recording the *hong bao* given by guests. A *hong bao* is expected even if you are the guest of honour—an even larger amount perhaps. During the dinner, the newlyweds will go from table to table and toast each group of guests.

New Houses
Taiwanese friends of your acquaintance may at some stage buy a new house. As with people the world over, this is a big event for the Taiwanese. They may have a housewarming party or a banquet. If they have a party, or you are invited over to see them soon after they have moved in, it is appropriate to bring a gift. Mirrors, pictures, paintings and so forth are acceptable. Never send a clock. (*Refer to 'Gift-giving' in* Chapter 3: The Taiwanese *on pages 44–46.*) If you know which household appliances they are lacking, you might send one of them.

New Businesses
Many Taiwanese prefer to be masters of their own fate and often leave employment with others to start their own company. If your friend and business associate starts a new business, branch or factory, it would be appropriate to send a gift. Again, mirrors, pictures and paintings are appropriate, but this time the gift may be ascribed to you or your business. This is often painted on the mirror or picture. If a sample of calligraphy is commissioned by you for the occasion, it may be attributed to you.

Infirmity
Illness is a touchy subject. It is not considered good manners to say to a friend who has otherwise proclaimed to you that he is in good health, "Really, I don't know, you look a little pale to me" or "You really should have that mole with the hair growing out of it looked at." To make such statements is to wish the ill that you are implying on the person. Discussion of preventative maintenance is similarly frowned upon, so, however good your intentions, don't say things like, "If you don't cut down on the cholesterol you're going to wind up with a heart attack."

The Taiwanese most frequently pray for success in their undertakings. When moving house or opening a new business, suitable prayers to the gods for prosperity will be made in the temple.

Discussions of wills are also sensitive, but the custom is that all undesignated property goes to the oldest surviving male in the family. Some people might even find a discussion about the purchase of life insurance rather touchy. Such insurance is a growing business in Taiwan but it seems that the selling strategy used by the insurance companies is to turn the policy into a bet of sorts, and Taiwanese love to gamble: "We bet you won't live X years. If you do, we pay $ Y. If you don't, well we pay $ Z."

When a person does take ill with a serious affliction, it is not uncommon for the family to approach the best specialist in the field and beg him to treat their relative. Gifts and red envelopes have been known to trade hands to get the needed appointment for surgery. If the doctor were to decline to take the gift on moral grounds, they would lose stature and face. He might be magnanimous and say he will do it cheaply or without being paid because they are nice people, but, should the relative survive, the family will still try to bestow the gift on him.

If you are made aware that a person has taken seriously ill and would like to see you, then by all means make the effort to do so. Talk about pleasant things: hope, recovery, your last golf game. Nice books or magazines, CDs or special foods and fresh fruit are appropriate. Another alternative is a living plant for long-term illness, but do not give cut flowers as they are used at funerals.

Funerals

Sadly, you might be called upon to attend the funeral of a friend during your stay in Taiwan. Funerals are a time when everything you have so far read about Taiwan comes into play: Confucian ethics and filial piety, face, traffic, the high price of land, *feng shui*, money in envelopes, communication with the spirits, *ren qing wei*, everything. You will certainly observe funeral processions during your stay in Taiwan. You may even be invited to participate in one. Even if you do not, it is important to spend some time understanding the beliefs behind funerals because, in Taiwan, how people die is a key to how they have lived.

Funeral customs vary between the Taiwanese and the *wai sheng* peoples. They are somewhat subjective and very extensive. Let's walk through a typical upper-middle-class death of a patriarch, realising that variations on a theme do occur.

Mr. Su dies at the age of 54 from a massive heart attack brought on by years of eating a lunch of stewed fatty pork on rice with a hard-boiled egg. He never even makes it to the hospital because the ambulance is delayed by afternoon traffic. He did not think himself ill, has no insurance and no will.

His wife is bewildered and not sure what to do, but well-intentioned relatives begin to tell her. Unfortunately, they do not agree on what would be the appropriate face to give her husband and she is soon made more upset and confused. Her son, 20 years old, gets leave from the army to help prepare the arrangements with her. In their mind, there is no question that Dad must be buried rather than cremated—no face in that. So they request the body to be transferred to a funeral parlour on Minchuan East Road. They pick out a casket—a fine hardwood model hewn from one log and with the traditional rounded sides and lid.

The body is dressed in many layers of clothing, six in his case. Clothes of natural fibres are preferred because they decay at the same speed as the body. The casket is brought to the Sus' home and a final viewing of the body is held. Then the casket is closed and painted. The paint acts as a seal to keep the stench of decay confined.

Tradition requires that mourning take place for 49 days (seven days a week, for seven weeks). Because they have a ground floor unit and can afford to do so, Mrs. Su opts to keep the casket in their parlour, which is converted into a place of mourning. A white sheet is suspended around the casket area and a prayer table with a brass censer and candlesticks is placed in front of it. Condolence gifts begin to arrive from friends, relatives, and business associates. These are either wreaths of artificial flowers with a message penned on a centre circle of paper, or pyramids of canned foods, beer, boxes of monosodium glutamate and rice wine. These also have messages attached.

Through the weeks, people visit to chat with the family, burn incense, ask about how the funeral plans are going, and throw in their unsought opinion about how the funeral should be handled.

Mrs. Su has asked her son and her husband's younger brother to pick out a burial plot. This is no mean feat. They must find a plot that has acceptable *feng shui*, is reasonably accessible for the yearly tomb sweeping, is allowed to be used for burial, and is affordable. For two days they search through the hills and valleys around Gwan Yin Mountain (just across the flood plain southwest of Taipei), talking to farmers, mountain men, tombstone carvers and funeral directors. They finally find a suitable location, but the asking price is NT$ 1,125,000 for an elevated piece of earth 11 m (36 ft) wide and 11 m (36 ft) across, with a view of a valley.

Fierce negotiation takes place and they finally wrest the plot for NT$ 1,100,000. Quotes are obtained from stonemasons and landscapists. Designs are weighed and selected.

In recent years, the cost of interment in a cemetery has risen beyond the reach of the average Taiwanese. Cremation has become increasingly common. For a booking fee plus annual maintenance charges, the urn of ashes can be kept in a labelled locker either in a temple or a purpose built, multistory mausoleum. These are usually located in mountainous areas with fine views and good *feng shui*. They have VIP floors, their own minibus transports from mass transit stops and a staff of attendants. Monks will occasionally burn incense and perform rites. In Mr. Su's case, the family is wealthy enough and feels such pressure to maintain family reputation that they opt for a cemetery.

The son and brother are expected not to shave during the mourning period. It reflects their sacrifice of personal material comfort, although, in modern Taiwan, some men opt for just growing a moustache during this period or even continue to shave. The men and women have all used a safety pin to attach a small piece of black cloth to their shirts and blouse sleeves. They also eschew brightly coloured clothes during this time, especially lucky colours like red. To wear them would be symbolic of celebration over the loss of the family member.

Meanwhile, plans for the funeral are under way. The guest list is drawn up and announcements printed on white cards are distributed. Mr. and Mrs. Su are nominally Buddhist, so some monks specialising in funeral chants must be hired. The funeral reception area has been extended out the front door and into a tarpaulin-covered area in the street. They have talked nicely to the local police constable to beg his forbearance and have sent a little card of apology to the neighbours for any inconvenience.

On a chosen day, several weeks before the funeral, the immediate family gathers to perform a *bai bai* (a ritual obeisance). Mr. Su's youngest sister, 30 years his junior, has just gotten married within the month and she is excused from all the ceremonies. During these grim affairs, relatives judge one's grief by how loud one sobs and how drained of tears one becomes. Traditional Chinese oboe and cymbal music, together with chanting, can be heard. At specific times, certain members of the deceased's family are expected to come forward, bow, kneel, prostrate themselves, kneel, stand, bow, and repeat the process three times. This is known in the West as 'kowtowing', but it is actually pronounced *koutou*, meaning to knock the head.

Seven weeks after the death, the family has another *bai bai*. This time the accoutrements necessary in the afterlife are made in paper miniature and burned after making an offering. Bales of spirit money, metallic paper Mercedes Benz cars, paper clothes, houses, mahjong sets, everything the well-heeled man with lots of time on his hands (an eternity to be exact!) would ever need. The spirit money is for those sundry expenses he is expected to run into. The fires of hell burn cooler and the doors to heaven open easier with a little grease.

On a different day, a *bai bai* is held for more distant relatives, friends and associates to participate in. This may also take place on the day of the funeral. On this day, the family performs an obeisance again. Traditionally, Taiwanese would dress from top to toe in coarse white fabric and burlap and wear rough woven rope sandals on their feet. This, again, is a symbol of grief and the sacrifice of personal material comfort. The Su family have opted for just a hood and cape of burlap worn over street clothes during the prayer and final tears over the coffin. One, two, sometimes three musical troupes will be playing during the funeral. They have employed just one.

You were a friend of Mr. Su's and have been invited to attend. At the funeral, similar to a wedding banquet, will be a table to leave money. This should be in a white envelope, not a red one. An odd amount, in excess of NT$ 1,000 is recommended. Follow the lead of those near the casket. Approach the person handing out incense and pay your respects. Feel free to ask questions. You may take photos, but ask first. You will be welcome to go all the way to the burial site, but it is not expected.

The family and friends accompany the bier from the residence to the funeral wagon. This brightly decorated truck has row on row of orange, yellow and green plastic flowers. Above the cab is a photograph of Mr. Su and his name. The family accompany the casket on this truck, followed by a procession of trucks with bands, participants and scores of plastic flowers. The procession goes around the deceased's neighbourhood, his old haunts, and then heads out to the burial ground. If the procession gets stuck in traffic, there is some concern because the coffin must go into the ground at the specific time chosen by the fortune-teller.

The relatives and friends will help to carry the coffin to the burial place. A fortune-teller has provided a list of which zodiac animals should not actively participate in the ceremony, so people born in those years must just observe the proceedings. One cousin of Mr. Su's, who pretends to be an expert on *feng shui*, saw the burial ground after it was bought and declared that the *feng shui* was bad. His implication was that the family were being unfilial. To counter this, Mr. Su's son and brother have hired their own *feng shui* expert. He declares the site sound as they put the casket in the ground and he instructs them on how to precisely align the box according to geomantic forces.

Before covering the casket with earth, it must be cracked open to release the spirit within and to admit a fresh supply of oxygen to help the corpse decay. All participants are asked to turn away from the coffin when this is performed. It is considered bad luck to look. There is a tradition in China that, after eight to 12 years, the remains are exhumed. The bones are scraped clean, dried and arranged in a special way in an earthen pot. They can then be stored at the burial site in a small mausoleum. We have also heard this is a *wai sheng* custom, adopted by those who hoped to return to Mainland China after their deaths.

After the casket is buried, spirit money is distributed and burned, and hard-boiled duck eggs are given out. One traditional custom was for a hard-boiled duck egg to be placed in the casket with the dead. The implication was that only when the egg hatched (i.e. never) could the deceased come back to haunt the living. This custom is modernised at Mr. Su's funeral, where the eggs are consumed at the site and the broken shells scattered over the grave.

RELATIONSHIPS

It should be clear by now that tradition, based on the guidelines laid down by Confucius and his followers thousands of years ago, is still influencing how the Taiwanese live their lives. This also applies to all kinds of relationships that exist among the Taiwanese. However, the fly in the ointment here is modernisation. Whether the Western liberal tradition is to blame, as many social critics trumpet, or whether this is the inevitable direction that a people take when faced with industrialisation and departure from the farm, is a debate sociologists can take up. But change is taking place and where old and new continue to chafe, sparks will inevitably fly.

Familial

In the family, this change frequently manifests itself as children who do not *ting hua*, or listen to their elders the way they are supposed to. The old complain that the young grow up, leave home and do not care about them or for them. Continuing the shame-based culture, they lay a 'guilt trip' on their children. In one respect, it is fortunate that the remnants of the extended family still prevail; it means the elderly are cared for by their children. There is no mandatory social insurance in Taiwan, so children must hope their parents have savings, or be prepared to take them in. On the other hand, parents frequently invest their savings in their children's education, with the explicit expectation that they are making an investment that will provide a return to them in their old age.

Gender roles are also affected by modernisation. Women work more and for longer hours, and they have greater expectations of freedom and voice in marriage nowadays. Women's rights have been protected by law since the 1940s, but it is very difficult to legislate equality when half the population does not agree with it and the other half is not in political control to enforce it. For sure, the situation for women in Taiwan is better than it has ever been and most women are content with the pace of change. Men trying to cope with the change find that old role models do not work anymore. Some are left confused and frustrated. Divorce, considered to be evidence of the weakness of Western values, is consequently on the rise.

Sexual Norms

Sexuality is also changing. While rather reticent when it comes to discussing sex, the Chinese are not prudes and have a long and colourful history of sexual techniques, experimentation and enjoyment. Sex is neither something to be displayed nor is it something of which to be ashamed. It is natural, it is enjoyable, it is not sinful, and it is the act that brings family and future to the world.

Traditionally, premarital sex was not unusual, if you include concubinage (which is now outlawed but still practiced informally). But the concubine could never compare herself to a 'number one' wife: she had no rights, her children were not the heirs of their father, except through special circumstances, and if her 'master' died, then she was chattel to be exhausted or disposed of. Not all concubines ended up this way.

Empress Wu Hou started at the bottom rung of the ladder in the imperial household in the 7th century AD. She was so beautiful and skilled in bedroom arts (as well as scheming!) that she became the emperor's concubine. When he died, she became his son's concubine, eliminated his first two wives, ascended the throne by his side, saw his death, and then became the first empress of China! She was, by historical accounts, an able ruler but she had such a voracious sexual appetite that she apparently exhausted to death many of the men sent to please her.

In normal life today, mothers hope that their daughters might marry a kind, well-to-do man and become his 'number one'. That means saving herself for him on their wedding night. Chinese mothers even today perhaps equate premarital sex with concubinage, or letting the man sample the goods before he has made a commitment, thus spoiling the girl's chance of finding a 'good' husband. They consider easy virtue to be a poor bargain—stupid but not sinful. Young couples in Taiwan do engage in premarital sex and occasionally move in with each other. Among more traditional or rural families, if this is discovered, the young couple may be forced to marry, even though the girl is not pregnant. More frequently, in modern city families, it is tolerated, but with a chorus of laments from mama.

Interracial couples certainly exist, both Western men with Chinese women and vice versa. Such couples must overcome the regrettable stigma attached to Westerners— the legacy left by the United States military after their use of Taiwan as an R&R outpost during the Vietnam War. Chinese women seen casually with Westerners at that time were irredeemably equated with whores, whether they were or not. Even recently, this meant that women who married Westerners had to maintain a very proper bearing in public, or be frowned upon by society. It was not until the 1980s that young women seemed to partially liberate themselves and could be seen relaxing with foreigners and having relationships with them. One would doubt, though, that they would ever admit such a past to a future Chinese husband.

What about homosexuality? It is legal between consenting adults over 16 years of age and as this book goes to print, President Chen Shuibian's backing of a bill that would make Taiwan the first Asian nation to recognise homosexual unions has long been stalled in the Legislative Yuan. However, if homosexuality is used as an excuse by young Taiwanese males to avoid military service, they must undergo two years of psychiatric evaluation. Traditionally, homosexuality is proscribed by Confucian ethic because it is a union that cannot result in male heirs and if practiced widely would represent an end to ancestor worship. The Taoist view is, as usual, more practical. It does not proscribe homosexual relations, but prescribes the exchange of *yin* and *yang* energies that takes place in heterosexual union as healthy and even therapeutic. This exchange of energies is lacking in gay sex and alternative sources must be found in order to stay healthy.

Friendship

Lifelong friendships among the Taiwanese seem to evolve between 17 and 24 years of age. During this time, young people are entering college or vocational training, going through military service and establishing a career. The friendships Taiwanese establish at this time, when they are first breaking away from the confines of the family, seem to be the ones that last into adulthood.

As for making friends with Taiwanese yourself, the best advice is to be sincere and aware. Try to understand what your social relationship is with the other person, act within the observed bounds of that relationship, but continue to strive for an increasingly sincere and communicative friendship.

THE HOUSE VISIT

Unlike in Japan, it is very possible that you might be invited to visit the home of a Taiwanese friend. This will be a nice opportunity to get to know this person's family better and learn more about the daily life of Taiwanese. They will certainly be lowering the curtain for you, revealing more of their inner lives to a foreigner, so it is important that you make them feel comfortable about what has been revealed.

If you are invited over for a dinner, it would be appropriate to bring a flower arrangement or a bottle of whiskey or wine. Present this to the person who invited you or the most senior resident family member if your friend lives with parents. Remember that in most Taiwanese homes, the wearing of street shoes is not permitted. Always make the motion to take your shoes off. Only if the host insists that you can wear them inside should you do so. If asked to remove your shoes, you may be given slippers to wear.

You will probably be led into the *keting* (living room) to meet everyone. Acknowledge the oldest person first. Greet them and get introduced, then do the same to the other people present. Expect a fuss to be made over you. Do you want a drink? Do you want a snack? Was it hard to find this place? Are you hungry? Are you thirsty? Do you want a cigarette? Here's some tea for you. Here are some snacks for you. Please sit. Don't stand up on my account. You will hear the phrase *bie ke qi* (don't assume a guest's airs) repeated again and again. In other words, make yourself at home. Relax, but remain courteous. Accept this attention with good-natured gratitude, as if you are unworthy.

If there are children, they may come over to have a closer look at you. Talk to them in Mandarin or English. It is bound to provoke a reaction that will lead to some laughter. Taiwanese love children and if they see you relaxing with them, it breaks the ice. Unless you are very close to this family, though, it is better not to hug or have the children sit on your lap. Anyone whom you have not met before is bound to ask a lot of questions, so be prepared.

A Note on Bathrooms

During your visit you may need to use the toilet. There are several things to note. Many apartments in Taiwan have only one full bath. If that is the case, you may find a whole family's toiletries in there. Because of the location of drains and hot water, you might also find the washing machine. The floor will frequently be wet. Take all this in your stride. Before you enter the bathroom, you may be asked to put on a different set of slippers. These are plastic bathroom slippers. They keep your feet dry and prevent you from slipping on the wet floor or getting your other slippers wet. Do not wear your house slippers in the bathroom or vice versa.

There are two varieties of toilet in Taiwan. Most apartments are now equipped with the Western-style 'sit down' toilet. Especially when outside the home, though, you may find a Japanese-style 'squat' toilet instead. These take some getting used to. Squatting is, however, the most natural and 'ergonomic' position for bowel movement. Without going into indelicate detail, suffice to say that you face the drain-cowling of the toilet, place your feet on either

TRIGG

side of the chasm, and squat. Make sure your cuffs are not in the way and have your toilet paper ready. Most toilet paper for home use in Taiwan is not on rolls. It comes in plastic bales pre-cut into approximately 25-by-25 cm (10-by-10-inch) single-ply sheets. These are normally kept in a vinyl box on the cistern lid. Return unused paper to the box.

If you are staying for an overnight visit, you may want to take a bath. Taiwanese homes do not have central water heaters. They utilise wall-mounted gas or electric spot heaters that heat water only when turned on and activated by water flow. If you have any questions, ask your host. Also note that many Taiwanese homes do not have a bathtub. They have showers with no specific cubicle, the water going down a drain in the floor. They do not usually take long steamy showers. Traditionally, the Taiwanese would fill a large plastic pan with water and use a dipper to ladle water onto themselves, soap up, then rinse off with the remaining water. In today's world of decreasing resources, this is probably the most environment-friendly way to bathe. By looking at the facilities available, you will be able to figure out what the appropriate bathroom etiquette is. For instance, if you have left soapsuds or hair on the floor, rinse it to drain them away. Do not worry about getting the floor wet!

We advise you to bring your own towel if you go to a Taiwanese house for the night. Taiwanese will normally only keep one small towel per family member and this is usually the size of a kitchen towel. It is quite thin and is used for both washing and drying, being wrung out in between. You will not find a closet full of thick fluffy white cotton towels here.

SETTLING IN

CHAPTER 5

'Taipei weather is like a stepmother's temper.'
—Popular saying

Historically most visitors to Taiwan arrived by sea. Keelung in the north and Kaohsiung in the south are still visited by cruise ships and there is a regular ferry service from Okinawa to Keelung. But it is far more common for modern visitors to arrive by air. Taiwan can be reached with direct flights from most Asian capitals, as well as from New York, Los Angeles, San Francisco, Minneapolis, Seattle, Portland, Schiphol, Frankfurt, Johannesburg and Zurich.

There are presently two international airports: Chiang Kai Shek Memorial International Airport in Taoyuan, about 45 minutes (traffic permitting) southwest of Taipei, and Kaohsiung International Airport at the south-western tip of the island.

Taiwan has two international carriers: China Airlines was established by the government (not to be confused with the Civil Aviation Administration of China, the airline of Mainland China) and EVA Air was more recently set up by the Evergreen Shipping Group. Of the two, EVA has a much better reputation for safety and innovation. China Airlines' record has been marred by a series of crashes, and their ad campaigns and reduced ticket pricing reflect their need to re-establish the confidence of travellers. On the other hand, EVA has a good safety record and initiated a new class of service—the Deluxe Economy Class—which is proving popular with expatriates returning home on a budget. Tickets cost about the price of a full-fare economy ticket and the food is economy class, but the seating is more spacious and the check-in less crowded.

VISAS

If you are arriving with a valid passport from a select 30 countries, you may enter and stay in Taiwan visa-free for up to 14 days, otherwise you will need to apply for a visa in advance. The visa-free eligible countries as of the time of printing are: Australia, Austria, Belgium, Brunei Darussalam, Canada, Costa Rica, Denmark, Finland, France, Germany, Greece, Ireland, Italy, Japan, Republic of Korea, Liechtenstein, Luxembourg, Malaysia, Malta, Monaco, the Netherlands, New Zealand, Norway, Portugal, Singapore, Spain, Sweden, Switzerland, the United Kingdom and the United States.

Because of its unusual diplomatic status, most countries do not have Taiwan Republic of China consulates or embassies. Instead, special correspondence offices in many countries function as unofficial consulates. In the United States, for example, it is called The Coordination Council for North American Affairs. Applications for a visa can be made by post or in person. In the latter case, allow a minimum of two working days for it to be processed, although the time varies from office to office.

Short-Term Visits

If you are visiting Taiwan only once and plan to stay no longer than six months, apply for a 60-day visitor visa. This visa can be extended twice at police headquarters in Taiwan. If you plan to visit Taiwan more than once, request a multiple entry visitor visa. For this visa, it would be good if your Taiwan business contact sends you a letter or fax requesting you to come to Taiwan on business. A visitor's visa allows you to study, tour, or engage in business, but not to seek employment without authorisation, which is difficult to obtain.

Strategies for Long-Term Stays

Whether by insidious design or otherwise, the visa procedures for foreigners coming to work and live in Taiwan are difficult and time-consuming to navigate. The work permit regulations are in a state of flux and, at the time of writing, have caused much anxiety within the expatriate community in Taiwan.

You should apply for a resident visa and work permit before you seek employment in Taiwan. However, you have to first gain approvals from 'appropriate government departments' in Taiwan and then make an application at a consulate or official office abroad, not in Taiwan. Generally, resident visas are very hard to get.

Many expats have through the years skirted these regulations. There are many foreigners who have ostensibly lived and worked in Taiwan for years, even decades, without resident visas or work permits, and without paying taxes. They are not just maids. Hundreds of Westerners have taught English or run trading companies this way. So, how

Notes on Immigration

The changes in immigration procedures recently promulgated also touch the following areas, which are structural rather than procedural. Residence or work permits, along with alien resident certificates and overseas applications are all still required:

- Foreign Investment-Approved and Foreign Branch Companies. If your employer in Taiwan fits this category, the issuance of work permits to foreigners has been relaxed. The employer must no longer demonstrate that certain capital or income requirements have been met.
- Capital and Income Tests. In order to be eligible to hire foreign workers (i.e. get approved work permits), companies must meet certain minimum requirements. If it is a local company, its capital must exceed NT$ 5 million. If it is a branch of a foreign company, then the figure is NT$ 2.5 million. Companies set up less than one year need not demonstrate income to

did they do it? They simply renewed their 60-day visitor visa twice and at the end of every six months they would take a brief vacation (sometimes as brief as the one hour needed to get on the next plane back!) in Hong Kong, Seoul or Manila, only to return and renew the six-month cycle. Sometimes whole families would do this. Now, however, the government is finally cracking down, with the result that lots of foreigners are scurrying for cover.

The government is trying to replace the old convoluted and protectionist system with one that encourages honesty. The new rules are so new that expats are not sure how efficiently or fairly they will be enforced. Therefore, the best solution in trying to secure your long-term stay is to pursue the open way first. Your prospective employer in Taiwan will have to help you and your family to apply for the resident visa and work permit approval at the 'appropriate

apply for a work permit. If set up over one year, they must demonstrate an average income exceeding NT$ 10 million per annum. Trading companies must demonstrate average annual imports and exports exceeding US$ 1 million or commissions on trading exceeding US$ 400,000.

- The Long-Term Resident. If you have managed to stay in Taiwan continuously for five years with 'good behaviour' (no one is sure whether this means that you have not been engaging in black market employment), you will have the right to a work permit.

- If this seems too mind-numbing a way to secure a work permit, then you might turn to your company's accounting firm. Most international accounting firms maintain consultancies which can provide assistance in wading through the bureaucracy…for a fee. The latest information from the government is available in English at http://iff.npa.gov.tw/fore-eng/en_index.htm.

government department' and then at the Ministry of Foreign Affairs. When approval is granted, you can then make an application to the consulate abroad.

If you are hoping to reside but not work in Taiwan, the best alternative is to enrol in a language course at an institution recognised by the government. You can then get a resident permit based on your student status. This does not allow you to legally work. You will need to travel abroad once more to get your resident visa processed.

Within 15 days of your arrival with your resident visa, you must still go to the Foreign Service Centre of the police and apply for your alien resident certificate. Before you depart Taiwan for business or pleasure, you must apply for an exit permit. This normally takes two to three days to process.

Customs and Immigration

Once you have secured the necessary visa and are finally on the plane to Taiwan, you will be given a three-part form. This is used both for immigration and customs. It should be filled out in pen prior to getting in line. At the airport, immigration counters do not distinguish between Republic of China and foreign passport holders, so you can line up at any counter.

From immigration you proceed to pick up your baggage at the carousel. At Chiang Kai Shek International Airport, there are free trolleys for use. At customs there are three categories of inspectors: those for Taiwanese, those for diplomats, and those for foreign passport holders. Produce your passport and the customs form that the immigration officer folded into your passport, and then put your bags up on the counter for inspection. Unlike some other countries in Asia, in Taiwan you will not be waved through without some scrutiny. Sometimes all your bags will be checked, sometimes only one.

On the customs form you should note anything exceptional that you are carrying. A list of restricted items is available from the customs, but needless to say the carrying of weapons, illicit drugs, and pornography will result in big trouble. Printed matter from Mainland China or anything which is critical of Taiwan might be confiscated, though this has been relaxed considerably. Gold bullion and large quantities of currency must be declared or it can be confiscated. Report the approximate amount of currency you are carrying. You do not have to account for every penny. If, however, you are carrying more than NT$ 40,000 (around US$ 1,600 at the time of writing), you are required to have a permit from the Ministry of Finance. Carry your allocated purchases of duty-free liquor and tobacco conspicuously to avoid delays.

There is a section of the form devoted to unaccompanied baggage. If you have household items being shipped separately that are already en route, check with your moving company for what the procedures are. You may have to attach a bill of lading or declaration onto your customs form. Also, if you want to leave some items at the airport or if the customs officer wants to hit you for duty on something you can temporarily live without, you can put the item in storage before going through the customs. Do not lose the receipt, and allow sufficient time when you depart Taiwan for the airline to claim it from customs and put it on the plane for you.

Transportation from the Airport

Kaohsiung Airport is located at the edge of the city, and if you are going to a hotel there, a taxi is your best option. From Chiang Kai Shek International, though, it is best to weigh your options. The bigger hotels maintain a limousine service that can meet you and take you right away to your hotel. If your company has a presence in Taiwan already, they may have special rates for this service with the hotel. Book through your company as this is otherwise the most expensive option. Taxis are also expensive, usually about US$ 48 to the city. There is not an orderly queue. Cabbies may try to hustle you into their car. Ask for the price before you get in the cab. Occasionally you can arrange to share.

There is a convenient bus service from Chiang Kai Shek International. Right after leaving the customs area, immediately ask for directions to the airport bus counters Buy your ticket first at a ticket window then walk outside to the boarding area. The current price to Taipei is NT$ 110 (around US$ 3.33). There are two choices of bus. One bus makes several stops on the way to the Sung Shan Domestic Airport in the north-eastern quadrant of the city. The other bus goes to the Santos Hotel and the Taipei Railway Station at the west and centre of the city. Pick the best one according to your ultimate destination. Get in the correct line, and when it is time to depart, you will be asked to put your bags beneath or on the bus, depending on your destination. Do not expect a receipt for your luggage. Buses depart every quarter hour and the air-conditioned ride takes 45 to 60 minutes. From the downtown drop-off point, you can easily get a cab to your destination, usually for less than US$ 8. There is a similar bus service to Hsinchu (*Zinzhu*).

Unlike in some other Asian countries, foreign-exchange counters at the airports in Taiwan offer fair rates for exchanging your currency. However, travellers should note that the black market for US dollars no longer exists.

RESTING YOUR HEAD

It has been a long flight and a long day. You will be glad you made the arrangements for your accommodations before you arrived. You didn't? In that case, when you come out of the customs area, walk straight across the lobby to a row of hotel representatives. This is not the best place to make a booking as you cannot negotiate with them and the choice, though ample, is limited to those larger hotels that can afford (because of their rates) to have a representative at the airport. Alternatively, you can lug your baggage downtown, make some phone calls, and hope for the best.

Taipei has a growing stable of first-class, international hotel chains. These hotels are centrally located in banking and business districts, have good, but absurdly expensive restaurants, and cater to your every whim with business centres, pools, health spas, and a concierge who speaks your language. Be prepared to spend at least US$ 200 per night for the pillow. Breakfast will set you back another US$ 20. There are also some home-grown five-star hotels. Staying with these hotels will save you 10 per cent, but you will probably get a 10 per cent reduction in amenities as well. A tax and service charge will inflate your bill by another 23 per cent at all 'nice' hotels. Between four-star and no-star hotels is a sliding scale of price and quality. Prices can range from US$ 140 for a single room and move down to US$ 40, including breakfast. Rooms will come with bath, TV, and air-conditioning.

Besides hotels, there are the 'rest houses' which rent by the hour for couples who want to get away from the in-laws. These rooms are also available for the night, but cash-in-advance payment is required and no breakfast is served. They are usually decorated for sexual adventure: mirrored ceilings, round beds, lacy this and that, and a lot of pink. If you are not carrying valuables (which might be stolen) and are on a tight budget, the price range of US$ 20–45 per night may interest you. These are not brothels, though you may indeed receive a phone call soliciting interest, as they are frequently located in 'entertainment' areas of the city. Also in this price range are the various guesthouses, YMCA and such. Prices are quite reasonable, but the availability of rooms is usually limited. Try to make the necessary arrangements before you arrive in Taiwan.

If you are travelling on a budget, you will be blessed if you have a friend already living in Taiwan on whom you can impose for a few days. This will allow you the greatest of luxuries: saving money while learning about the country from someone in a similar situation to yourself. A week in such circumstances would be worth a month searching for your own options. One such option might be to stay long-term in a Buddhist monastery. This would, of course, represent the most fully immersed yet severe lifestyle possible for a foreigner. We are aware of only one person who had the guts to do this in Taiwan, but she was a fluent Mandarin-speaker and Chinese physician!

SURVIVING YOUR FIRST IMPRESSIONS

Unless you come from more chaotic places like Chernobyl, Calcutta, or South LA, then your first impressions of Taipei will more than likely be unfavourable. Even though Chris had studied Chinese language and culture for two years before coming to Taiwan, he still found much of what awaited him to be discomfiting. Many daunting 'first impression' images come to mind: traffic congestion, noisy diners, red and seemingly tubercular expectorations dotting the sidewalks (betel nut juice), air pollution, a garnish of Western values. All these are apparent on the surface, and if you do not look beyond what is apparent, you will miss the beauty, simplicity, cultural depth, and kindness that do exist here. To a certain extent, that is the purpose of this book: to guide you in what to expect and what to look for, so you can survive your first impressions and get on to the good parts. Read thoroughly, keep your eyes open for the good things that happen around you, and be patient.

ACCOMMODATION

If you are moving to Taiwan to work or study, you will want to find permanent accommodation quickly. If your company is transferring you and your family, it is wise to ask for a house-hunting trip. This will allow you and your spouse a chance to look at the local situation clearly before making the big move. It will also allow you to arrange for accommodation prior to packing and moving, understand better what things to bring and what to leave behind, give you a chance to get the work permit application prepared if necessary and will help to minimise the time you spend in a hotel after you arrive. There are, however, some service apartments and 'residence inn' type hotels which offer a midterm alternative while looking for your own place.

The Right Place for You

Before trying to find a real estate agent, it would probably be wise to tour the city, get the lay of the land, understand where your office is, where schools and recreation are located, and what types of areas cater to people with your budget. If people from your own company or expatriate friends could accompany you on this tour, all the better. Ultimately, only you know how close you need to be to the foreign community support net, how much short commutes mean to you, etc. In this chapter the focus is on Taipei, since that is where most expatriates wind up. However, if you are destined for Hsinchu, Taichung or Kaohsiung, it would still be useful to read on.

A Note on Locations

Volcanic fissures are abundant in Taiwan and have created the many soothing hot mineral springs people enjoy here. However, in northern Taipei especially, they add a heavy mineral content to both the air and public water supply. This rapidly and thoroughly tarnishes silver, silver plate, and lower carats of gold. Unless you enjoy polishing silver, have a maid to help or must bring your silver set for business entertaining, then we suggest you either leave it at home or move to a different part of the city.

Buy, Rent, or Share?

Taiwan real estate prices have been growing rapidly. Fortunes have been made and lost in land speculation in

Taiwan. If you have a resident permit, a fat bank account and a taste for risk, you might consider buying an apartment. The prices are high compared to almost anywhere else in the world, but if you are already from a major city or capital, you won't find them too daunting. Shop around carefully for the right area, compare prices and understand that you will most probably have to pay cash.

Renting is the option most people pursue. If you are interested in sharing, you can put a notice up in the American and other foreign clubs, in *The China Post* and *Taipei Times* (the two local English language newspapers), and at the many larger English cram schools where lesser-paid English and American expatriates tend to hang out.

Recent Property Rental Rates

Here are some recently quoted monthly rental prices for a range of three-bedroom apartments:

Taipei Business District	NT$ 50,000–80,000
Taipei Residential Area	NT$ 23,000–35,000
Taipei Suburb	NT$ 12,000–18,000
Taichung Residential Area	NT$ 12,000–25,000
Kaohsiung Residential Area	NT$ 7,000–10,000

The Real Estate Agent

This profession has a perhaps deserved reputation worldwide for being less trustworthy than the average citizen. In Taiwan, real estate agents are no different, but the rules of the game are new to you. The real estate problem in any country is the question of whom the agent acts for and how much they are obliged to disclose. In Taiwan, the agent receives commissions from both the landlord and the tenant. Keep your own interests in mind and speak to the agent as if they are the landlord. Do not 'show your hand', and do not let them know that your 'company is paying the whole bill and you just want to find a great place, to hell with the cost!'

If you look for rental apartments and agents only in the classifieds of the two papers mentioned above, you are sure to get stuck with only the most expensive expat-targeted units to view. Nevertheless, if you have not learned any Mandarin yet and have no one to help you with translation, these English-speaking agents may be your only recourse. It does not hurt, though, to shop around. Once you have selected a suitable location to live in, find a real estate agent in that part of the city. The hotel concierge or your office staff can help you here. Ask them to call to see if the agency has any English speakers; you may get lucky. Also remember that the more specific you can be about what is most important to you and your family, the better.

In Taiwan, for large, luxurious executive expatriate accommodations, landlords may demand six, 12, or even

What to Ask the Real Estate Agent

Before you meet with the agent, try to decide on the relative importance of the following:

- **Proximity to**
  Schools
  Expat shopping
  Work
  Entertainment and recreation
- **Environment**
  Spacious or small
  Green
  Suburban
  High-rise
  Detached house
  Urban
- **Price**
  No limit
  Budget
  No budget
- **Others**
  Car park space
  Security

24 months' rent in advance. For so much upfront cash, it is important before you place a deposit that you make sure what repairs or improvements need to be done to the place. These improvements may involve painting, woodwork, sanitary fixtures, lighting, air-conditioning, security systems, additional power points, satellite TV reception, kitchen equipment, and cabinets. The contract should specifically detail the required improvements, the quality of materials, who is responsible for what level of repair after you have taken over the property, who pays for supplementary expenses (guard, parking space, etc.), and the conditions of the deposit return at the end of the lease. Contracts should be in English and Chinese. For basic apartments, a one to three month deposit is customary.

Landlords are generally willing to accommodate renovations, but in return expect a long-term commitment from the tenant. Only place a fraction of the final payment (perhaps one month's rent) with the landlord or agent on signing the contract and reserve the remainder until all the work is done to your satisfaction. Expect the agent to help you negotiate, but do not let them know what your 'final offer' is until you reach that point and keep yourself fully involved in the negotiation. Expect the agent to 'ride shotgun' on the landlord to see that he honours all the terms and conditions of renovation.

For more information, you may check out http://www.poagao.org/phousearch.htm. An excellent website written by an American who has rented apartments in many places in Taiwan, goes into the detail of this ritual.

Ping-pong

The *ping* is the unit of measurement for floor area in houses, apartments and offices. Termed the *tsubo* in Japan, the *ping* corresponds to the floor area occupied by two *tatami* mats, an area which covers approximately 36 square feet. An advertisement might say, '48 *ping*, expat quality apartment, 3 bedrooms', which means that the square footage is about 1,728 square feet.

Home Appliances

Standard wall voltage in Taiwan is 110V, suitable for most appliances used in North America. A limited number of 220V sockets are normally installed for air conditioners and heavy appliances.

Not all apartments are equipped with ovens as Chinese cooking involves little baking. Know your budget, tour prospective homes before you move and find out what you will need to bring from home since you are not likely to find exact replacements of your favourite kitchen equipment.

You can operate TV sets from the United States and Japan, but not European PAL standard sets unless they have a multi-system function. Cable television is popular in Taiwan and your apartment might come equipped with it. HBO, CNN, Discovery, Star and other popular channels have Taiwanese versions (which are in English but subtitled in Chinese). To make a legal application for cable TV, call the News Bureau of Taipei City [tel: (02) 2728-7535] and request for a list of licensed operators in your residential area. Charges are generally NT$ 600 per month with an initial NT$ 1,500 installation fee. No ID or Alien Resident Certificate is needed. 'Pirate' cable operators charge a fraction of the normal cost but may shut down or disappear with your deposit. Hi-speed Internet is widely available in apartments. To subscribe, you will need your resident certificate number and the fees are about NT$ 900 per month.

Taiwan is one of the most modern mobile phone markets in the world. Like Korea and Japan, it is a market watched by the giants Nokia and Motorola to see what consumer trends and uses are driving mobile phone adoption so they can anticipate changes in other parts of the world. You can buy a new phone outright in a store, or buy it at a discount with a subscription plan or buy a used phone. Keep in mind, however, that to activate it, you will need to have a resident permit and local payment method (bank account or credit card).

GETTING DOMESTIC HELP

Taiwan is not the paradise it once was for expatriates, who could previously afford the luxury of a driver, houseboy, gardener and '*a-mah*' (housemaid/cook). The standard of living has increased so rapidly for all levels of society that it is difficult to find people to work as domestic help. If you are intending to hire a full-time, English-speaking Taiwanese maid, you are probably on a full-blown expatriate benefits package, but you must be prepared to spend considerable time finding the rare person who will be willing to work for you. There are, however, a few alternatives.

Previously, Taiwanese and expats alike had created a growth industry for imported Filipina, Vietnamese and Indonesian '*a-mahs*'. In recent years, the government has cracked down on the hiring of imported domestic help. Taiwanese may now only hire them if they have children under seven or parents over 75 who need tending. The barriers are set absurdly high for expats who seek this kind of help. Your company must have either a capital of NT$100 million or sales of NT$500 million, or your salary must exceed NT$3 million.

And this gets an imported domestic helper for only the CEO of the company! For detailed requirements and charges, see http://www.7777.com.tw/eng_qualifications.asp.

A better option may be to hire a part-time maid. Both Taiwanese and Filipinas perform these services. The best place to start looking is through friends, referrals and bulletin boards. The latter are maintained at some grocery stores serving the expatriate community in Tienmu and at clubs like the American Club. Expatriate families moving away will frequently put up a notice trying to help a trusted maid find a new employer.

Handling Domestic Help

Remember that a maid will have access to everything in your house and might be entrusted with your children's safety. Referrals or a discussion with the previous employer is strongly recommended. During the interview, explain fully what responsibilities, hours, time off, privileges, meals, holidays and rules are expected of the candidate, so you can determine if there is any resistance.

If you expect the 'a-mah' to help take care of the children, then it is best to have your kids meet her to gauge their acceptance. Finally, when you have made a selection, make up a weekly schedule of what is to be done and when. During the first week, help the maid understand how you want things to be done.

It is a good idea to agree in advance on a one-month trial period, during which time both parties can get to know each other. If this is your first overseas assignment, it is possible that this is also your first household help. Adjusting to managing the house rather than doing it yourself can be a shock (whatever you may think about housework!). Understand that this may be the result of your own frustration in dealing with the maid and don't blame everything on her. However, if either party finds the work unacceptable, pay for the number of days worked and resume your search. If after the one-month trial things turn sour, make a determination quickly and settle the matter with surgical immediacy. Make sure keys are returned and then change the locks. Be prepared to pay severance of 5 per cent of the total salary paid to date. Despite having to ask the maid to leave, be as positive as possible about the termination to preserve the 'face' of the employee.

If you are fortunate enough to have a yard, you may need to hire a gardener to help you. Maids do not do outside work. When looking for a gardener, you should follow the procedures outlined above.

BANKING AND MONEY MATTERS

If you are working and earning money locally, you may want to keep it safe in the bank. After you have your work permit or resident visa (required by most institutions), take your passport to the bank. If you do not have a Taiwan ID card, you may require a Taiwanese co-signer as a guarantor. Note that checking accounts are not common, local businesses do not want to accept them, so you will be issued an ATM card and wind up carrying cash around with you. Also note that most post offices have savings banks and ATMs. When your account is established, you can sign up for an auto deduction program to pay for your utilities bills. Some bills and traffic fines can be paid at 7-11 convenience stores. For more information and banking hours, see http://www.gio.gov.tw/taiwan-website/2-visitor/quicklook/1_facts/fact1_2.html#2

Taxes

In Taiwan, if you are employed you will be called on to make your contributions to the government. Taxes need to be filed by May 31 and can be paid through your bank. If you are employed in Taiwan for less than 183 days, your income is taxed at a flat 20 per cent. If you are employed in Taiwan for more than half a year, your income is taxed according to the table below.

Annual Income	Tax Rate
Up to NT$370,000	6 per cent
NT$370,001 to 990,000	13 per cent
NT$990,001 to 1,980,000	21 per cent

NT$1,980,001 to 3,720,000   30 per cent
NT$3,720,001 upwards   40 per cent

A lucid explanation of the tax situation, complete with tax office contacts in various cities can be found at:

http://www.englishintaiwan.com/taxes.htm.

SHOPPING

The routine of going out to procure the daily necessities of life can either be a frustrating and disgusting experience, or else a source of adventure, amusement, and cultural awakening. Most Westerners who venture to Taiwan will have been raised in a relatively sterile, pasteurised, processed, packaged-for-convenience, fixed-price world. Meats, for instance, have no relation to the animal they came from by the time we see them. They are filleted, breaded, cubed, ground and marinated. We are divorced from the source of our foods, the smell of anything but fresh meats and vegetables, and the rigors of bargaining for even small items.

Taiwan is a land of entrepreneurs. It is almost everyone's wish to be their own boss, to have a pushcart, stall, restaurant, shop, company or major corporation all their own. In Taipei, a walk down almost any avenue, street, lane or alley will take you past shop after shop after shop. The sequence of these small shops might go like this: cafeteria, stationery, pharmacy, clothing store, bakery, convenience, tire, hardware, video, clinic, repeat, repeat. Inside the stationer's, you can get newspapers, pens, all manner of paper and envelopes, file folders and usually some little toys and sports equipment. Occasionally they also sell stamps. The bakery will sell milk and soft drinks. The clothing store may sell fish from dawn to 10:00 am. Welcome to the real world of shopping in Taiwan!

Though the modernisation of consumer retailing is rapidly changing the way the Taiwanese shop, there are still many opportunities to enjoy the 'traditional' shopping experience. The *Yellow Pages* in Taiwan are available in English from Chunghua Telecom subscribers in limited quantities at no cost. When you register for your phone, make sure you inquire. Looking at the various guidebooks on Taiwan can provide you with the addresses of shops that sell the items you want. Copy the Chinese address down, or take the book along, and carry the phone number in case you get lost. An easier option is to make friends with local people who can show you around their favourite shopping haunts.

THE ART OF BARGAINING

Because they are their own boss, the Taiwanese entrepreneur can make decisions about prices and terms of sale right on the spot. This facilitates the 'culture of negotiation' in Taiwan. The art of the negotiated purchase is ancient and venerated here. Much zest is injected by the Taiwanese into any major acquisition by the thrust and parry of bargaining. Some Westerners from certain countries and cultures are more equipped than others to readily mesh with the bargaining scene in Taiwan.

A Bargaining Encounter

So, you have decided to purchase a TV and you have been to three stores to check the price of brand X model Y. You return to the shop that quoted the lowest and tell the shopkeeper you want to ask about the price again. He

---

Unwritten Rules for Bargaining

- Always start at a price lower than the price at which you expect to get the item.
- Know as much as possible about what you are getting and its relative value before going into the final negotiation. The merchant will respect the knowledgeable opponent and making outlandishly low offers or extravagant claims will insult the art.
- Keep your cool when negotiating. There is really nothing about which to get uptight. Smile with a firmly resolved face. Threats will not help.
- Remember there are things besides cash to be negotiated: delivery, installation and accessories should be included in the bargaining.

quotes you the same price. Ask what that includes. He
indicates that it includes an antenna, a remote control and
a one-year manufacturer's warranty. "What about delivery?"
you ask. "Where do you live?" he asks. You tell him and he
agrees. Now, tell him you are willing to pay the price less
15 per cent. He makes a large groan and grimaces, maybe
smiles, shakes his head, and refuses. "What is your best
cash price?" you ask. "Price less 5 per cent," he replies.
Offer the price less 10 per cent. He refuses. Ask if he can
include some video cassette tapes or a VCR hook-up cable.
He agrees. Offer the price less 7.5 percent. He refuses. Ask
him when he closes for the night, then make an effort to
leave. He may stop you. If not, keep walking. Go back to
store number two and try to get better than the price less
5 percent. If the manager of store number one does ask
you to stop, then smile and say you really want to buy it
with cash right now and you are just asking for 2.5 per cent
discount (the price less 5 per cent is now the established
price from your point of view). He may now agree.

Where and When to Bargain
With the advent of Western-style retailing, where and when
to bargain on prices has become clouded. About 20 years

ago, some shops began displaying signs that read *Bu Er Jia* (no second price, in other words, a fixed price shop). The shop owners' hope was to stop eroding margins by claiming that they would not countenance bargaining. However, most of them would lower the price if the purchase was right or if a local was buying, so the signs were largely ignored.

Now, though, with Western-style convenience, hyper-market and department stores, bargaining is definitely out. You could still try in other large stores, if you have the guts, but we can't guarantee the reaction of the store assistant. Some shops, like the occasional bookstore, might give you a discount, even if you do not ask!

Bargaining

Below is a guide (that is by no means complete) which serves to demonstrate the trickiness of this question.

Item or Type of Shop	When Bargaining is Accepted
Automobile	Required
House Rental	Required
Major Appliance	Required at small shops At larger retailers, negotiate for extras. This includes computers.
Small Appliance	Acceptable at small shops, not at larger retailers
Restaurants	Never, unless preparing for a banquet
Hotels	Room rates can be negotiated prior to checking in
Repair Services	Acceptable
Supermarket	Unacceptable
Department Store	Unacceptable
Small 'Mom & Pop' Shop	Acceptable if the purchase is above NT$ 1,000
Small Specialty Retailer	These might be selling shoes, clothes, toys, hardware, lighting, art, antiques. Acceptable for purchases of over NT$ 1,000
Street Vendor	Acceptable, except food vendors

A final word about bargaining. If you have finally managed to get the vendor down to the price you want and then whip out your American Express card, you will leave for home without it (the purchase that is!). Credit cards charge 1–3 per cent to vendors for purchases made with a card. Either be prepared to pay cash, tell the man up front at the beginning that you intend to pay by card, or allow him to put the several per cent charge on top of the purchase price.

GROCERIES

You have four choices in buying your groceries. These are listed on the following page, with comments about their relative convenience and expense.

- Home Delivery and Import Grocery Stores. The medium-sized grocery stores in expatriate enclaves have delivery services. This is both convenient and costly. They charge you the same price as if you bought at the store, but it is more expensive because, unless you specify the brand, they buy the more expensive imported label for you. These are the stores you will have to patronise to get specialty items for seasonal expatriate use, like turkey roasting pans and stuffing, for example.

- Convenience Stores (7-Eleven, Nikko Mart, President Bakeries, Family Mart, etc.). These stores have spread like termites throughout the major cities, eating away at and displacing the 'mom & pop' shops. Their opening hours are great and, while they sell many different types of items, you often find that there is only one or two of each thing on the shelf. Prices are also about 10 per cent higher than elsewhere.

- Supermarkets. Smaller than their Western cousins and increasingly popular, these are still 'super' on the Taiwanese scale. They carry a complete selection of fresh and packaged goods, meats, and dry goods. Prices tend to be fair and stable. But note that locally made packaged goods from these supermarkets will probably not have English labelling.

- Vegetable Markets (*cai shi chang*). This category deserves special attention on its own. For obvious reasons, other parts of Chinese-speaking Asia refer to these as 'wet markets'. If you go to one, do not dress up or wear a nice pair of white shoes. The concrete floor is frequently wet, either with rinse water or the effluent of raw foods (blood, slime, scales, etc.). Be prepared for a smell like nothing you have smelled in the grocery store at home. It is worth getting used to, though, for this is where the Taiwanese traditionally shop for all their food needs on a daily basis. This is where you and your children can be given free street courses in biology, dissection, vivisection, and animal anatomy. It is also where the full bounty of Taiwan's fields, orchards, streams, and seas is on display in all its freshness and glory. These market areas are usually set up by the government and the stalls are rented out to vendors who take the same spot every day with their fresh produce.

A Stroll Through the Wet Market

You will enter from the sidewalk, usually into a poorly lit area of rows and rows of small stands. Each stand usually comprises a table, around 10 feet by 5 feet, which has an array of goods displayed on it. Vegetable vendors are lined up together. Their tables might display many different kinds of leafy vegetables, for example *bai cai*, also known as *bakchoy* (cabbage), *kong xin cai* (kangkong) or *jie lan* (Chinese spinach). Alternatively, the stall might specialise, selling only garlic or chillies or sweet potatoes.

The meat vendors are also together; beef here, pork there, cooked chicken and duck at another stall. But do not come here to buy a New York-cut sirloin steak or, indeed, any recognisable cut of meat, beyond *pai gu* (pork chops). The Taiwanese use limited beef in their cuisine and do not use cuts that will be familiar to you. At the pork stall, you can see whole heads, sides, legs and accessories. Taiwanese pork is fresh and excellent, and you can get ribs, chops and loins. Only 30 years ago, in poorer times, the only meat many people could afford on a regular basis was sow's ears. Times have changed.

At one stand you can buy fresh chickens. Inside rows of cages are live pullets and roosters, clucking and crowing about. You can select a regular chicken or a *tu ji* (literally

Being a tropical island, Taiwan's fish markets are filled with fresh and delicious seafood.

earth chicken, i.e. free-range chicken) which Chinese chefs and nutritionists prefer. Don't worry about having to pluck the feathers. Pick out the chicken you want and the vendor will put it into what Chris calls the 'Wonderful Chicken-Stripping Machine'. The vendor will remove the chicken from the cage and deftly slit its throat. While being drained of life it is put into a device that looks like a spin washer. It is a stainless-steel barrel with rubber nails lining its internal surface. When the motor engages, the chicken bounces about inside at high speed (bing-bing-bong-bong!), while the vendor pours a scupper of boiling hot water onto the bird. Forty-five seconds later, a denuded bird emerges. The vendor will clean the guts out for you and give you the bird (head, claws and all), still at body temperature, in a plastic bag.

In the seafood section, you will see very fresh whole fish, squid, octopus, crustaceans and shellfish on beds of ice. Pick out what you want. A fish will be gutted and scaled while you wait, but will still be delivered to you complete with head. Note that vendors charge you for the weight of the whole fish before gutting, even if you ask them to cut off and discard the head. However, the fishmonger only charges according to the weight of the selected piece for choice cuts like a swordfish steak.

Then there are the soybean curd vendors. Bean curd, known in the West by its Japanese name tofu, is called *doufu* in Mandarin. Chris refers to it as 'The Cheese of the Chinese' since bean curd truly fulfils the nutritional requirements in the Chinese diet that dairy products fulfil in the West. It is also just as versatile. Most Westerners know bean curd as a whitish, soft, flavourless, custard-like substance. It is made from ground soybeans and water.

The Taiwanese eat *doufu* in many different ways, depending on how much moisture is removed. As a soup (full water), it is called *dou jiang* (bean sauce). Fermented *dou jiang* is called *dou zhi* (bean juice). Thicken and ferment it in a different way and you have Japanese miso paste, used as a flavouring and fortifier for a number of dishes. With the water squeezed out, it becomes large slab-like cakes. These are cut up and sold in smaller cakes. If it is extruded now, it becomes *doufu sz* (bean curd threads). If it is marinated and dried further, it becomes *doufu gan* (dried bean curd). If it is fermented, it becomes *chou doufu* (smelly bean curd). If it is deep fried, it becomes *zha doufu* (fried bean curd). Dried in sheets it is called *doufu pi* (bean curd skin).

At the vegetable market, you can also buy prepared foods: roasted chickens and ducks, barbecued sausages, pickled and salted vegetables, roasted peanuts and peanut candy, dried fruits and fish, etc.

Slim Jins

Supermarkets and convenience stores use the metric system for weighing goods and packaged foods. However, at the traditional market, the Chinese weights and measures system is based on the jin, for some obscure reason called the 'catty' in English. A comparison chart of the various metric, imperial, and Chinese weights and measures is listed below.

- 1 *jin*   1.32 lbs
- 1 lb   0.75 *jin*
- 1 kg   2.2 lbs
- 1 kg   1.66 *jin*
- 100 gms   3.52 oz

- 1 *jin*   0.6 kg
- 1 *liang*   1.32277 oz or 37.5 gms
- 1 *da*   1 dozen
- 1 *cun*   'Taiwanese inch' 3 cm
- 1 *chi*   'Taiwanese foot' 10 *tsun* or 30 cm
- 1 *gongsheng*   1 litre
- 1 *gongjin*   1 kg
- 1 *gongke*   1 gm
- 1 *gongli*   1 km
- 1 *yingli*   1 mile

Goods in the vegetable markets are sold either by units (for example, four oranges for NT$ 100) or by weight (NT$ 30 for 1 *jin*). Many displays of produce have signs made with scraps of cardboard and felt-tip pens that indicate how goods are priced each day. If you do not see a sign, ask before you have the vendor load up the bag or cut the meat to your requirements. The question to ask is, "*Yi jin duo shao qian?*" (How much is one *jin*?)

Generally, you cannot bargain at the vegetable markets. There are, however, many vendors of any particular item and we encourage you to spend your first day perusing the merchandise, asking how much, how much, and 'comparison shopping'. Some will let you squeeze and smell the merchandise, but some will be fussy and could complain if you do. Once you've familiarised yourself, settle on a group of vendors who will get to know you, know how you want your fish prepared, your ribs chopped, your pineapple shucked—whatever your pleasure. They will begin to anticipate your patronage and look forward to seeing you, even helping you to pick out the sweeter or juicier stock.

No White Sales

With the advent of large foreign retailers operating in Taiwan like Carrefour, it is much easier to find household sundries like towels and sheets. Keep in mind, though, that there is no single international standard for mattress sizes, so measure your mattress before you buy sheets. If you like a warm bed on a cold winter night, don't forget the electric blanket! A table of mattress sizes appears below (remember that in Taiwan, the package might be listing Taiwan inches rather than Imperial measurements.

Beds and Sizes	
Bed Type	Size in Inches
US King	72 x 80
US Queen	60 x 80
US Double	54 x 75
US Twin	39 x 75
US extra-long Twin	40 x 80
Taiwan King	72 x 74.4
Taiwan Queen	62.4 x 74.4
Taiwan Single Bed	36 x 74.4

CLOTHES

Dress standards depend on the industry or business you are in. In many offices, suits are rarely seen and a shirt and tie is sufficient. Leisure suits and sports jackets are popular with locals. But please note that Taipei and most of Taiwan has four seasons. Though this is a 'tropical island', you would not know it in the middle of a cold and dreary Taipei evening in February. Most homes and many offices are not heated. This means you will need lots of layers of clothing, but probably not the heavy, winter sort, which will make you overheat.

During the hot, humid summers from mid-May to mid-September (often 32°C /89.6°F, 90 per cent humidity), you need light cotton clothes. The spring and autumn periods are usually warm and pleasant, but the cool dreary winters in February and March (17°C/62.6°F , 80 per cent humidity) require woollens, underwear of natural fibres (which allow your skin to breath under warmer clothes), sweaters, and flannel.

The Ubiquitous T-Shirt

Taiwanese men will almost always have a singlet or T-shirt on under their polo or business shirt. This applies even in the summer, especcially if working in an air-conditioned office. Chinese medical theory warns against sweating and being subjected to drafts. After many summer colds, Chris adopted this custom of wearing a minimum of two layers of clothing all year round. Sure enough, we saw the colds and sinus problems vanish, without an increase in heat discomfort or body odour.

Buying Clothes

Designer clothes and fashions are not cheap in Taiwan, despite the fact that many branded clothes are made in Asia. Moreover, the clothes that you do find locally (priced reasonably or not) will probably not fit, unless you are sized and shaped like the average Taiwanese. If you are a 'supersized' American or European, make sure you bring enough clothes with you. If you still need or want to shop for clothes in Taiwan, your best bet will be casual and sports clothes. Hit the streets and scour the stalls. Also go to the night markets and department stores during the change of season sales when you may pick up a bargain or two. Do not rely on the size indicated in the clothing or shoes. There are many international systems to express clothing measurement, and Taiwan has its own system which is not used consistently. Always insist on trying on before you purchase. The below guide introduces some popular shopping areas and the types of items typically on sale there:

- Kuanghua Market — Computers and electronics
- Shihlin Night Market — Local food stalls and young fashion clothes
- Shihlin and Tienmu — bamboo and rattan furniture, pottery, expat grocery stores, reproduction artwork
- Hsimending Market — Department stores, shoe stores, handicrafts, costume jewellery, cameras, nightlife
- Chungshan N Road — Chinese furniture, porcelain and antiques, tailors, boutiques, English language book stores
- Taipei 101 — The area around the world's tallest shopping complex offers high-end brand name boutiques, eateries, fast food and the island's biggest Cineplex with 18 screens.
- Neihu — Neihu is a new hi-tech city that has sprung up across the Keelong River North of Taipei. Here, within a three-block radius, you will find a Costco Warehouse membership store, Tsann Kun's flagship home electronics outlet, HOLA home furnishings and accessories, Carrefour and RT Mart hypermarts, Eslite Bookstore, Caves Bookstore and other furniture and clothing stores. A mile from this location in another part of Neihu one will find the Miramar Cineplex and ferris wheel.

CONVENIENCE STORES AND BANKING

In Taiwan, 7-11, Nikko Marts, OK, High Life and other convenience chainstores truly provide convenient services. If a bill is delivered to you with a bar code on it (telephone, utilities, traffic and parking tickets, income tax etc), it is likely you can pay it in the store. Besides the limited selection of food and sundries stocked, they are normally equipped with a cash ATM. The transaction fee for withdrawal from local banks with a cash card on these machine is either free (if your card is the same bank as the machine) or NT$7.

To get that local ATM card, you will need to open a bank account. To open a bank account, you will need an Alien Resident Certificate. Many ATM's will give cash against an overseas card, but note that you will pay local and overseas service charges. It is important to note that outside of large department and chainstores, credit cards are not universally accepted, cash is King, so make sure you carry sufficient amounts with you.

THE THREE M'S

The above comments about climate and clothes tell you three more things: Mould, Mildew and Moths! These three M's are the scourge of clothing and a big problem generally in Taiwan. Wallpaper frequently moulds or peels off and anything made of leather or fabric not regularly used can develop a living ecosystem of its own. The only way to handle this is to use sufficient mothballs in storage and to pack away clothes and blankets at the change of seasons. Pick a dry, hot summer day and let the items dry and freshen outside before packing them away. Alternatively, put them in the dryer and iron them immediately before putting them in a box or chest. Dampness forms around floorboards and corners, so be careful to store boxes in dry areas.

With the growth of environmental awareness, the Taipei city government has recently instituted a garbage separation and recycling program. Garbage must be separated into colour-coded plastic bags for plastic, glass, paper, and other trash. Bags are available at 7-Eleven and other mini-marts. As part of the same green drive to prevent the proliferation of plastic garbage, retailers can no longer give away plastic carry sacks for your purchases. Consequently, you may be asked to buy these for NT$ 1 each, or you can bring a satchel in which to carry your purchase home.

If you live in Taipei, garbage is collected only at certain hours specific to each neighbourhood. You are to bring your tied bags out to the curb just prior to that time or out to the truck when you hear the blaring of its distinctive melody. Ask your neighbours when the pick-up time and where the pick-up place is.

TRANSPORTATION
Expect the Worst

Taipei Traffic

On one occasion, an expat was rear-ended in Taipei traffic. The Taiwanese driver of the offending vehicle insisted that it was the expat's fault; he had stopped too suddenly to avoid another collision. In such circumstances, if the two parties can reach an agreement right there, cash-out-of-pocket, or through an exchange of cards and addresses, then there is no need to call the police. If the police are brought in, the offender must pay a procedural fee. The two could not agree and so the Taiwanese man insisted on calling the police. When the police arrived he rushed over to them and explained he had called them. "Whose car is the one behind?" the cop asked immediately.

"Mine," the Taiwanese said.

"And you called us?" the policeman asked incredulously.

Yes, the concept of right of way is legally alive in Taiwan, but it is not too healthy in the minds of drivers. Prepare for the worst and learn to look left, right, up and down before you cross the street.

Although it has significantly improved over the past ten years, Taiwan traffic is reputed to be among the worst in the world. It is not just that roads are choked for 20 hours a day with too many cars, motorcycles, and buses, all competing for miniscule advantage. It is not just that there are not enough traffic police and they do not seem to give out tickets for anything but highway speeding. On top of all this, there is the Taiwanese-Confucian sense of responsibility to one's family and to hell with others. If the traffic rules or right of way do not suit the circumstance of the person driving, they are ignored.

Taxis

If you do not have a car, you will immediately begin to rely on *jichengche* (taxis). Taxis are plentiful during off-peak hours, metered, and reasonably priced (NT$ 75 for the first kilometre).

Taxis are known to drive much faster than the traffic allows, causing much concern to the uninitiated passenger. Learn to say, "*Qing man yi dian*," (A little slower, please) to the taxi driver.

It is very possible that when you alight, the driver will ask you for more than the fare on the meter. He is probably not trying to cheat you. The authorities revise fares periodically and rather than get new meters, they will carry a conversion chart around. If this happens to you, pay the higher fare. During Chinese New Year and when going to distant or difficult places, drivers will sometimes demand negotiated fares.

Thankfully, Taiwan now has radio-alerted taxi fleets. But note that they will add NT$ 10 to the meter for this service. Unfortunately, we are not aware of any English-language phone service for these fleets, so you will either need help to call them or will have to learn to speak Mandarin.

For long-haul taxi trips (Taipei to Taichung or Kaohsiung), there are the so-called *yejiche* (wild chicken taxis). It is a name well-earned by these coarse speed demons who will try to get a full complement of four paying passengers to squeeze into their cars for a fast and risky ride. These fellows are reputedly 'hopped up' on stimulants and make as many trips as they can squeeze into the day or night. They wait for prey at the rail, bus and downtown air terminals. Best to either book long-haul trips with someone known to your company, drive yourself, or take the bus or train.

Automobiles

Owning and operating an automobile in Taiwan is an expensive affair. Although local prices of imported cars have dropped over the past decade as the government liberalised import duties, the New Taiwan Dollar has appreciated, thereby making the foreign currency price (your home price) still high. Expect to pay close to double what the automobile would cost in the United States, Europe, or Japan.

To legally own and operate an automobile or obtain a local driver's license, you must have obtained your alien residence certificate. If you do not have this, you can still lease a car. But be sure to have a valid driver's license from your home country before you come. It will allow you to legally drive in Taiwan for the first month of your stay and then you can readily apply for a local license. You can get a local license even if you have no valid international permit, but it is time consuming, involves medical examinations (even the teeth!), and application forms in Mandarin only. For a detailed explanation of how to get a driving license, please see http://www.englishintaiwan.com/getting_around. htm#DRIVERS%20LICENSE

Used automobiles are available. Make sure you get all the proper documentation, which should include a contract of sale, certificate of previous ownership, and automobile registration papers. The car dealer should be willing to assist you with all the paperwork. Make this a condition of purchase. Ask the dealer to brief you on the various inspections and

Alternatives to Finding Parking Space

- Buy a space in your office building. This might cost the same amount as the car itself.
- Hire a driver who worries about the parking for you—an even costlier option.
- Queue up to use hourly underground and surface parking decks.
- Comb the streets for an open space in a public parking area. These are either metered, at NT$ 20–40 per hour, or attendant-based. Look for the attendant when you park and pay them. If you leave your automobile before they get to you, they will put a parking ticket on the window. Pay this when you return to your car or face a stiff penalty.
- Try to find a free but questionably legal space in an alley or lane.
- Park it illegally.

There is frequently gridlock on Taipei;s roads which, coupled with the fight for parking spaces, makes driving in the city far from convenient.

taxes you will be expected to pay and when. Also shop around for your insurance and be sure to buy it, preferably maximum coverage. Driving in Taiwan is not a picnic. Accidents do occur, the locals are underinsured, and they do go for higher claims when a foreigner is involved. In a court settlement, the aggrieved can prevent you from leaving the country until the claim is settled.

Finding a parking space is a true nightmare as construction companies have studiously ignored city planning edicts to include sufficient parking space in their building projects. Time is wasted in search for a space every morning.

Fines for public parking are paid at any of the aluminium parking attendant booths throughout the city. They look similar to some stalls that sell bus tickets and magazines, so learn to differentiate them.

If you parked your car illegally and it disappears, it was probably not stolen. Check the sidewalk for chalk scribbles of your automobile number and its new location and recover it with your automobile registration papers and driver's license. The fine will be NT$ 1,500 if you recover it immediately. They add NT$ 200 for each day the vehicle remains in the lot. If you cannot find your car,

With narrow streets such as this, parking is a nightmare in Taipei.

call 2505-7631 on a tone phone (which will give you instructions in English), then press the # button followed by your license plate number. The location of your car will be explained to you in Mandarin!

Gasoline is expensive and sold by the litre. The government-owned China Petroleum Corporation's monopoly on legitimate *jiayouzhan* (pumping stations) has been eliminated with significant benefits to the consumer: there are more stations, and these are better marked and brighter. The competition has led, if not to price-cutting, at least to other incentives. So, if a bikini-clad maiden wearing a clear plastic raincoat in the dead of winter coyly fills your tank and gives you free bottles of mineral water and energy drink for the road, you know to thank the laws of supply and demand!

A small but sturdy car will certainly ease your drive in Taiwan city. For a lot of freeway travel, a stronger, more protective automobile is advised. Smaller cars can thread through the minute openings in the traffic and can park in the half-spaces that are often the only options.

Give yourself plenty of time to get to destinations. Stay cool and try to laugh at the insanity you see around you. There is a method in the madness. An essayist once wrote that there is a *Tao* to the traffic, which flows like water, the molecules of the liquid flowing closely packed, but softly moving around obstacles. Taiwan drivers, just like nature itself, abhor a vacuum. If there is an empty space in front of you on the road, two cars, a bus, and a motorcycle will be sucking themselves into it. A two-lane road becomes a conduit for three lanes of cars and one sliver of motorcycles. Without such Taoist driving, there would be only gridlock. There are just too many vehicles for the road system.

On the highway, do not expect more road courtesy. The melee is merely sped up and with higher stakes. Always stay alert when you are driving. Be aware that the north-south freeway is not free at all; it is a toll road. A single toll is NT$ 40. Prepare change or buy a book of 10 tickets at the tollbooth or post office. Freeway rest stops have been established at several of the exits. They sell gasoline and snacks and have toilets.

Motorcycles

An alternative to owning a car, especially if you are single, have no children, or are on a tight budget, is to buy a *mwotwoche* or *jiche* (motorcycle). Taiwan reportedly has the highest per capita ownership of motorcycles in the world. Any major intersection during the day looks like the starting line of some urban motocross race. When traffic lights are on red, motorcycles will weave their way up

This sign indicates that in order to turn left, you must first stop in a box on the right, then proceed to another box across the intersection on the right and finally proceed when the light is with you.

through the lines of densely packed cars and deposit themselves right at the front. In the crowd it is not unusual to see a family of five balancing on a Vespa. Junior is standing between Dad's legs, Mom sits behind Dad carrying the baby, and Big Sis is clinging on behind Mom. By the time the light changes, as many as 50 to 100 motorcyclists may be revving their engines as they race off in clouds of blue smoke.

If you are planning to join their ranks, be aware that motorcycles are the second-class citizens of the road in Taiwan. When a slow lane is allocated for turning traffic, motorcycles must use that lane only. In any event, motorcycles are not allowed into the fast left-hand lane. At many intersections, motorcycles are not allowed to turn left because that would necessitate being in the fast lane. In this case, they are required to wait for the green light, go through the intersection (staying to the right), and then pull into a special waiting box sometimes painted on the road in front of the pedestrian crosswalk. Here they will await the light to change again.

You can legally drive a motorcycle under 50 cc if you are over 18, show your International Driver's Licence and take a written test. They will add an endorsement to your IDL allowing you to drive in Taiwan for 30 days. For a Taiwan driver's license, you will still need to take a written and road test and have an Alien Resident Certificate. They will give you a local license. The cost of a small, used motor-scooter is only NT$ 7000 to 15,000. For larger bikes, you will be required to take a road test and a written test, as well as a physical examination.

Many expatriates (especially those who do not have work permits and alien residence certificates) buy motorcycles. However, they often do not get licensed, do not have insurance, and ride around for years on their iron horses. But be warned that it is illegal and you could be in big trouble if you have an accident. Judge for yourself.

Mass Rapid Transit

The North–South line runs from Tamshui to Hsin Tien; the East–West line travels from Taipei City Hall to Hsin Pu. These two lines intersect at the Taipei Main Train station in the centre of the city. Stations are modern and clean, ticket machines have destinations indicated in Romanisation and while riding on the subway, upcoming stations are announced in Mandarin, Taiwanese, and by a foreigner who knows neither language, so listen for your stop.

Unified, stored value 'You-You Easy Cards' are for sale at the MRT stations. You must purchase the cards with a minimum value of NT$ 500, but will get a 20 per cent discount on fares when using it on the rapid transit and bus lines. You can also use it at government managed car parking decks or parking meters for parking fees. Fares on the rapid transit line run from NT$ 20–80. To recharge the card, you may add value at MRT stations. A one day pass is available for NT$ 180 and allow a single passenger unlimited journeys for one day. For more information see http://www.tscc.com.tw

Inter-City Trains

The first locomotives were delivered to Taiwan in 1888 under the Qing Dynasty and the network was improved on by the Japanese Colonial administration. Today, Taiwan has an excellent and improving train network that links all major towns down the West coast and up the East Coast. Tickets can be booked on line via an English language website http://www.railway.gov.tw/en/index/index.aspx. Taiwan has recently inaugurated service of a high speed rail line. These ultra modern high speed trains zip from Taipei to Kaohsiung at a top speed of 300 km per hour and cover the 345 km in 90 minutes.

City Buses

There is no single bus service procedure in Taipei. There are both government buses and over a dozen local bus companies. The Mandarin for bus is gong gong qiche or gongche. Bus routes are differentiated by numbers and stops are marked with signs in different shapes and colours, with destinations and further stops written in Chinese only. Fares are based on the number of sectors travelled in the city and the type of bus. Depending on the bus company, a lighted sign at the front door above the driver will indicate whether you pay your fare when you board (上 shang) or when alighting (下 xia). For particularly long sections, you might pay both when boarding and alighting. The deduction will be made from your 'You-You Easy Card' or you can pay with exact change. On all buses, the fare for adults is NT$ 15 per sector and it can be paid in exact change or with an Easy Card. Initially it is best to ask for help and to have someone write destinations in Chinese for you. People in Taiwan are usually friendly and approachable, and if they are waiting for a bus they will help you to pick out the best one to take. When you see the right bus approaching, flag it down. You can show the destination to the ticket collector and he or she will sometimes help to alert you when it is time to get off. To alight, pull the bell cord or push the bell button to tell the driver to stop at the next stop. Be sure not to miss the last bus home (usually between 11:00–11:30 pm).

Tour Buses

If you want to tour the island city by city, a good transport option is tour buses. These are comfortable, modern and dependable. From Taipei you can get buses to the east coast,

or head south. For details, see http://www.taiwantourbus.
justtaiwan.com.

Bicycles and Walking

As medium- and short-distance alternatives, these
environment-friendly modes of transportation are effective
in Taiwan. But exercise maximum caution when travelling this
way on the road. You may be moving more slowly than the
rest of the traffic, but we urge you to wear a bike helmet.

As befitting the country with the world's biggest bicycle
company, Giant, Taiwan has some great bike tours to be
enjoyed. In the Taipei area, over 20 km of bike paths and
landscaped park lands have been set aside between the flood
control dikes and the Keelong and Damsui Rivers. Along the
Damsui River, one can ride from the Grand Hotel Vicinity
all the way to Danshui, or cross the Kuandu bridge and ride
on to Bali. There are many bike riding clubs and impromptu
groups out on the bike paths and touring mountain roads on
the weekend. To facilitate access to good rides, for a fee the
MRT service on select routes and at select stations during
the weekend allows cyclists to carry their mounts on-board
the trains.

NAVIGATION

Many expats have found trying to use local maps a complete
nightmare. Fully detailed maps are only in Chinese and the
semi-detailed maps (such as the ones found in the free *This
Month in Taiwan* guide) are adequate only to orient yourself
and to find major roads. With help, you may be able to use
them to get to desired destinations. Give yourself lots of time
and exercise maximum patience during the first few months
when you are venturing out to appointments. There is an
online mapping utility for Taiwan addresses available at http://
www.taiwan-map.com. This website has improved over the
years and now can show maps of addresses typed into the
English form in 16 major cities on the island. The accuracy
is dependent on the Romanisation used and if it does not
recognise the location you have entered seems to deposit you
somewhere in the mountains north of Taipei. The 'landmarks'

function works better, allows the selection of various kinds of landmarks, hotels, embassies, coffee shops, tourist attractions for which accurate maps are immediately accessed.

The Center in Taipei has recently produced a hand-drawn, bilingual, easy to read, *Map of Taipei* available for NT$ 200 at its Tienmu location. More information can be found at www.community.com.tw

There are two elevated freeways that run north-south through Taipei city. These are called Shinsheng and Jiankuo roads. Both of them have public parking stops built underneath them. The Civic Boulevard connects the Chunghsiao bridge in the west, across town to the eastern reaches of the city.

Street Names

As part of its socialisation program when the Kuomintang recovered Taiwan from Japan, they rewrote the map of Taipei city. If you know the geography, philosophy, and political history of Mainland China, it will help you with street names. Many major boulevards are named after social and political principles, or famous people: Chungshan Road (after *Sun Zhong Shan* aka Sun Yat Sen); Minchuan, Mintsu, and Minsheng roads (named after Sun Yat Sen's Three Principles of the People); and Renai and Chunghsiao roads (meaning benevolence and loyalty to country and family respectively). North, south, east and west, Taipei has streets and lanes named after cities or geographical features in China. They also correspond to their relative location in the Mainland. Emei, Chengtu and Kunming are all in Sichuan province in the south-west of China and, as streets, are all located in the south-west quadrant of Taipei city.

Addresses

The details of addresses written in Chinese come in declining order of magnitude. They roughly follow this format, although they may not include all the graduations below:

- Country
- City
- District
- Road or Street

- Road Section Number
- Lane or Alley Number
- Building Number
- Floor Number
- Door Number
- Company or Person

When translated into English on name cards or advertisements, this is somewhat reversed, but the information often gets jumbled up and confusing punctuation creeps in. For example:

Wholesome Goodies Pte Ltd, Rm. 1025 Shin Shin Bldg., 96, Chungshan N. Rd. Sec. 2, Taipei, Taiwan
or
Noodle Trading Inc., 20 Floor, No. 26, Lane 76, Tachih St., Sanchung, Taipei, Taiwan 241

If you are confused, ask friends and colleagues to clarify which numbers refer to the building, street, postal district, etc.

PUBLIC FACILITIES AND ASSOCIATIONS

Because Taiwanese culture and language have represented such a barrier to Westerners in the past, an extensive variety of clubs and associations have sprung up which cater to the needs of the expatriate. There are clubs for everything from bridge to bungee jumping. There is the American Club, the Correspondents' Club, the Bankers' Club, the Australian/New Zealanders' Social Group, and many more which you can find out about through the larger expatriate clubs and associations.

Welcoming Services

There are several organisations in Taipei that are devoted to helping English-speaking expatriates settle in. They can be invaluable in helping to ease your family into its new lifestyle.

The Center in Taipei (http://www.community.com.tw) is the compiler of the indispensable *Taipei Living* guidebook now in its eighth edition (see further reading at the back of the book), in which you will find complete details and addresses for all the public facilities, clubs, associations and schools in Taiwan. The centre is a non-profit organisation located in Tienmu and is open on weekdays during normal business hours. They offer newcomer orientation programs—very helpful in getting settled in. Even after you have read this book, remember the Chinese saying, 'A thousand words are never as good as a look'. Having someone to personally introduce you to Taiwan in situ is so much more helpful. The centre also offers cross-cultural training, various classes and professional counseling. Small outings to nearby spots are also organised, additionally, The Center has great resources on day-trips around Taiwan. Their address and phone and fax numbers can be found in the resource guide.

Libraries and Translation Services

A limited number of private and public lending libraries with extensive English-language resource materials do exist in Taiwan. In addition, several companies offer translation services for written documents or conversations, which may be of use to you at some time. However, these services tend to be expensive. In the long run, it is better to try to learn the language or employ staff who can cope in a bilingual environment.

Schools

Various nationalities within the expatriate community and missionary organisations have set up a growing number of international schools, such as the Taipei and Taichung International Schools and the Christian Morrison Academy with branches in Chiayi, Taichung and Kaohsiung.

Depending on the ebb and flow of expatriate transfers, obtaining tuition at the school of your choice can be problematic. Contact the school prior to accepting your assignment in Taiwan to ensure that a space will be available for your children. Enrolling your child in a school that has a curriculum similar to your home school will help to ease the culture shock the child might experience. For a complete listing of educational institutes catering to foreigners with links, please see http://english.moe.gov.tw/ct.asp?xItem = 626&CtNode = 421.

Teaching English

Perhaps you did not come to learn, but to teach. Taiwanese parents have a penchant for investing in their children's schooling and many foreigners who hail from English-speaking countries make a modest living in Taiwan teaching their mother tongue.

The largest chain of language schools is Hess Educational Organisation (http://hess.com.tw) with over 100 language schools and 60 kindergartens. There are hundreds of other schools in Taipei alone, so it pays to visit a number of them and negotiate the best terms for yourself, especially if you have TESL (Teaching English as a Second Language) credentials.

Employment contracts are typically for six to 12 months. The school will either help you arrange your visa or you do the 'Hong Kong Shuffle' to renew your 60-day visa. After you are settled, you can also try to arrange some more lucrative private tutorial sessions. We know people that have found better paying tutorial jobs independently through university bulletin boards, online social networking websites, and even being approached on the street. For the low-down on teaching English in Taiwan, visit the website Teaching English and Living in Taiwan (http://www.tealit.com) or English in Taiwan (http://www.englishintaiwan.com).

Helping Your Family Stay Sane

What causes culture shock? It is basically an accumulation of stress caused by a lack of the familiar. Familiar cues received from the environment (for example, telephones that ring a certain way, signs that communicate in a certain way, toilets that look, feel, or flush a certain way) are suddenly gone. Familiar cues received from people in our own culture are also gone, and familiar stress-relievers (like a talk with your mother, your favourite soap opera, even your favourite brand of aspirin) may be absent.

Culture shock can hit the young, the old, the experienced, the naive. It can hit early or late during a tour overseas. It might only be a fleeting moment of melancholy, or a brief loneliness, but it can also be a profound and deep depression.

Understanding what it is can help us to prepare for its onslaught and we can immunise ourselves by slowly immersing into the host culture. Just as one can get used to a hot or cold bath by slowly easing into the water and not shocking the system, so one can slowly ease into the new culture.

We have advised that, given the opportunity, you should take a house-hunting trip to Taiwan. This initial visit as a half-tourist, half-house-hunter, will give you a much better idea of what to expect. You will have a chance to return right away, sharing your adventures and concerns with friends and relatives, and feeling their support and sympathy. This is not to say that a tour of duty in Taiwan is a death sentence, but there are sacrifices to be made. You will not fully appreciate the rewards until you have spent some time in the country.

Talk with each member of your family about the move well in advance of the departure. Perhaps assign different family members to do a book report or some research on different aspects of the culture, history, or customs of Taiwan. They can then present the report to the family. You could rent Chinese videotapes, eat Chinese food, get some copies of the English language daily papers from Taiwan so they all can read about what is going on.

The next step for immunisation is to allow yourself to bring some familiar items with you when you move. These need not be irreplaceable family heirlooms or have a high value. More often than not, they will be mundane things: a blanket with a familiar smell, the well-seasoned cast iron skillet you have used for years, your favourite author's books. Just as Superman has his 'Fortress of Solitude' with familiar things from his home planet, so you should make your home a 'familiarity retreat'.

Recreate familiar routines as much as possible. If the family ate together at 6:30 pm before, try to maintain that in the beginning. Be patient and listen to your children and spouse, but lend a strong guiding hand. Maintain communication with your relatives back home and encourage your children to write to grandma and grandpa.

The next step is to acknowledge that there will be stress and stress symptoms. Everything will be changing for all of you. The air you breathe, the water you drink, the food you eat, the way you get around, the people you see and everything you hear outside will all be new and different. Symptoms of stress can include withdrawal, changes in eating habits, aggression, absent-mindedness, regression of habits (toilet training, bed wetting), etc. Take the time to talk through these manifestations with family members.

Indeed, the most familiar and warm thing you can bring with you from the old home is, and should be, your intra-familial relationship. Strengthen it. Spend more time with your children and spouse, not less. The temptation is to dive into work. Set aside time for your family until you can see they are well settled. Try to get them into regular activities of interest to them, such as scouting, gymnastics, bridge. Finally, share your feelings of shock and loneliness with each other. Let them know that you are feeling the same things that they are, and that you understand and care about their feelings too.

Expatriates have commented that culture shock Taiwanese-style falls heavily on the non-working spouse or parent. This is usually the wife, who may be used to working in her native country. Her children fit quickly, albeit with varying degrees of stress, into the routine of school. Her husband is busy with the business that sent them to Taiwan. She may find herself lonely in a strange country. Her family needs to be aware of this and work together to try to make the transition less stressful. Thankfully, Taiwan is the one of the world's most 'wired' countries and expatriates can be online with family and friends in their home countries via webcam or computer for only the cost of Internet connection time.

Explore your environment. Tour scenic areas with the family. Take long walks together through your neighbourhood, and initiate conversations with people. Check out the expatriate meeting areas and meet new people. There are several community centres and aid organisations just for the expatriate community. Contact the several newcomer services that exist. Enrol in language classes and paste up vocabulary stickers in Mandarin all around the house, where they can be in constant sight and make learning easier and more fun. Soon the strange will become the familiar and angst will become appreciation.

STAYING HEALTHY AND HANDLING EMERGENCIES

As so many platitudes have proclaimed, prevention is easier than cure. However, when you find yourself in a foreign land, not only are many dangers alien to you, but the handling of possible emergencies is also different. Our advice, then, is to read this chapter before you have any necessity for the information contained.

HEALTH

It is easy to let your health deteriorate when you move to a foreign country. You arrive and have jet lag, new routines, new demands and maybe an initial bout of intestinal flu. You go to bed every night feeling spent. You wake up facing a frustrating day ahead. On top of this you are experiencing culture shock.

Be kind and gentle on yourself. Take time to recover from illness. Force yourself to change your pace so you can finish the race, rather than letting the race finish you. Try to maintain your usual exercise routine. If you jogged, or played tennis or golf at home, find out about clubs and facilities open to you in Taiwan. Get into the network of new friends and associates with whom you can share your interests.

The climate is probably different in Taiwan than in your home country. It is hot and very humid in the summer, not affording many natural options for cooling down. People come to depend on air-conditioning, but this can lead to 'summer colds'. To prevent these, follow the local custom and learn to wear undergarments year round. Winter is troublesome because most homes and many offices are not heated. Again, you must learn to mix and match several layers of attire to stay in good health.

Water

Water is a basic element required in copious amounts by everyone living in Taiwan. The country is very hot in the summer and it is important that you do not become dehydrated. But, in answer to the never-ending question, "Is the water safe to drink?", the Taiwanese themselves never drink tap water that has not first been boiled or filtered. Chris drank unboiled tap water in Peitou for years without ill effect. However, we do not encourage you to try it.

Besides bacteria and viruses, a more subtle but no less dangerous component of the water might be chemicals (such as complex pesticides) and heavy metals. These cannot be removed by boiling and are not passed through the system. They accumulate in the body and, therefore, even trace amounts over time can become deleterious to your system. Filtering and boiling is recommended for cooking and drinking water. Many locals and expatriates have bottled water delivered to their premises. Check on the supplier of the bottled water and do shop around. Some suppliers have been hit on by the health authorities and consumer associations for supplying water which is substandard to the tap variety!

Food

As with all things, there is a *yin* and a *yang* to food. During your immersion in Taiwan, food can be a source of life-giving vitality, or a draining, energy-sapping scourge.

Taiwan reputedly has some of the 'cleanest' pigs in the world.

The locally available foods are, by and large, very healthy. Delicious fresh fruit and vegetables are various and plentiful. They will provide you with nourishment, roughage and vitamins. It is important, however, that they are cleaned properly before consumption. In Taiwan, it is still customary to protect small vegetable plots with chemicals and fertilise them with unprocessed natural fertiliser (human and pig night soil). Until only recently, DDT was being used in Taiwan, and other very harsh and environmentally unsound chemicals can still be found. Vegetables should be soaked, washed, and cooked thoroughly. We have not had stomach problems with salad ingredients, providing they are properly cleaned. Fruit should also be soaked and washed, but can be eaten raw.

The Taiwanese commonly rinse off a fresh piece of meat or seafood bought from the vegetable market prior to freezing it. We second this custom. You can buy freezer bags at the market. All meat and seafood should be thoroughly cooked, unless, of course, you are having *sushi* and *sashimi* (Japanese raw fish recipes).

Also be aware that buffets, cafeterias and roadside stalls, though they may have a different ambience and different price tags, can all serve up food that is tainted. This is not to say you should avoid them like the plague, but rather use caution in your selection of foods from them. It is always best to eat food that you are reasonably assured has been recently cooked or can be cooked to order.

At buffets, avoid eggs, mayonnaise and foods that have a glazed-over or stale look. A friend came down with his worst case of intestinal flu shortly after having a breakfast buffet at a major five-star hotel. He ordered an omelette to be prepared to his taste. Raw whipped eggs were poured into a pan from a pitcher but, while cooked to his liking, the inside of the omelette was not well done and the eggs were obviously not fresh.

Having said this, Chris also attended a buffet at a hotel restaurant and experienced something entirely different. At the end of the buffet was a carving table with a huge baked ham on the bone. When Chris got to the chef he was surprised to find him asking how he would like the meat (medium-rare or well done) as if it was a piece of beef. Chris declined to make a choice, but asked his business counterpart to advise him. He was told that Taiwan has some of the world's healthiest pigs which do not have the diseases (i.e. trichinosis) that must be cooked out of American pigs. This pristine reputation was damaged in recent years with an outbreak of foot and mouth disease. Let the diner take their own risks where this is concerned! However, if you do want to choose how your meat is cooked, note that the Taiwanese do not actually use the terms 'medium' or 'well done'. They use a point system and literally ask, "How many points done?" Ten points is well done, seven to eight points is medium, and four to five points is rare.

Another thing to be aware of in Taiwanese cuisine is a food additive called monosodium glutamate (MSG). This tenderiser and seasoning is sometimes used as a flavor enhancer in Western food, but it was invented in the Orient and is known locally as *weijing* (flavor essence). It is used by restaurants in copious amounts, being sprinkled over the food like salt during marinating or cooking. Some people develop a reaction to MSG, which often takes the form of runny nose and eyes soon after eating food containing the flavoring. If you are sensitive to it, you may ask chefs not to use it in your dishes. Say, "*Qing bu yao jia weijing.*"

It is a good idea to bring your favorite stomach remedy with you from home. Products like Pepto-Bismol, Kaopectate, and Alka-Seltzer are not as readily available in Taiwan as they are in the West. However, an excellent local remedy for vomiting and diarrhoea is *baojiwan* (Po Chai Pills). This traditional herbal preparation comes in convenient plastic vials. Take the whole vial of tiny brown pills in one gulp with a glass of warm water. However, if your vomiting or diarrhoea occurs more than three times, you should try to see a doctor. Be sure to replace lost body fluids rapidly.

Pollution

The city of Taipei is geographically set in a 'bowl' surrounded by mountains. In fact, this positioning once prompted a friend of mine to quip during my visit to Taipei, "So, when are you 'flushing out' of this place?" The point is that, being set in a basin surrounded by mountains, Taipei holds in the fumes from traffic, industry, and cooking. These build up until they choke even the insensitive and weaken the strong.

It is therefore conceivable that your usual morning jog would become excruciating in downtown Taipei, as well as hazardous from the traffic point of view. Try getting up very early (like the Taiwanese do) to exercise in the parks before the pollution count gets too high. If you jog or ride a bike or motorcycle, you may want to adopt the local custom of wearing a gauze face mask and glasses. Although the masks are too coarse to stop gaseous pollutants, they do prevent granular media from getting lodged in your nose, lungs, and eyes. If you are a contact lens wearer, wash your lenses religiously and carry a bottle of eye drops with you at all times—you will definitely need them!

Smoke Stack City

The Taiwanese like to smoke cigarettes. The habit is common among young men. Many women do not smoke because it was formerly associated with vice among women. One of the friendliest and most common ice-breakers a Taiwanese will use with a foreigner who does not speak Chinese is to hoist out a pack of butts and proffer one. To scowl and refuse, as some non-smokers in the West might, would be seen as rude and devoid of cultural flexibility. The most polite refusal is to hold the outstretched fingers of your hand to your lips, as if you are making a one-handed prayer. While doing this, bow your head and say, "*Xie xie wo bu xi yan*" (Thank you, I do not smoke).

The consumption of cigarettes is discouraged by the government and health authorities. Smoking in offices, restaurants and many public places has been banned in Taiwan. Note however, that the government owned Taiwan Tobacco and Liquor Corporation produces the ever popular Long Life cigarette brand with annual sales approaching US$1 billion!

Diseases

- **Conjunctivitis** is a severe eye inflammation caused by reaction to airborne pollutants. Also known as 'pink eye', it is highly contagious. Considering what we have just said about pollution in Taipei, it would not be surprising if you contracted this complaint. We have found that over-the-counter preparations, like Bausch and Lomb Allergy Drops, can put a stop to reactions before they develop into conjunctivitis, if they are used early enough. Otherwise, go to the doctor for treatment.

- **Hepatitis** is a significant health hazard in Taiwan. Type A is transmitted through food and water. When eating out, choose clean restaurants with good food and water sanitation. Use only plastic or wooden disposable chopsticks (*weisheng kuai zi*) when dining out. Reusable wooden ones cannot be adequately washed. Hepatitis B is more severe and more common, and can cause liver disease or cancer. Like AIDS it is transmitted through body fluids. Oral transmission is rare. You can protect yourself with a series of vaccinations.

- **Tuberculosis** is a greater threat in Taiwan than in most Western countries. This disease attacks slowly, usually focusing on the lungs. It is transmitted through the sputum of infected individuals. The germs can live in dried spittle for months. This means that, again, when eating out, use only safe chopsticks and clean utensils. Use the serving spoon, rather than your own spoon, to serve from the dishes.

- **Sexually transmitted diseases** are a cause for concern, particularly if you choose to partake to the full in any of the sexual amusements available to men on the island. Even if you have only one partner, you should be aware of the need to protect yourself and whoever you are having sex with. Although probably not as serious as in the 'play-for-pay' centers in Manila and Bangkok, possible infections run the gamut from syphilis and gonorrhea, to herpes and AIDS. There are many well-advertised clinics specialising in the treatment of foreigners with sexual diseases. They exist for a reason. Protect yourself.
- **Sudden Acute Respiratory Syndrome (SARS)** struck Taiwan with deadly effect in the winter of 2003. Scientists believe it originated in the exotic animal slaughter houses of Guangdong, China, and after jumping to the human population spread to Hong Kong, Taiwan, South-east Asia and Toronto, Canada. Symptoms overlap many of those seen in flu and pneumonia, and can include a fever, body aches and pain, chills, nasal congestion, and shortness of breath. Its onset is sudden and it does not respond to antibiotics. The outbreak in 2003 resulted in 84 fatalities in Taiwan alone. Health authorities scrambled to respond and it was only in July that year was the emergency declared over. However, the World Health Organization (WHO) advises everyone to remain alert for a recurrence of SARS, especially in the colder months. If you travel to Taiwan during the flu season, be prepared to have your temperature taken (quickly and effortlessly) at the entrance to immigration, department stores, restaurants, and train stations. You might also notice bottles of antiseptic solution with which to cleanse your hands and a proliferation of face masks. Take your own precautions and if you have flu symptoms, see a doctor.

Snakes, Bugs and Mosquitoes

It has been said that, during World War II, Taiwan was a major Japanese research center in animal-based poisons, especially snakes' venom. They apparently released their stock of toxic lovelies at the end of the war. We do not know if the story is based on fact, but it is true that the island is home to cobras, vipers, coral snakes, and 'hundred-pacers' (so called because, if you are bitten by one, you die within the time it takes to walk 100 steps). For this reason, you should take precautions whenever you walk in grass, especially high grass. Make a lot of noise when walking so that snakes are startled into going about their own business, or you could use a walking stick to clear the path ahead. Carry a flashlight at night.

Beware of any snake you come across. If someone is bitten, kill the snake if possible, or at least get a complete description of its size, colour and markings. If you can, take it in a bag to the hospital so they can see what antidote to use. In the meantime, keep the victim still. You can get snake bite kits for your first aid box which show you how to extract venom, but if you don't have one, you can always pack the bite in ice to slow down the spread of the poison. As soon as you can, go to the nearest emergency room, where antitoxins are kept in stock and can be administered, providing you know which kind of snake struck. Veterans General Hospital has a special toxicology unit if you have further questions. Foreign community centers also have more information about local snakes and what the venomous ones look like.

> If you live near any burial grounds, be aware that on Tomb Sweeping Day, Taiwanese will be busy cutting down all the high grass in the tomb area. Bereft of their homes, snakes will seek new shelter, possibly behind your shoe box or under your car.

Mosquito-borne diseases like dengue fever and Japanese encephalitis are also a concern in Taiwan. It is a very good idea to put up screens in the doors and windows of your home, as well as checking on a weekly basis for any standing water that could be turning stagnant around your house. This includes flower pot trays, vases of flowers, and even toilets that are not regularly used or flushed. Repellent devices you could try are those green mosquito coils which slowly burn like incense, or their modern electric equivalent which plugs into the wall socket and releases a vapor. If you live in an area plagued by mosquitoes, you might consider getting mosquito nets for your beds, especially those of your children.

Medical Insurance

In 1995, Taiwan instituted a national health insurance program (NHI) under which all citizens can be covered for their medical costs for a modest monthly sum. More recent legislation has made it so that all holders of the Alien Resident Certificate must also subscribe. The subscription fee is based on your income level. With a NHI card you will be able to see clinic and hospital doctors for as little as NT$ 150 per visit. Dental is included. For more information, see http://www.nhi.gov.tw/english/index.asp.

Hospitals

Hospitals around the world seem to be getting increasingly bureaucratic, to the detriment of health care. In the culture that invented the very concept of bureaucracy, do not expect this to be any less so. When you go to a hospital in Taiwan, take plenty of cash, your identification card (passport or alien resident certificate), and lots of patience. Be prepared to be shuttled from one desk to another, to wait, and to pay for each service in advance as it is called for by the doctor.

For instance, you have an ear infection that is driving you batty. Your spouse takes you to the hospital and you go to the reception desk. After describing your problem briefly to the clerk and requesting an English-speaking doctor, you are told you must first register and pay a registration fee. Then you will be given a queue number and a receipt that must be produced again before you go to the doctor.

After paying, you proceed to the waiting area. Show your number and receipt to the nurse in attendance. She will tell you where to wait. When your number is called, you can go in to see the doctor. He checks you over, examines your ear, asks a few questions and gives you a prescription. When you have paid for this, show the receipt to the dispensary and you will be given your medicine.

Some hospitals now take credit cards. They will give you a small card informing the staff of each section that you are paying by credit card. They will then send the separate bills to a central desk where you can pay for them all together.

Certain hospitals also offer V.I.P. (read 'expat') services which include scheduled appointments, reduced waiting, English-speaking services, and generally less of a runaround. Expect to pay for it, though!

Clinics

Economic alternatives for mild symptom ailments are the hundreds of small clinics that line the major city roads. There are also various specialty clinics (ENT stands for 'Ear, Nose and Throat', not 'ENTerologist'). These are licenced by the health authorities and are usually run by one or two doctor-cum-entrepreneurs. They are open at convenient times, accept patients without appointments, but usually do not have English-speaking staff. You might get lucky and find a doctor who understands the vocabulary of anatomy, fever, cough, and discomfort. Otherwise, they should know what they are looking at! They will dispense a selection of pills and liquids for your problem, typically a three-day supply. The average visit will cost you about NT$ 500–1000 if you book an appointment.

Seeing a Doctor in Taipei

'The doctor was a tired, overworked man who had just peered down at least one hundred throats and two hundred ears, had sprayed and swabbed all of them with the same elixir, and sent the patients on their way with a prescription and an admonition. Behind him were the tools of his trade: a reclining seat, various stainless steel bowls, stainless steel tools bathing in sterilizing fluid and stainless steel sprayers and suction devices. We were the last patients of the morning shift.'
—Taipei clinic scene, Chris Bates, *Unwanted Vocabulary*

Pharmacies

Pharmacies in Taiwan are not controlled by the government and health authorities, the way they are in the West. Many types of medication that are only available by prescription in the West, can be bought over the counter in Taiwan, assuming you know how to ask for them in Chinese. This has its advantages and disadvantages. If you have a recurring problem, like allergies, and you know the medicine you need, you don't have to keep going to the doctor to get a supply. On the other hand, the ready availability of certain drugs, like Valium, means that they can just as easily be abused. Hospital dispensaries, however, will only supply drugs on the doctor's advice.

CHILD SAFETY

Your children will be in a whole new world in Taiwan. Small children, especially, are naturally outgoing and gregarious, so make sure their discoveries are safe ones.

You should make your home as childproof in Taiwan as it was in your native country, perhaps even more so. Be aware that many cleaning liquids and hazardous chemicals are produced for the local market without safety packaging and perhaps with colorful or attractive markings that young children would find new and interesting. Be sure to store all hazardous chemicals out of reach of little ones.

We have commented earlier about the traffic. In Taipei, you should never rely on drivers to stop in time not to hit you or your children. Motorised vehicles have the right of way for all practical purposes, so do not let your children play in the street. If they are used to riding their bikes on the road at home, take them out with you first and train them in the realities of the road in Taiwan. They should ride defensively, wear helmets and not pull stunts. Also, familiarise your family with the appearance of local snakes and insects. Children should be taught never to play with them.

It is a good idea to establish an 'emergency center' in your home with the phone numbers of English-speaking police, doctors, hospitals and clinics kept close at hand. Know where the nearest hospital is and perhaps make a visit to the emergency room so you know where, what, why and how. Remember, you are in a foreign land where the delays of language and uncertainty can mean the difference between life and death in an emergency.

Crimes against foreign children are not as prevalent in Taiwan as they are in other countries in the region, like the

Philippines. Still, you should not drop your guard, especially if you have come from crime-ridden Western cities which make Taiwan seem comparatively harmless.

Within school there is the same possibility that your child will fall in with a 'bad crowd', and gangs of expat children do exist, whatever you may imagine about their affluent backgrounds. You should be aware of your child's whereabouts and insist on a level of personal responsibility appropriate for their age. If you have teenage children, make sure they are aware that the laws and administration of justice in Taiwan are not the same as in their home country. The concept of habeus corpus and 'due process' are not the same, and the fact that they are foreigners will not protect them should they be found breaking the law.

Drugs such as marijuana, cocaine, heroin, PCP, speed and various pills are illegal and yet still available. Penalties are stiff for possession or sale of them, but there is a growing demand. This is not to say the threat reaches anywhere near the scale of the drug problem in the West. You should be aware, though, that drugs are available and be sensitive to the signs that show your children might be trying to cope with the stress of culture shock in this way.

CRIME

Taiwan has several criminal elements. Staying clear of them is largely a matter of minding your cultural Ps and Qs and staying out of areas or situations where you are likely to stub their toes. Criminals can be roughly stratified into three groups: organised crime syndicates, disorganised youth gangs and individuals (thieves, pickpockets, toughs and dealers).

Organised Crime

Taiwan's organised crime groups evolved out of the secret societies of the Qing Dynasty which were patriotic organisations trying to re-establish the Ming Dynasty. They turned to crime as their cause gradually became redundant. Nowadays, they deal extensively in extortion, racketeering, prostitution, smuggling, endangered species trafficking, and live entertainment. They have also established ties with the

Japanese Yakuza underworld. Unless you really look for trouble (trying to do business with them, or beating up a prostitute), you have little reason to be alarmed about them.

Gangs

Youth gangs may be of greater concern to you because their actions are driven by emotion and they are therefore less predictable. It should be noted that Taiwan protects its citizens with laws like the death penalty for armed robbery. When the rate of violent crime escalates, the officials have been known to take certain convicted felons, 'whack 'em', and (remarkably) the crime rate drops! Therefore, you are not likely to be confronted with a hood armed with more than a knife, screwdriver, or his drunken ego. That is not to say he won't be dangerous, but gentle (not groveling) persuasion, coupled with some 'face-giving' may talk you out of the mess, if, of course, you speak Mandarin! Otherwise, give them what they want, rather than 'letting them have it'.

Theft

Your house should always be properly protected, however safe you think your neighborhood is. Change the door locks once you have moved in. If you want to live in a ground floor or low level unit with access from the street, make sure it has security grills on the windows. The locals use them for a reason. Even 'controlled neighbourhoods' with their own security guards still have break-ins. We recall an incident, several years ago, which occurred in a supposedly secure up-market enclave, where thieves drove a moving van up to the house, emptied it entirely of its possessions, and drove off!

There is little hope of recovering stolen items. Make an inventory of all the valuable and irreplaceable items that you own, preferably with photos, valuations and receipts. Then get a good insurance policy.

On the Road

On the road, the chance of falling victim to crime is much higher. For example, if you have a mishap, accident or disagreement with a taxi driver, don't be surprised if he

comes after you armed with a screwdriver which he wants
to plant in your intestines. Also note that citizens treat the
road or area in front of their house or shop as their own,
whether it is zoned for parking or not. The nicest of them
will place a sign that says in Mandarin, 'Please Do Not Park
Here', while the worst will put all manner of obstacles out
on the road (old chairs, cinder blocks, tires and the like) to
prevent their space from being taken.

If you foolishly do not heed their warning, you will
probably find a long, deep, rather expensive scratch or two
on your car hood or door. Don't even bother reporting it to
the police. Just take it to the garage workshop and call your
insurance man.

If you are robbed, are in an accident where someone is
injured, or your property is vandalised or stolen, call the
police. Minor traffic accidents can usually be cleared up
between individuals through an exchange of name cards and
other details, if both parties are amenable. This information
also proves you did not flee the scene of crime if the case ever
ends up in court. Calling the police only involves a procedural
fee that increases the cost of solving the problem.

FORCES OF NATURE

Two forces of nature strike Taiwan with alarming regularity:
earthquakes and typhoons. The word 'typhoon' comes
from the Mandarin *taifeng*. Typhoons are formed by a
massive rotating weather system that is born over the
Pacific, southeast of the Philippines, and they generate fast
winds and heavy rains. In the Atlantic Ocean they are called
hurricanes. Typhoon windspeeds can exceed 150 km per
hour, the rain falls almost horizontally, and cars can be blown
off bridges.

Needless to say, public services are disrupted and water
and power can be cut off for days. ICRT reports on the steady
progress of typhoons approaching the island during the
typhoon season in July, August and September.

Several days before a typhoon is due to hit, make extra
ice—you will need it to keep food fresh should the power go
off. Keep a 'typhoon kit' in a cardboard box set aside for that

purpose. You should keep in it a flashlight and spare batteries, a battery-powered radio, candles, matches, a 'sterno' or camping stove with extra cylinders of gas, some tape for taping up windows and some empty collapsible containers to put water in and some dried food that can be cooked up, like instant noodles. This first aid and emergency kit should be kept handy.

During the typhoon, stay inside. As the eye of the typhoon passes over, calm and clear returns, but only temporarily. The other side of the storm will hit soon. Don't be caught out in it and stay away from windows.

Taiwan is part of the Pacific Rim of Fire, the chain of volcanos and fault lines that encircle this ocean. It is prone to earthquakes and they can be severe as evidenced by the major trembler that hit Taichung in September 1999. Even some buildings in Taipei were leveled by this Richter 7.6 shock wave. Over 2,000 people lost their lives on the island and 400,000 were left homeless. There were widespread power outages and production at Hsinchu's Technology Industry park took weeks to restore causing a major run-up in world semiconductor prices. This was Taiwan's most severe earthquake and quakes of such size are rare, but smaller quakes do occur regularly and you should take precautions. The same emergency box you have created for typhoons will come in handy if a 'big one' hits. When you feel a trembler, move away from windows as they may shatter, stand under doorways or get under a desk. Do not board an elevator to exit the building; take the stairs.

But don't let these warnings deter you from visiting Taiwan. The Taiwanese have thrived on this island for several centuries, despite the earthquakes, typhoons, snakes and gangsters. They are a happy people, always ready to face up to the challenge of their future, and building a better society along the way. They will welcome you, and if you in turn welcome them into your heart, all culture shock can be overcome.

CUISINE OF ILHA FORMOSA

CHAPTER 6

'Food is as much a backdrop as a recurring symbol.
Chu's failing taste buds parallel his loss for the zest for life.
Jia-Chen's love of cooking harkens back to a frustrated
childhood desire, and Jia-Ning's work at a Wendy's makes
a statement about the infusion of Western culture
into modern-day China.'
—Review of Taiwanese director Ang Lee's
Eat Drink Man Woman by James Berardinelli

EATING CONSTITUTES A MAJOR PREOCCUPATION, concern and form of enjoyment in Taiwan. You would expect this coming from a nation that has had its share of famines, hard times, and overpopulation. In Mandarin and Taiwanese a way of asking, "How are you?" is to enquire, "*Ni chi bao le ma?*", meaning literally, "Have you eaten your fill (yet)?" Happily, food is now plentiful in Taiwan and both Taiwanese and Wai Sheng chefs are masters at its preparation.

Once you are settled, you will definitely want to get out and about and enjoy at least some of the vast variety of food available. But, before you venture into Taiwanese restaurants and hawker centres, you should be prepared for what to expect. There is one word that describes what Taiwanese seek in dining and entertainment. That word is *re nao*, which translates directly as 'hot and raucous'. This means that, while Westerners going to a French restaurant will seek a quiet repose, Chinese going to a restaurant are looking for noisy, happy diners enjoying their repast and the company of friends. Loud and sometimes aggressive toasting takes place. The noise of the food being prepared in the kitchen is heard clearly in the dining room. The plates and bowls being removed from a neighbouring table clang and bang. All of this is part of the enjoyment.

Some foreigners take umbrage: "Why can't I just enjoy a quiet meal out?" Go to an expensive Western restaurant, then! For the Taiwanese, *re nao* is part of the enjoyment of eating and being alive. If they had to eat a Chinese dinner in regimented silence, they would not be happy. We had some Canadian friends who had lived in Japan for 10 years and had become immersed in the formality of the culture. We went with them to a Japanese eatery in Taipei. The *lao ban niang* (manageress) came over and served our tea and appetisers, banging the cups and saucers on the table in a happy rush. My friend, who was used to the formal, non-obtrusive silence of Japanese service, was incensed. There was, in fact, no use getting angry; the manageress was not insulting us, she was just trying to efficiently get the job done, get out of our way, and on to the next table.

THE MEALS OF THE DAY

Most Westerners, when thinking of Chinese cuisine, immediately think of rice, rice, rice. Indeed, in Mandarin and Taiwanese, the word *fan*, literally meaning rice, may be used to refer to meals and food in general. However, this may be a good time to point out that not all rice is equal. The rice consumed in Taiwan is the same as the Japanese Calrose variety—short-grained and sticky. It is better than the rice you will eat in Mainland China and different from the long-grained, fragrant rice favoured by the Chinese from Thailand through to Singapore.

Breakfast

Taiwanese like to eat three 'squares' a day and then snack now and again. Breakfast is called *zao can* (early meal) or *dzau fan* (early rice) and is normally taken between 7:00 –9:00 am. If the family is Western-oriented, they might have a glass of milk with a slice of bread, into which has been folded either *rou song* (pork floss) or a fried egg. Sometimes it might be prepared buns from the local bakery. These buns often have fillings that can be an annoying or pleasant 'surprise' for Westerners expecting a plain bun. It might be sweetened condensed milk, pork floss, tuna fish, sweetened bean paste or a hotdog. If you aren't sure of the freshness, take care. This is especially true of some 'cream horns' or prepared sandwiches with mayonnaise. However, we must also comment that we have had some excellent croissants and pastry from local Taiwanese bakeries as of late.

If the family prefers local taste, breakfast can be one of several things. Mandarin *jou* or Taiwanese *buh* (rice porridge) is served with side dishes of peanuts, salted duck egg, pickled seaweed or cucumber, preserved fish, or canned fried gluten. Northern *Wai Sheng Ren* brought with them their *shao bing* and *you tiao* breakfast breads.

Shao bing (roast cakes) are a flaky crusted bread pocket with sesame seeds sprinkled on the outside. *You tiao* (oil sticks) are deep-fried Chinese crullers. The chef will put a long thin string of dough into an immense oil-filled wok standing over a large flame. The string will balloon out to make a thin golden brown and crispy rod. This is folded in half and inserted in the *shao bing* pocket. It is frequently accompanied by *dou jiang* (soybean milk soup), which is served hot or cold, sweet or salty. The white sweet type is common and can be found everywhere. The hot salty type is made by taking raw soybean milk and adding a spoonful of dried pickled radish, sesame oil, chilli oil, salt, bits of broken *you tiao*, and shallots. It tastes like a divine cream of chicken soup. Worth looking out for.

Lunch

For students, office workers, or factory people, *wu can* (lunch) or *wu fan* (noon meal) is usually eaten between 12:00–1:00 pm and is frequently in a *bian dang* (lunch box). This term is not used in China and came from the Japanese o bento. The *bian dang* was traditionally brought from home and heated at the school or office. Today there are small eateries that sell them 'to-go' in styrofoam containers. They will also deliver to local offices.

Usually the meal contains steamed white rice and a fried pork chop, or fish, a chicken drumstick, or stewed pork, stir-fried vegetables, mustard greens, dried bean curd, etc. An alternative is the *zi zhu can* (self-service meals) which are served in small cafeterias. In the late morning, the chefs will busy themselves cooking up vast aluminium trays of food: fried and steamed fish, eggplant, bean curd, greens, pork chops, fried eggs—usually 12 or more dishes. You are asked first if you want rice or porridge and then you can just point at what you want on top. The lady will heap it onto your disposable tray. A weak soup is also available.

Dinner

The ideal Taiwanese family will eat dinner together. The meal is called *wan fan* (late rice). They will usually have soup, two vegetables, and chicken or seafood—enough for a typical family of three. More dishes will be prepared if Grandma is around to help cook and eat. Today, though, Dad is out entertaining, Junior is off to cram school, so Mom eats a specialty at a pushcart to remind her of the flavours of her youth.

When they have all returned home they might go out together for *xiao ye* (midnight snack). This might be a bowl of noodles, or *chou doufu* (smelly bean curd—they say it smells like a sewer and tastes like a dream; bean curd's equivalent to Blue Stilton cheese). Or it could be *lu rou fan* (ground meat sauce on a bowl of rice), *rou geng*

Street stalls sell a wide variety of food and this is just one of the many street stalls that the Taiwanese frequent for their *xiao ye*.

(breaded, deep-fried bits of meat in a thick sauce) or *rou zong* (glutinous rice, egg, mushrooms, dried shrimp and pork mixed together and steamed in a leaf). Tomorrow, they have decided to go out for dinner. With so many hundreds of eateries and restaurants to choose from, the only problem is deciding where!

REGIONAL STYLES

The island's history as an entrepôt, the arrival of the two million *Wai Sheng Ren* from every corner of China in 1949, not to mention the bounty of local vegetables, fruit, and meat, all meant that Taiwan was destined to become a gastronomic paradise. A brief introduction to the regional cuisines is in order:

- **Taiwanese** (*Tai Cai*). The cuisine of the local population is best known for its seafood, pork, chicken, light soups, and use of crushed or sliced garlic. Look for *ti pang* (stewed pig trotter), *hai gua zi* (clams fried with soy sauce and garlic), *qie cai hua zhi* (squid cooked with celery), *san bei ji* (three-cup chicken), *jia chang doufu* (homemade-style bean curd), and *cai pu jian dan* (omelette with preserved radish or oyster).
- **Hakka** (*Kejia Cai*). The Hakkas settled in Taiwan centuries ago and their cuisine is now very similar to the above. Specialties include *niang doufu* (stuffed bean curd), *jiu ceng ta qie zi* (eggplant basilico) and *tieban doufu* (teppanyaki bean curd).
- **Sichuan** (*Chuan Cai*) and **Hunan** (*Xiang Cai*). These cuisines from the south of central China both make liberal use of minced garlic and hot chillies. You can order the food to be prepared more mildly (*bu yao tai la*), but we have found this spicy food to be manageable by most of our foreign visitors. Look out for *suan la tang* (hot and sour soup), *gan shao xia* (sauteed shrimp with hot sauce), *yu xiang qie zi* (fish-flavored eggplant), *ma po doufu* (Ma Pwo bean curd), *bang bang ji* ('bang bang' chicken), *zhang cha ya zi* (camphor tea-smoked duck), *gong bao ji ding* (kung pao chicken), *la dou ban yu* (whole fish in hot bean sauce), *gan*

bian si ji dou (dry cooked string beans) and the famous numbing *ma la huo guo* ('spicy fire pot').

- **Cantonese** (*Ao Cai*). The Cantonese brought their style of cooking to the United States when they were used as forced labour on the railroads. Their cuisine became synonymous with Chinese food until the 1970s. However, it has been greatly damaged in the transition to the United States and you should try this popular cuisine of southern China to get to know 'the real thing'. Cantonese cuisine occasionally uses heavier and thicker sauces, is milder than other Chinese food, and is very colourful. Some popular dishes are *yao guo xia ren* (shrimp with cashew nuts), *gu lao rou* (sweet and sour pork), *cha shao rou* (roast pork), *dung gua pai gu tang* (pork ribs with winter melon soup), *hao you jie lan* (abalone with Chinese broccoli and oyster sauce).

- **Peking** (*Jing Cai*). This is Mandarin cuisine from the north of China. Look for more noodles and breads, and less rice. Famous dishes are *Beijing kao ya* (Peking duck) and *shuan yang rou* (rinsed mutton chafing dish)—a dish which is either cooked or kept warm at your table by means of a small, portable spirit stove.

- **Shanghai**. Cuisine from Shanghai and its surrounding areas features a lot of seafood and fish dishes. In particular, try *ninybo shi shan yu* (Ningpo-style eel) and *xi hu cu yu* (West Lake vinegar fish).

- **Vegetarian** (*Su Cai*). China has some marvellous vegetarian cuisine, thanks to its Buddhist heritage. It tries to make vegetarianism for hard-core omnivores a little easier to endure by making some dishes look and taste reasonably like meat—*su e* (vegetarian goose), for instance. Other popular dishes are fried gluten, *fa cai geng* (hair vegetable stew) and *su chun juan* (vegetarian spring rolls).

- **Mongolian Barbecue** (*menggu kao rou*). The concept of the barbecue is said to have evolved from the travelling kitchens of Genghis Khan's mounted forces. A large metal shield would be placed over a fire, game slaughtered, and local vegetables rounded up. Popular with both foreign visitors and locals, the barbecue in Taiwan is an all-you-can-eat buffet-style affair. Pick out your choice of raw meats, vegetables, and sauces, then watch the chef cook it before your eyes.

■ **Steamboat** (*huo guo*). This is a cook-at-your-table, chafing dish. Pick out a selection of raw meats, seafood, vegetables, won ton, and noodles. They will either be cooked in a *shi tou huo guo* (stone pot) or just a stainless steel pan at your table. Be sure to ask for Taiwan's famous *sha cha jiang* (literally 'sand tea paste'). It is a delicious, not too spicy sauce, into which Taiwanese will add a raw egg and maybe some soy sauce. Cooked food is then dipped into the mixture.

■ **Dim Sum** (*dian xin*). Normally associated with Cantonese cuisine, there are actually several regional *dian xin* traditions. It is also known as *yin cha* (roughly meaning tea time). Expect *dian xin* only between 10:30 am— 2:00 pm. It is a boisterous substitute for lunch and comprises a variety of freshly cooked items served in round bamboo steamers. Waiters and waitresses will busily push carts loaded with these steamers to and fro through the aisles of the restaurant, where they are eagerly snapped up. Feel free to stop a waiter to ask to look at what he is selling. If you are not interested, just say, "*xie xie, bu yao*" ("No, thanks"), though you will find that it's all quite edible and delicious. Chosen items will be marked on a tally kept at your table. Popular *dian xin* are *cha shao bao* (steamed pork buns), *feng zua* (chicken claws), *pai gu* (steamed pork ribs), *xia jiao* (shrimp dumplings) and *chun zhuan* (spring rolls).

Regional Specialities

As you travel around Taiwan, it is worth noting that each area has its own local specialty foods to be eaten or taken back home as a souvenir. Although modern transportation has made many of these items more universally available, they still make excellent gifts to give your Taiwanese and Western friends when you return home. They demonstrate *ren qing wei* and can lead to discussions about Chinese food preparation and things you saw on your trip. The list below

A purveyor of roast chestnuts happily tends to his treats.

is by no means comprehensive and we hope you may make your own discoveries of other specialties!

- *Taiyang bing* (sun cakes). These are found in Taichung and are a flaky layered flat bun, white in color. In the centre is a thin layer of sweet paste. They can be bought singly or by the box.
- *Dan dan mian* (noodles). This dish is a specialty of Tainan and is usually eaten at the stalls where it is cooked. It is made of yellow noodles, the size of spaghetti, which are cooked in a broth and then served with a crown of fragrant stewed ground pork. A dash of fresh coriander tops it off.

Ask for a *lu dan* (Shandong egg) on the top. This is a very hard boiled egg that has been shelled and marinated or cooked in ground pork broth.

- *Wulung cha* (oolong tea). The world's finest oolong tea is grown in Taiwan and the finest Taiwan oolong is grown in Tungting.
- Fresh apples and pears from Lishan are particularly good and worth buying.
- Peanuts and peanut candy are a specialty of Hsinchu.
- *Zhu sun gan* (dried bamboo shoots). These are found in Hsitou. Taken home, soaked and stewed, they make an excellent appetiser.
- *Guancaiban* (coffin burger) are a street food consisting of a juicy ground pork centre in a baked bun.
- *Fuzhou hujiao bing* (Fuzhou pepper bread) is a peppery pork filling surrounded by a crispy sesame seed draped crust.
- *Pao mo cha* (bubble tea) took Taiwan by storm several years ago, spread throughout Asia, then died down. Select the base for your drink (tea or fruit flavors), whether you want milk or not and bubbles (large sweet chewy tapioca pearls). They will add ice and seal the plastic cup with a plastic top. You can suck up to this delectable drink by stabbing the lid with the sharp, large diameter straw they will give you.

The International

The range of international cuisine has improved greatly over the years from intercultural exchange as travel to and from Taiwan increases. Twenty-five years ago, a pizza comprised the bottom half of a hamburger bun with a slice of Spam, American cheese and ketchup toasted in a broiler. Now one can choose from international fast-food chains such as Pizza Hut and Starbucks; fast food of all description has infiltrated the Taiwanese diet, so the Westerner will not want for a Big Mac or Dominoes. Restaurants serving Greek, Italian, French, Spanish, Mexican, American and even British food can also be found. Prices can be steep but the following cuisines are relatively more affordable and available.

- Japanese (*Ri Ben Liao Li*). A colony of Japan for 50 years, the Taiwanese learned to cook and enjoy Japanese food. This, coupled with the booming trade and tourism links with Japan, means that authentic Japanese food is readily accessible. The Japanese names for some of the most popular styles are *sushi* (rice, seafood, and seaweed hors d'oeuvres), *sashimi* (raw seafood), *yakiniku* (barbecued meat on a stick), *teppanyaki* (meat and vegetables quickly grilled in front of you), *tempura* (seafood and vegetables, battered and deep-fried) and *udon* (thick noodles in a broth).
- Thai, Indonesian and Vietnamese. Overseas Chinese from various areas have gone to Taiwan to set up eateries serving ethnic cuisine. The foods are refreshingly spicy and reasonably priced.
- Italian Pasta (*Yi Da Li Mian*). Since Marco Polo is reputed to have brought noodles to Italy after his journey to China, it is fitting that pasta has become very popular and affordable in Taiwan. Many small eateries (frequently identified with the Italian Tri-colore of red white and green) serve up a choice of pasta with red, cream or white wine sauce and seafood, bacon, beef, clams or vegetables. A decent dinner, complete with bread, soup and a drink will set you back only NT$ 200. Pizza is also increasingly popular with Pizza Hut, Dominos and the local Napoli chains deep dishing it out, as well as many upscale Italian bistros.
- Coffee Shops. Formerly monopolised by Japanese coffee chains and frequented by well-heeled young lovers, coffee shops are now ubiquitous around the island. Besides the global powerhouse, Starbucks, you can enjoy your java at Barista, Dante, Doutor, McCafe, Mr. Brown and the economical favourite 85° C. Besides coffee or tea, you can enjoy cakes, tarts and in some locations sandwiches.

List of Restaurants

An excellent list of local Chinese and foreign restaurants is available at

http://travel.yahoo.com/p-travelguide-6916771-taiwan_restaurants-i

THE BIZARRE, THE MACHO AND THE ILLEGAL

Every nation has its strange and macho foods: prairie oysters (raw testicles) in the United States, *balutte* (semi-incubated duck eggs) in the Philippines, *fugu* (the poisonous puffer fish) in Japan. Frequently, it is expected that their ingestion will improve one's sexual performance, or at least one's vitality. Translated into Taoist theory, such foods are very *yang* or create a lot of energy. Below are some foods which you may see on a menu or find being served to you during a night out with the guys.

- Sea Cucumber and Jellyfish. Neither item is considered bizarre or macho by the Taiwanese. Sea cucumber is frequently served cooked in thick sauces, while jellyfish comes on cold platters. Sea cucumber is gelatinous and innocuous; it takes on the flavour of whatever it is cooked with. Jellyfish is usually served cold and shredded in a chilli, sesame and vinaigrette seasoning. It has a chewy, rubbery consistency.

- Whole Fish or Poultry. Fish and poultry are frequently brought to the table in a state of wholeness that Westerners find shocking. That means cockscomb, head, eyes, brains and feet (or fins). Of course, they have been gutted. Chris distinctly remembers the dinner he had, three weeks after arriving in Taiwan, when the lady of the house served up a boiled chicken, its head limply hanging over the rim of the pot, staring him straight in the eye. Superior flavour is the reasoning behind this custom. Feel honoured if your host serves the meat from the fish's gill shield to you—it is reputed to be the tastiest.

- Cracked Bones. Chinese chefs, either before or after cooking, will cut a piece of chicken or pork clear through the bones. It is felt that greater flavour and nutrition is imparted to the dish this way and Taiwanese can frequently be seen gnawing on the marrow. However, this means that sometimes the dish can have sharp shards of bone in it, which you should be careful of. Bone pieces can be removed from your mouth with your chopsticks or spat onto your plate. Follow your friend's lead.

- Braised Ox Phallus or Rooster and Tom Turkey Privates. Enough said!

- Snake's Blood Soup. This is available mostly at Snake Alley, where vipers, cobras, and hundred-pacers (all very poisonous snakes) are milked of venom, vivisected and squeezed dry of blood and bile. This is often served as a cocktail, mixed with potent *gao liang* (sorghum spirit). Alternatively, it can be boiled up as a soup with strips of snake meat.

- Bear Paws. It is said that when bears go into hibernation they store nutrients for the winter in their paw pads. Blissfully asleep, they lick the pads and are slowly fed. Consequently, the Chinese feel that, being so full of vitamins and minerals, bear paw pads make an excellent tonic. However, bears are endangered in China and, indeed, around the world. This is a very expensive dish and it is best to steer clear of it. If asked whether you will eat it, you might reply that your Chinese physician has told you only to eat eel as a tonic, not bear.

- Turtle's Blood Cocktails. Again, these can be had at Snake Alley, or you could watch the movie *Farewell to My*

TRIGG.

Ready to eat grilled cuttlefish, barbequed skewers of chicken and fish cakes.

Concubine to see how it's done. Turtles have long lives (well, not at Snake Alley!) and phallic-shaped heads, so they are presumed to be very *yang*. To make the cocktail, the head of the turtle is pulled out of the shell and chopped off. Then the shell is peeled back slightly (legs are still moving) and *gao liang* is poured into it, mixed, and then poured out with the blood. Bottoms up!

- Dog Meat. Called *xiang rou* (fragrant meat) in Mandarin, it is actually illegal to sell it in Taiwan. Pets still disappear, though, and signs will occasionally appear on the street, saying 'Fragrant Meat for Sale'. Curiously, the Chinese view this as a 'heaty' tonic food to be consumed in winter, while the Koreans see it as a summer tonic. Whatever your belief, it certainly gives a new meaning to the song 'How Much is that Doggy in the Window?'

- Betel Nut. Betel nut is chewed like tobacco and sometimes referred to as 'Chinese chewing gum'. Traditionally sold at roadside stalls, these are brightly lit, air-conditioned glass-windowed kiosks 'manned' by attractive, revealingly attired young women called *bin lang xishi*, perhaps formerly engaged in the barber salon or massage parlour trade. A betel nut is wrapped in a betel pepper leaf, after being smeared with an alkaline paste. When chewed, the result is a blood-red mess in the mouth, which is frequently spat out onto the sidewalk and can be mistaken for rather nasty tubercular expectorations. The effect of the juice is a mild narcotic high, which is nevertheless legal. Addicts can be readily picked out of the crowd by their stained teeth and bloody grin.

TEA TIME

Tea drinking is a culture unto itself in Chinese societies and this is especially so in Taiwan, with its splendid oolong, jasmine, chrysanthemum and *tie guan yin* varieties. It is interesting to note that, in all languages around the world, there are only two words for this beverage that originated in China, and both names are Chinese. *Cha* is the Mandarin name, which found its way into Japanese as *o cha*. *Teh* is the term in the Hokkien dialect, which of course found its way into English, French and other languages.

There are many places where you might enjoy tea and the etiquette involved might vary. If you are invited to have tea or coffee during a business meeting, you might reply that you want Chinese tea. If it is served to you in a Western teacup and there is no evidence of leaves, then it was brewed in a bag. If, however, it comes to you in a tall cup with a lid, it will probably have the leaves still seeping in hot water. The proper etiquette is to hold the cup in one hand and gently remove the lid with the other, holding it over the cup and sweeping the condensation from the tea back into the cup in a soft circular motion of lid against lip. Then, with the cup brought to the nose, lift the lid and smell the perfume of the tea. Finally, look at the surface of the water. Are there leaves still floating on the surface? If so, wait a minute more. After that, repeat the process, but this time either gently blow the leaves away from the area you wish to drink from, or use the lid to push them out of the way.

Another privilege you may enjoy is to go to a teahouse or the house of a friend to enjoy *lao ren cha* (pensioner's tea), so called because old folk like to sit with friends, sipping, chatting, snacking, sipping, chatting, snacking, and so on.

The home-grown oolong tea is of very fine quality and can be appreciated at one of the teahouses in Taiwan.

During *lao ren cha*, a small teapot, usually from Yixing (a town north of Shanghai which is famous for its teapots), is stuffed with tea leaves and placed in a small terracotta bowl in which tiny demitasse cups rest. Water which was boiled about 10 minutes before is poured into the pot, allowed to activate the leaves briefly, then poured onto the cups, ostensibly to rinse and heat them up. The cups are rolled around in the tea water, then removed with a pair of bamboo tweezers, and stood up in a row.

When the leaves have steeped, the tea is poured into the cups and your host will probably present your cup to you with some ceremony. Again, take the time to savour the aroma of the tea. There will be no leaves in it to blow away, so take a sip and roll it on your tongue. If you are drinking a quality oolong, you may taste a slight bitterness behind the fragrance. After you have swallowed, however, you will most likely taste the sweetness of the saliva in your mouth. The Chinese believe this is good to swallow as it helps to build *chi*. The process of steeping and savouring is repeated as often as ten or 12 times for a quality tea, the taste varying to the connoisseur's palate each time round. In between, snacks designed not to interfere with either the enjoyment of the tea or the meandering of the conversation, are enjoyed.

It is enjoyable and worthwhile acquainting yourself with Chinese teas. They are a source of pride to the Taiwanese, can provide plenty of opportunity to break the ice and get to know people, and may become a lifelong obsession for you as well.

DINING OUT
The Invitation

Invitations from Taiwanese are normally warm, sincere, and spur-of-the-moment. Do not expect a week's notice for an informal dinner. You might be on the phone with a Taiwanese friend at 3:00 pm and be asked out to dinner that night. Let's say you are free and want to go. Return the warmth and sincerity of the invitation in your words and voice. For example, "That sounds great. I have never been to that restaurant before. Thank you." Make sure you get the time and place properly noted. If there is any question, ask to be met at a more obvious popular landmark.

If you are not free, do not just say, "No, thank you". This does not show *ren qing wei*. You should preferably have a reason for not going that is bigger than the face of the person asking. That way, he or she does not lose face. This is especially important if the invitation is given in person in front of a group. For example, you are invited to dinner with a business associate, but have another business dinner planned. If you just say ,"I'm sorry, but I have a dinner planned with Mr. Y of company Z," it may chill relations. You may not know the inviter's relation or relative status to Mr. Y. What you are saying indirectly is, "He is more important than you." Better to say something like, "I wish I could come, but I have bought tickets for my daughter's play/have to be at the school to give a test to students/have to wait at the hotel for a long conference call with my boss."

Since many invitations are spur-of-the-moment, it is not appropriate to add, "But can we go next week?" if you must decline. Better to say, "But I have left Monday night open and planned to invite you and your staff to dinner." Your invitation will probably be turned down, but it leaves the door open. Note that, because of the sincere persistence required of *ren qing wei*, some excuses will not do. For instance, you are invited to play a round of golf, a game you have admitted to having played before. If you refuse, using the excuse that you don't have your shoes, they will say, "We can rent shoes at the clubhouse." To say you do not want to wear rented shoes is too stuffy. If you say no because you do not have a handicap yet, they will say, "No matter, we can fix it up with the club to let you play." You really must think of a good reason not to take up the invitation.

Invitations to weddings, *man yue*, *man sui* and company New Year's banquets will be issued in writing or in advance. A *xi jiu* (wedding banquet) invitation is normally red with gold lettering. Invitations to company banquets, on the other hand, will usually be relayed by word of mouth.

The Casual Meal

A typical casual business lunch is described in Chapter Nine. Expect the same situation in any Chinese restaurant which is a step above the cafeterias. Ordering is usually done off the menu. If you are with Taiwanese, avoid the temptation to order for the group. Unless you have been in Taiwan for a long time and know the specialties of the restaurant's regional cuisine, then you should ask your Taiwanese friends to order, even if (perhaps especially if) you are the host. Out of courtesy, they may ask you to order. Politely insist that they order. Do not even peruse the menu; this implies you want to have some say. Turn it over to the 'big shot' at the table.

Why? Invariably they will know the *zhao pai cai* (house specialty). They also know the quantities and proper mix to order. Letting them select gives them face, it says you trust them, and, if you are the host, it lets them order things they will enjoy. It also saves you the embarrassing problem of having ordered too little or too many 'cheap' dishes. So far, our Taiwanese friends have not abused this trust by ordering only the most expensive things and, moreover, it reaps more *ren qing wei* points.

When you insist they order, you should advise them that you do not like, for instance, sweet and sour pork or cream of *sum yung gai* (yes, it's a joke alright!) because otherwise they may order according to what they think a foreigner's taste is. But you should ask them specifically not to order a certain dish, only if you really can't handle it (that means you are allergic to it!). Who knows, maybe this restaurant has a tastier way of preparing *hai zhe* (sea cucumber)? It is completely appropriate to ask what they have ordered and to review the dishes one by one as they come. Individual dishes frequently have stories behind them and this can become one of the most interesting things about the repast. It also lets you prepare for what kind of food will be set before you.

How do Taiwanese order foods? They will normally order one dish per person, plus a soup and rice or noodles. If the meal is for four people, they might order, for example, one meat, one fish, two vegetable dishes, one soup and plain white rice. Certain styles or types of dishes are not repeated. For instance, two sweet and sour dishes or two shrimp dishes will not be ordered together. Unlike in the West, Taiwanese do not order for individual diners. This goes back to the practice of the family always eating together as a group. Unless you are eating lunch box-style, the dishes are almost invariably shared. You will be expected to try everything. Respond enthusiastically to dishes that you like and give a reasoned explanation of why. Likewise, politely say that the things you do not like are not to your taste, but be sure you have tried some first. Anyway, they will know what you do not enjoy by watching you, so it is best to be upfront.

Mind Your Manners

During the meal it is possible that the host or your neighbour will serve your plate. He or she will do this either with the serving spoon or *gong yong kuai zi* ('public-use' chopsticks), the usage of which was promoted by the government 15 years ago to prevent the spread of hepatitis and tuberculosis. They should be returned to the dish they came from. Alternatively, they might deftly reverse their own chopsticks and use the back end. Thank them for their hospitality. Though it is not expected, you may return the gesture with another dish later, but make sure you use the public-use chopsticks and return them to the platter afterward. If you aren't so deft at using chopsticks, it is probably best to sit this one out, rather than risk dropping food over your host (it has happened!).

When serving yourself, you should again use the public-use chopsticks or serving spoon, if provided. If they are not provided, you may ask for public-use chopsticks to be brought to the table. Your friends will not think this queer and may possibly commend you on your knowledge of Taiwanese eating habits. If it is a very informal group of friends, and they are using their own chopsticks to serve themselves, then you may do so. However, do not dredge your chopsticks or spoon through the food looking for a choice morsel. Do not even reach across to the opposite side of the plate to get that nice-looking shrimp. It is considered selfish and greedy. Select a piece near to your side of the plate and go for it.

Chopsticks should not be used as drumsticks to bang or tap the table with; nor should you plant them in your serving of rice so that they stand up. This reminds Taiwanese of incense sticks in a censer, used when praying for the dead, so it is not a good sign at the table. Depending on the class of company you keep, loud belching could be considered rude, acceptable or naturally expected. Taiwanese are uninhibited at times and belches are frequently heard in mid-sentence: "Hey, Chris, did you—belch—go to Taichung yesterday?" No apology proffered or expected.

Toothpicks will either be on the table or brought to it at the end of the repast, sometimes stuck in pieces of fruit. The Chinese like picking their teeth, be it for hygiene or to get full value from the meal. However, do not open your yap and dig in; the Taiwanese do not want to see your tonsils. In fact, they usually cover the mouth with the left hand, while industriously mining away with the right.

The Fight for the Check

Even if you were the one to invite your Taiwanese friends or colleagues out to dinner, drinks, karaoke, and the rest of it, expect a fight for the check. This is not a fight because nobody wants to pay, but the fight of who has the privilege to pay. Frequently, you will see perfectly happy diners suddenly erupt into a flurry of emotion and hand-waving. You wait for them to come to blows as the volume increases. Don't be alarmed. This is merely proper gamesmanship. If it was clearly your invitation to them, make sure you win. Do not let them pull the tab out of your hands and just say, "Okay, thanks." If they have invited you, make a show of trying to get the tab, but eventually yield it to the host, otherwise he loses face.

Sometimes the fight for the check begins at the time of the invitation. The scenario may go something like this. You invite several friends out to dinner. They have already treated you before. One of them insists that he invite you. The frequent ruse given is, "This is my country. When I come to visit your country, you can invite me out." The best reply to this is to jovially (never brusquely) insist that: a) they treated you last time; b) you have been in Taiwan for a while and this is now your second home; and c) without question, you expect them to visit when they come to your country and let you treat them, so this is just your pleasure to take them out now.

One strategy to ensure that you win the fight for the check (if it is known to be your treat) is to discreetly leave your credit card with the cashier before or during the dinner. The same blizzard of grabbing hands will fly when the bill comes, but they will realise at a glance that it is too late, and have to commend you on your artifice. Express your gratitude that they accompanied you for the meal.

BANQUETS

You know from Chapter Three what kinds of gifts to bring to certain types of banquet celebrations. If it is a banquet in your honour, or just a large group of diners joining together for a good meal, you might consider bringing a gift. A bottle of whiskey (Johnnie Walker preferably) is reasonable and may well be opened at the banquet to be enjoyed by all. Give it to the host, though.

The banquet table is always round and seats ten to 12 people. Expect to find it in an individual room for your party. The guest of honour will sit to the right of the host in a chair which faces the door and has its back to a wall. This harks back to Chinese chivalric courtesy: the safest and therefore most honoured seat was the one with no entry behind you and a view of your enemies ahead. If you are not sure if you are the guest of honour, wait to be shown to your seat.

At each place-setting, expect to find:
- a soup bowl
- a small plate
- a chopstick-rest and spoon-rest
- chopsticks (sometimes the wrapped, sanitary type)
- a metal serving spoon
- a ceramic soup spoon
- a napkin or cold face towel
- a teacup
- a shot glass
- a juice/beer glass

The table usually has a tablecloth and a 'lazy Susan' at its centre. The lazy Susan (a small revolving platform at the centre of the table) rotates either way to give you access to the many dishes that will be delivered. Do not play with it or spin it too fast. When you arrive, it may already have some *xiao qi* (little snacks) on it, such as peanuts or dried watermelon seeds. Follow the lead of the Taiwanese to gauge when you can begin to eat these. You may have to wait for the guest of honour, host or other big shot to arrive. He or she may be late. Spend the time chatting with your friends and asking them the rules of banqueting. Unless the person is extraordinarily late or you hear the Taiwanese complaining, it is best not to comment on punctuality.

When the guest of honour has arrived, the first course—normally an assorted cold plate—will be brought to the table. In some restaurants, a waitress will serve a helping of each course onto individual plates or bowls. At other places, you serve yourself. Go with the flow. In all, ten or 12 dishes and soups may be served. Pace yourself. Try not to 'chow down' the first two courses because you are hungry, only to end up wishing you had room to squeeze in a taste of the last three courses.

The last main course (and it is a signal that things are slowing down) is usually a rice, fried rice or noodle dish. Other culture guides to Taiwan state that you should not eat this at all. We have not found that to be true. You will see the Taiwanese eating it. However, it is considered bad form to finish your helping or, especially, to ask for more, no matter how good it tastes. To do so signifies you are still hungry, that the host was terribly remiss in not ordering enough, and that you are going home unsated. Shame on your host!

After rice, a plate of fresh fruit will normally be served. At some northern-style Chinese banquets either a sweet steamed rice and *ba bao fan* (preserved fruit dish) or crepes with sweet bean paste filling might be served. Other than this, do not expect or ask for dessert.

If you are the guest of honour, it is important to know when to leave, as they will be waiting for you to make a sign. No more than 15 to 20 minutes should pass after the last course and fruit is brought out. You should then thank the host profusely for the bounty they have provided, for the thoughtful attention they showed in ordering such delicious foods, and for the friendship shown during all the toasting. If things are going well and you are so inclined, it would not hurt to invite the host out for further partying at a bar or karaoke lounge, but not for a snack, cake or other food.

Banquet Drinking

Depending on the function of the banquet, different types of toasting will take place. At family milestone banquets (weddings, *man yue*, *man sui*), the hosts will go to each table to toast a glass. Usually this is beer or *shao xing jiu* (amber-coloured Chinese rice wine served warm or at room temperature, frequently with rock sugar or a dried plum in the glass).

At a company function, the boss will toast each table. Toasting will also take place among the guests at each table. Indeed, it is considered poor form to take a drink of alcohol (or any drink besides tea) without it being a toast. The man across the table from you may raise his glass to you. He is honouring you. He is also thirsty. It would be unthinkable not to salute him with your glass. The usual toasting salutation is a boisterous *gan bei* which has the same characters as the Japanese *kam pai*, meaning 'dry glass'. At some time during the dinner, the toast should be returned. Just think of it: nine people toasting you, plus nine returns make 18 glasses of beer or shots of wine. And we haven't even counted the people from other tables in the banquet who may come over especially to toast the foreigner!

Banquet Drinking

At one banquet (a source of fond memories for Chris and his Taiwanese host), the host announced to the group that he knew Chris did not like to drink too much, so he had brought him a special glass. He popped the tiniest of shot glasses on the table top. He continued amid laughter, "And I have chosen a special plum for his glass." He then put the largest of dried plums inside. There was hardly any room left for wine! You might try a similar strategy.

The Taiwanese, especially men, like to drink and think they are good at it. Indeed, they generally hold their liquor better than Japanese, but have the same genetic tendency to turn red in the face with their first beer. They like drinking with foreigners, are eager to introduce you to the local spirits and appreciate a good drinker. Some women drink moderately, but those who can 'put it away with the best of them' are generally considered 'bad' (i.e. morally loose or even a prostitute). This attitude is changing among college-age girls, but as they age, they still do not want to be associated with 'darker elements'. Foreign women who can drink heavily will be held to a different standard than local women and might be an amusing fascination to the other dinner guests. The impression left is risky though. Temperance is advised.

Temperance Strategies

For the person who does not want to drink alcohol, there are several alternatives, depending on the function. If you never drink because of religion or health, just say so. Juice is available to toast with. This excuse means they should not find you with beer in hand next week. Alternatively, if you are driving, you can try the 'designated driver' excuse; explain what it means in the West, and hope they do not think you too much of a wimp. If you can take a little alcohol, but not too much, do not drain your glass with every toast. The person who toasted you will point it out, but you can smile and laugh it off, and they will understand.

We also know a high-powered American executive who brings with him to banquets his own 'designated drinker' (a company employee who takes the successive belts for him). For heavy duty banqueting this might give him tremendous status, but he does not get any of the face from being able to loosen his tie and commune with the locals in their most relaxed state. He admits, too, that even with the designated drinker, he occasionally gets roped into drinking bouts.

A final note about banquets: there is never any question about who picks up the tab and hence no fighting for the bill!

ENJOYING TAIWAN

CHAPTER 7

'Trekking in Taiwan is not for the faint-hearted.
The Central Mountain Range is steep and wild, and much
of it is covered with thick forest. Summer thunderstorms rise
unseen, temperatures can drop below zero, and facilities
are few and far between. But for those willing to carry their
own gear, the treks are among the most beautiful in Asia.'
—Brent Hannon, *Hiking in Taiwan*

WHETHER YOU HAVE COME TO TAIWAN on holiday or to live and work, you should try to get to know the people. The more you travel around the island, the more you introduce yourself to the regional cuisines and appreciate the many and varied outings and holidays that you can have, the more you will have a chance to interact directly with the friendly people here. There is so much to do, see, eat, and enjoy that no time need be spent lonely or unoccupied.

Taiwanese work hard all day: night-time is when they play. As with dining, Taiwanese entertainment revolves around *re nao* (literally, 'hot and raucous', but a term generally indicative of lively and noisy activity). Everywhere is *re nao*: on the streets the hawkers selling clothes, sausages, fruit, teapots; the roar of hundreds of motorcycles; the endless shop signs setting the evening alight. Similarly, the Taiwanese like their movie entertainment to be *re nao*: kung fu movies, *The Matrix*, Schwarzeneggar, slapstick. In the movie theatre, don't be surprised if the couple sitting next to you are noisily enjoying fried chicken or leathery dried squid, or if rather loud laughing and chattering are going on. The audience are simply enjoying themselves as well as the movie!

Perhaps this kind of behaviour dates back to the spectacular Chinese opera shows in 1920s China. Half the spectacle was actually in the audience, as pastries, tea and hot towels were delivered and consumed during the performance, the towels being thrown through the air, back to the towel boy.

Most religious observances are also *re nao*. *Re nao* is pageantry and spectacle, colour and emotion, the noise of large gatherings of people enjoying themselves. "Why can't we just take a little quiet respite from the noise of this life here?" a tired Westerner laments. But you must remember, for the Taiwanese, respite from the noise in this life is death. They are in no hurry. Try to enjoy life with them, their way, especially if they invite you to do so.

ENTERTAINMENT

Though you may get the impression from all the full restaurants you see around you that the only entertainment in Taiwan is eating, you would be missing out on half of what goes on.

Hot Springs

As long as you are living on the Pacific Rim of Fire, you might as well enjoy one of its delights, bubbling hot mineral spring baths. Taiwan's hot springs have been famous for a century since the Japanese created retreats in the hills of Peitou, and infamous during the days of Vietnam War R&R (rest and relaxation) revelry. Today one can enjoy these in a range of ways. Taipei area, Hualien, Taitung and other towns boast high-class spas. There are also rustic resorts, traditional hillside bathhouses and even 'au naturel' spots, such as the hidden springs emptying into the cold rushing gorge an hour's hike from the enchanting Tienhsiang resort. In recent years a row of high-class restaurants cum hot spring bathhouses have sprung up on Hsing-yi Alley 300, up above Tienmu in the Taipei suburbs. Here you can dine on good Chinese, Taiwanese, and Japanese cuisine, and, for a reasonable minimum per head dining charge, take in the baths in luxurious private cabanas. Towels are provided.

We advise you not to wear silver or low karat gold jewellery into the baths as they will be tarnished. For more information, see http://www.gio.gov.tw/taiwan-website/gogo/goen_31.htm.

Cinema

Movies are popular in Taiwan. Western films are usually in English with Chinese subtitles. A European movie, however, might be in the original language without English subtitles, so beware. Chinese movies normally have both Chinese and English subtitles.

Chinese films fall into several categories: serious dramas of high quality (these are rare); action movies (which include police, soldier, military chivalric and kung fu themes); banal comedies; and 'cry me a river' tear-jerking family dramas. Hard-core pornography is not screened publicly.

Beginning in the early 1980s, auteur cinema took hold in the form of movies such as Hou Hsiao Hsien's *City of Sadness* and Edward Yang's *Taipei Story*. In the 1990s, Ang Lee and Tsai Ming Liang became the most recognised directors succeeding the first wave of Taiwanese cinema. The Taipei Film Festival is the largest international film event in Taiwan and screens both emerging domestic talent and established foreign directors. Held in the early summer, tickets are sold out quickly so it is advised to book tickets well in advance. Contemporary art house films are regularly screened at the Spot Taipei Film House. For information see http://www.spot.org.tw .

Movie theatres are spread around the city now. The Times Square of Taipei is *Xi Men Ding* (the Point of the Western Gate), where ten or so theatres and several department stores are clustered within 10 minutes' walk of each other. Also like Times Square, this part of town has a reputation for low-life, prostitution and drugs. Beware. In the eastern part of the city, just past the World Trade Centre, Warner Bros. has built a new cineplex right next to Taipei 101 called Warner Village where trendy people go to catch the latest releases in theatres equipped with the most modern sound systems.

Modern theatres, like Miramar and Warner Village, have online booking facilities and advance ticket sales. Older, or down island, theatres may adhere to an earlier practice. Movie tickets can only be bought one hour in advance of the show time. At the right time, a curtain will open at the ticket window and the attendant will let you choose which seats you want. Each person is only allowed to buy a maximum of four tickets per visit to the window. So, if you have a large group or family, make sure enough people stand in line to buy the required number of tickets.

This ticketing arrangement creates its own problems. When blockbuster movies hit town, the ticket scalpers (low-life, all) emerge from the woodwork. In Mandarin they are called *huang niu* (yellow cows). A clique of them waits in line for every show. Though the ticket line may extend around the block, somehow the regular folk near the front merely complain, but otherwise tolerate the shenanigans of the *huang niu* who continually break back into line with their cronies. When the ticket window curtain is closed, all the seats sold out, the *huang niu* disperse through the disappointed crowd selling their tickets with a 50–100 per cent mark-up. It is not wise to argue with them; they are a group and are sometimes lightly armed. Try to find a policeman instead. Or save the hassle by booking your tickets by phone at Warner Village, tel: (02) 2757-2345.

In the standard theatres of today, popcorn and hotdogs are usual food fare. Squid jerky, corn on the cob, and bottles of sarsaparilla used to be bought from sidewalk vendors and shared among friends. Street food has expanded to include international interpretations, with small brown paper bags of tempura straw mushrooms and miniature Belgian waffles, new portable snacks for the discriminating theatregoer.

Did you manage to get a ticket? If you did, you will notice that the theatre seats are divided left and right into *dan hau* (odd numbers) and *shuang hau* (even numbers) respectively. Before the movie starts there will be some commercials for things like juice, motor scooters, or life insurance, along with some movie previews if you are lucky. Lastly, try to look around the theatre before the lights go down and make sure you know where the *tai ping men* (emergency exit) is located. Note that smoking is not allowed in the theatre, so if the guy next to you lights up, feel free to point out the sign to him.

Clubs and Pubs

Taiwan's nightlife spans an encyclopedic range of genres. From velvet-rope danceclubs in the Taipei 101 area to mirror-walled billiard halls in university districts, going out in Taiwan caters to every taste intrepid enough to find it.

KTV

This stands for Karaoke Television. Karaoke, you may well know, is a Japanese term that literally means 'empty orchestra'. It is an advanced sing-along system. In Taiwan you will frequently see signs for KTV and you can take your family, friends or business associates along. You can get a private room, have snacks served up, and order songs to croon to in the relative privacy of your own soundproof room. The lyrics will appear on the screen, along with a video to go with the music. English, Mandarin, Taiwanese and Japanese songs are normally stocked. Check the charges per song and for snacks before you take the room, otherwise you might be in for a surprise at the end of the evening! More recently some KTV joints have begun to overlap into hostess bars, so check the place out before you bring the kids. There are also karaoke pubs which are basically bars with a karaoke rig, except here you sing to a crowd of inebriated strangers. The choice is yours!

Golf

If you are a visiting duffer, you can enjoy numerous challenging and mature courses throughout the island. Club memberships are expensive and treated as investments by Taiwanese businessmen, who sell them later for a profit. If you have business contacts, inform your Taiwanese counterparts of your interest in the game and an invitation will probably come your way. Post-game activities at down island courses might include hot springs or jacuzzi, sauna, massage and a meal.

Light Gambling

Although illegal in Taiwan, certain forms of gambling are ignored by the police. Mahjong *(majiang)* is an example. This is similar to a Western card game, but is played with tiles instead of cards. There is a whole culture of gambling etiquette established around mahjong and many movies in recent years have glorified the prowess of mahjong gambling kings. The Chinese will bet considerable amounts of money on mahjong and some sit up until the small hours playing this addictive game.

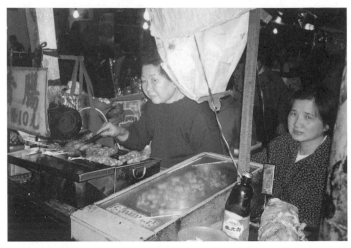

Try your luck at *pachinko* (pinball) and win a juicy sausage, but don't count on getting a free dinner this way. Chris has never won a sausage yet!

The government runs its own ingenious numbers lottery for a distinct and practical purpose. Like most business people, Taiwanese are averse to surrendering their tax dollars. Businessmen often kept two sets of accounts: one showing deflated earnings and the other the real situation. Then the government instituted the *Tong Yi Fa Piao* (Unified Invoice System). On a monthly basis, all businesses must purchase a booklet of these numbered invoices from the taxman. The populace is encouraged to ask for their receipts when making purchases as a monthly grand prize draw is made with the invoice numbers. The winning numbers are posted in the newspaper. Ask your secretary to help you keep track if you want to win.

On some streets in Taiwan you may also see an old man with charcoal brazier and a homemade *pachinko* board on the back of his bike. Cooking on the grill are nice, fat, juicy Taiwanese sausages. Try your luck—probably about NT$ 10 per try. Chris has not won a sausage yet and has always ended up asking the man to sell him one!

Other Diversions

Bowling is a popular and affordable indoor recreational activity among the young and old. Modern multi-storied complexes can be found in most major cities and suburbs. Shoes can be rented.

Fishing, a traditional hobby has now been updated. Try your luck for an hourly fee in concrete ponds stocked with fish or shrimp. These establishments frequently have kitchens that will cook up your catch.

For Culture Vultures

Cultural entertainment of some sort takes place every week in Taiwan. Several excellent ballet troupes perform original and classical works. Try, in particular, to see the Cloud Gate Ensemble while you are in Taiwan.

Traditional opera of several regional varieties is also performed. It used to be that, during festivals, a stage would be erected in the middle of a back street for several days so that *ge zai xi* (Hokkien opera) and *bu dai xi* (puppet shows) could

A stall selling some of the traditional puppets used in street shows.

be performed. You may still see that occasionally, but more often a screen is draped over a line across the road and films projected onto it for the whole neighbourhood to see. *Ping ju* or *Jing ju* (Beijing opera) is performed in theatres. Do not count on being able to understand the words, but the music, colour, acrobatics and action are sufficiently stimulating.

With increasing frequency, big-name pop acts are stopping in Taiwan. Listen to ICRT (the local English-language radio station) for details. Tickets are expensive and sell fast.

FESTIVALS AND HOLIDAYS

We have already stressed the Taiwanese love of *re nao* and this is nowhere more clearly seen than during festivals and holidays. The various festival celebrations that occur during the year allow them to stretch into ever louder and more raucous celebrations. Festivities and holidays revolve either around those that are religious or cultural, or those that are political and governmental. The dates of the former are determined by the farmer's calendar (the lunar *nongli*) and the latter are determined by the solar (Western) calendar. Here they are discussed in the order in which they fall in the solar calendar.

National Holidays

The ROC government has eliminated many national holidays associated with Chiang Kai Shek and the Kuomintang. The other holidays (2005 example) are:

Jan 1	Founding Day of the Republic of China
Feb 8-11	Lunar New Year (dates change every year)
Feb 28	Memorial Day
April 5	Tomb Sweeping Day
June 11	Dragon Boat Festival (dates change every year)
Sept 18	Mid-Autumn Festival
Oct 10	National Day

Founding Day of the Republic of China

Conveniently celebrated on New Year's Day (of the solar calendar), this holiday commemorates the founding of the Republic of China on 1 January 1912, following the overthrow of the Qing Dynasty.

Chinese New Year

Also called *chun jie* (Spring Festival), parts of this celebration occur over a six-week period, from the eighth day of the last month of the farmer's calendar to the 15th day of the first month. Chinese New Year's Day will normally fall between 10 January and 19 February. It is the grandest holiday for all Chinese around the world and is celebrated in many ways during the course of the season, depending on your age, sex, and marital status. It celebrates the birth of a new year, a time for renewed hope, the coming of spring, and fresh crops. Three days of official holiday are given around the change of the year. Depending on how outgoing you are and whether or not you have Taiwanese friends, it will be either a splendid and culturally enriching time or your loneliest week spent in Taiwan.

Prior to New Year's Eve, businessmen and individuals will feverishly crisscross the city settling old accounts. It is considered bad luck to have debts and accounts due when the New Year arrives. Pawnbrokers do a bumper business as people try to turn assets into paper money for the purpose of renewing credit. It is important, too, for businesses and individuals to collect what is owed them, for expenses peak during the New Year.

A business will normally have a banquet for its employees at this time. The cost can run into the tens of thousands of dollars for a medium-sized enterprise. At the banquet, there will normally be some sort of prize draw. The prizes are subsidised by the business, donated by the owners, or contributed by major suppliers. If your company is asked to contribute a gift to another company's banquet, figure on spending a minimum of NT$ 3,000–10,000. Cameras, household appliances, and gift certificates are appropriate. Employees also expect to receive a New Year bonus. This amounts to a minimum of one month's extra salary, or more if the company is doing well. Some companies will plan company trips before or after New Year as another employee perk. Even a medium-sized enterprise might book a trip for all its employees to go to Bangkok, Hong Kong or at least Kenting.

The individual also has increased expenses. On New Year's Eve the whole family will gather for a sumptuous dinner at home. Unmarried children receive *hong bao* (see chapter three) with *ya shui qian* (literally, 'push the year money') inside them. The children will visit relatives in their homes, run up to them, and politely demand, "*Gong xi fa cai! Hong bao na lai!*" (Congratulations and be prosperous! Hand over the red envelope!)

When visiting Taiwanese friends during the holiday, you should keep a pocketful of *hong bao*. Put one bright red NT$ 100 note in each so you are ready in case the children come to you. If they are too shy to come forward, it is very *ren qing wei* to ask them, "Aren't you going to ask for your *hong bao*?" It is also good manners to bring baskets of fruit, especially mandarin oranges, for they look like gold and are consumed by merrymakers during the 24-hour snacking that takes place.

Inside homes and offices, you might see black or gold Chinese characters painted on red paper and pasted to the walls and doors. If you are really astute, you will see the character *chun* (springtime) pasted upside down on the wall. This is because the phrase 'Spring turned upside down' has a similar sound in Chinese to 'Spring has arrived'. You will also see images of fish, especially goldfish, everywhere. This is because the word *yu* (fish) sounds like the word *yu* (surplus)— in other words, prosperity. Many New Year greetings revolve around this twist of words. At midnight on New Year's Eve, the staccato thunder of dozens of strings of exploding firecrackers can be heard across the city. Your sleep will be intermittently interrupted until about 3:00 am by this noise, designed to welcome the new year and scare evil away.

On the first day of New Year, it is appropriate to have new clothes ready for everyone in the family to wear. The day is spent visiting relatives, seeing movies, snacking, gambling, and playing mahjong. Even children join in on the betting, as older siblings try (often successfully) to win *ya shui qian* from the younger ones in games of dice-in-a-bowl and poker. The clickety-clack of shuffling mahjong tiles can be heard coming from second-story windows everywhere.

In the weeks leading to the Chinese New Year period, many shops will sell greeting cards, ornaments such as firecrackers as well as other auspicious items to usher in the new year.

On the second day of New Year, it is customary to allow one's wife to visit her family. In decades gone by, the wife became the virtual property of the husband, as well as fair game for ill-treatment from her mother-in-law, whose viciousness is legendary in Chinese culture. But at New Year, the wife was freed to go back to her family for a day. The plight of the modern Taiwanese housewife is not quite so bad these days, but the custom persists.

You might decide to join the crowd of thousands who want to see one of the blockbuster movies released at New Year (the equivalent of Hollywood's Christmas releases). Be aware that pickpockets and *huang niu* are working overtime during the festive season and will be in line with you.

On the third day of New Year, it is considered better luck to stay indoors. Morning, noon, and night the TV stations will be broadcasting New Year specials, none of them very much different from the other, nor from last year's offerings. You will be inundated with choruses of '*gong xi, gong xi, gong xi ni ah!*' (congrats, congrats, congrats to you!), until you will feel like screaming. Before you do scream, just remember that any Taiwanese visiting, for example, the United States during Christmas time will be buried under drifts of Bing Crosby's White Christmas and the like.

During the holiday break, the opening of stores, restaurants, and other businesses is at the option of the owner. Many small shops might take up to two weeks off, so don't get caught with an empty fridge or with all your laundry at the dry cleaners'! Ask in advance if the shops you regularly patronise will be taking time off. Convenience stores, cinemas and many department stores may stay open, but banks and government services are definitely off for the three days. Wet market food prices go up 15 to 25 per cent as the stallholders dig deeper into everyone's purses for New Year cheer. Taxis become more scarce and may demand a quoted fare rather than a metered one. If you decide to leave Taipei or Taiwan altogether for a break, you will not be alone. Book way in advance; six months beforehand is not too soon. You may also be asked to pay a peak season premium at many regional resorts.

Lantern Festival

This marks the last day of the New Year Festival and comes two weeks after New Year's Eve, on the 15th day of the new moon. In old China, this was a magical day, the only day when virtuous young maidens were allowed to go out alone into the evening carrying beautiful delicate paper lanterns, there to be espied by prospective suitors under the golden glow of the candle light. Today, it is just another part of New Year, not a national holiday, and is celebrated by youngsters of both sexes, carrying plastic battery-powered lamps in many shapes. Traditional lantern contests are still held at the Lung Shan Temple and Guandu Temple.

Other Holidays

Memoruial Day is held on 28 February. It remembers the Taiwanese who died during the 228 incident or were political prisoners under Kuomintang rule.

Tomb Sweeping Day is observed on 5 April as a national holiday. In Chapter Four, under the section on funerals, we commented on the expense and trouble to which Taiwanese go in order to find a proper and auspicious burial place for their relatives. Chinese cemeteries are not managed the way they are in the West, with a yearly upkeep fee and hired gardeners. Most tombs are left to go to seed with tall grass and weeds during the year. But in the West, the graves are rarely revisited by the whole family. In Taiwan, it is a yearly ritual to hike out into the mountains, following the lonely path that leads through tall grass and hundreds of other tombs, to find the one belonging to your relative. Once there, the family set it right by cleaning, sweeping, cutting down the grass, burning incense before an offering of food and burning paper money in the small chimney built into the tomb.

Labour Day
Observed on 1 May around the world and in Taiwan.

Beigang Matsu Festival
Held once a year on the goddess Matsu's birthday (April/ May of the solar calendar) at her principal temple in Beigang (four hours' drive south of Taipei), this festival is a sight not to be missed. Teams of devotees from all over the island bear their local gods on palanquins (enclosed litters borne on the shoulders) as spiritual ambassadors to participate in

Devotees bearing their local god on a palanquin pause to let off firecrackers during the Matsu Festival.

the celebration of the birthday of their liege. This amounts to literally hundreds of palanquins. As they approach the temple they set off string after string of firecrackers to scare evil spirits from their path. A blue-gray haze fills the air as you wade ankle-deep through the paper of spent firecrackers. Mountains of spirit money and forests of incense are burned. At night, you can see *dangki* (trance mediums) go into trances and flagellate themselves with swords and nail-encrusted wooden rods.

The Dragon Boat Festival

Celebration of this festival during the month of June includes perhaps the only sporting event in the world to have been inspired by a drowning bureaucrat. In 221 BC, the famous poet-scholar and counsellor Chu Yuan began to advocate a policy of resistance to the unpopular emperor Chin. He found his opinions spurned and rival courtiers began to plot against him. In protest, he drowned himself. The people were so taken by his expression of loyalty to his principles that they threw *zong zi* (rice dumplings) into the lake so the fish would feed on them rather than the patriot's body.

Today the festival is celebrated with the famous Dragon Boat races that can be watched in many countries where Chinese have settled. They symbolie the attempted rescue of Chu Yuan. In Taiwan, this has become quite an organised event, with teams coming from as far away as Australia and the United States to compete in eliminations and final rounds. Rice dumplings are also eaten at this time.

Ghost Month

Traditional beliefs indicate that on the first day of the seventh lunar month, the gates of hell open and allow the spirits condemned to the netherworld a chance for a break. We have earlier explained the influence that spirits have over the world of the living, the importance of appeasing them and keeping them properly fed and financed. Particularly cautious Chinese will be very careful in their undertakings during this month: weddings are not held, new business not started and so forth. On the 15th day of the month, a feast is prepared for the ghosts at home. The table is set and dishes brought out on the lazy Susan. Then incense and paper money are burned. After waiting for an appropriate time, to let the ghosts have their fill, the family sits down to enjoy the 'leftovers'.

Confucius' Birthday

The celebrated scholar-philosopher's birthday is remembered on 28 September with festivals. At Confucian temples, special and very solemn rites are held in traditional costume and with traditional music. Tickets are available for you to attend, but must be arranged way in advance.

Mid-Autumn Festival

The vast majority of Chinese have traditionally been farmers. The Harvest Moon Festival, as it is known in the West, is also celebrated in Chinese tradition at the happy end of a period of summer sowing and reaping. The actual day of celebration falls on the 15th day of the eighth lunar month. By this time the grain would have been traditionally dried and stored, and all things would be ready for the winter. It was a time of rejoicing before the long, cold months arrived, the last festivities before the coming of the new year in spring.

Today the Mid-Autumn Festival is celebrated by families going out to view the full moon, drink Chinese tea, and eat mooncakes—small, round, rich cakes filled with a variety of sweet pastes, nuts and egg yolks. Firecrackers and sparklers are also popular with the children. It is a national holiday, the date of which is established on a yearly basis.

National Day and 'Political' Celebrations

National Day falls on 10 October, hence it is also known as 'Double Ten' Day. It is a public holiday in Taiwan and commemorates the fall of the Qing Dynasty, which led to the establishment of the Republic of China. Grand parades with marching bands, floats, and military hardware are reviewed by the president in front of the presidential building downtown.

HOBBIES TO ENJOY

Throughout the book we have discussed various aspects of Chinese and Taiwanese culture. If any of these dovetail with a personal interest of yours, you might delve more deeply into one of them. Indeed, undertaking a hobby is one way to overcome culture shock and get to know the local people better. Some popular hobbies foreigners frequently pursue are listed here.

Martial Art

Chinese Martial arts of Shaolin and Taoist lineage are trained in the parks in the mornings and in private academies at night. Look around for a system you like by watching several classes at different schools, then join in. Japanese martial arts, such as kendo, aikido and judo are also practiced and Korean taekwondo is popular because it was adopted by the ROC military for training. In recent years, the local martial arts scene has been supplemented by foreigners teaching martial arts such as Brazilian Jiu-jitsu, Capoeira, Philipino Arnis, Indonesian Silat, Western Boxing and, yes, even Chinese Martial Arts.

Calligraphy and Painting

Chinese have been painting and writing their ideograms for several millennia with the charcoal ink stick and brush. Teachers are not hard to find and learning these arts can be directly connected to any study of Chinese language you undertake.

Hiking

Taiwan's mountains offer refreshing day hikes close to Taipei, as well as challenging weeklong alpine backcountry excursions. Check online references for trails and excursion dates. Information about hiking in Taiwan can be found at http://www.hikercentral.com/regions/asia/taiwan.html.

Scuba Diving

There is excellent diving off of the northern coast and Lanyu islands east of Taiwan and off the southern tip. Diving conditions in the Taiwan straits is generally murky. Visit http://www.taiwanscuba.com

White Water Rafting

This activity can be booked on the east coast of Taiwan in the Hualien area.

Antique and Curio Collecting

After familiarising yourself with the 'good stuff' at the Palace Museum, you can search the many antique and curio stores on the island and build your own collection. Buy things you truly like and negotiate thoroughly because the chances are what you are buying is not an investment grade antique.

Kite Flying

Chinese have flown kites for thousands of years and if you are lucky you will see some of the huge hundred foot long dragon kites soaring majestically in the sky. You can learn to fly them too.

Cooking

Community associations and clubs frequently put on local cooking classes. This is a chance to learn how the locals create magic in the kitchen.

THE SIGHTS AND MUST-SEES OF THE ILHA FORMOSA

Taipei has much to be explored in itself. There are several good guidebooks listed in the further reading section at the back of this book which will be of help in planning your excursions. Here, we will point out things you really should endeavour to see in order to enrich your understanding of Taiwan, but we will leave other guides to give you the details.

Lung Shan Temple Area

This is a very traditional area of Taipei, just south-west of the city's government centre. It is known as *Wanhua* (the 10,000 Glories). Of central interest is the Lung Shan (Dragon Mountain) Temple. Originally built in 1738, it has been rebuilt on several occasions, following fire, earthquake, and bombing. However it still retains a very traditional flavour. Because the temple was such an important social hub in centuries past,

A Tour of the Taipei Area

Your driving tour around Taipei might go like this:

- Start the day with a drive up Yangmingshan. This is a mountain to the north of Taipei, popular with the wealthiest locals and expatriates. Here you will pass many private villas, all with yards or gardens, some with their own swimming pools or tennis courts. The air is relatively fresh, the homes spacious, the view desirable, and the prices astronomical. Shopping is not particularly available, nor is access to schools, though the American Club is not too far away.

- Drive down the opposite side of Yangmingshan to Wellington Heights. This is an old community built up on a quiet and green hillside, for the most part facing away from Taipei. Prices are slightly less than in Yangmingshan for stand-alone houses. Since the area is secluded, public transportation is rather infrequent and taxi drivers grumble about going all the way up the hill to drop or pick up passengers.

- Next stop is Tienmu. On the way to Tienmu you will pass through Shihpai. This is primarily a Chinese community, though some foreigners may spill over into it. It has become a more attractive alternative with the completion of the Taipei Mass Rapid Transit system (MRT) which goes through Shihpai. The unofficial demarcation line between Shihpai and Tienmu is the stream just beyond Veteran's Hospital.

- Tienmu, at the end of Chungshan North Road, is half an hour north of the city. It is the most conspicuous foreign ghetto. Here you will find the Taipei American and Japanese schools, and the Taipei Youth Program Association (a foreign youth community center). Many grocery stores, like Jasons and Matsusei are well supplied with foreign foods and specialties. The bus terminus for Chungshan Road is part of the heart of this suburban city. Accessible public transportation, and taxis are readily available.

- Tienmu is convenient for schooling, socialising, shopping, and living. There is a wide variety of housing, from high-rise apartments packed in alleys, to smaller villas on the side of hills, to ground floor walk-in units in small side streets. Prices vary widely. Air quality is better than in Taipei but not as good as in Yangmingshan. If your office is in Taipei, count on an hour to get to work, or double if you take a bus and need to change lines downtown.

- Between Tienmu and Taipei is Shihlin. This used to be a local enclave but has grown by leaps and bounds in recent years. The Taipei French, English and German schools are located here. The MRT has a stop in Shihlin. It borders on Taipei yet is not too far from the foreign schools, and the prices are better than downtown. The air quality begins to deteriorate the closer you get to the city.

- Far on the other side of the city is a rapidly growing area with many new apartment complexes, popular with wealthy, trendy, and young Chinese and expatriates. It is the Chunghsiao East and Jenai Road areas. This is a location for people who like to be in the middle of everything and probably do not have school-age children. It is convenient for entertainment, shopping and many of the major modern office complexes that have sprung up here and on Dunhwa Road.

- Of course, if you are adventurous, on a very tight budget, or your primary purpose in coming to Taiwan was to learn about the language and culture, then you can really look anywhere. Having a car also widens the horizons. The Taipei city folk are expanding out across the rivers to Lujou, Yungho and Hsindian. Take a look at these suburbs if you require more reasonably priced local living in new apartments and don't mind a considerable commute.

the area surrounding it became a bustling trade centre. Now it is best known as one of the 'licensed quarters' where prostitution is legally pursued. Snake Alley is also only one block away and is crowded every night with tourists, diners, and gawkers who come to see the vivisection of turtles and snakes served up fresh for culinary adventurers.

Jenai Road and Chunghsiao East Road

Over the past decade, this area has blossomed. Thirty years ago, Ling-li went to a new junior high school built in the area that was in the midst of a papaya and mango orchard. Now it is high-rise offices, apartments, hotels, memorials and boutiques.

Travelling east from the Presidential Office Building on Chieh Wu Road, you will first hit the northwest corner of the Chiang Kai Shek Memorial. Step in and learn more about this important figure in modern Chinese history, then continue down Jenai Road. The tall and beautiful trees on this road and on Dunhua Road were left standing for a reason. It was the route taken from the Sungshan Airport to the Presidential Office Building when visiting American statesmen came to see how their foreign aid was being invested.

A long walk past hotels and boutiques will take you to the Sun Yat Sen Memorial Hall where this Chinese patriot is remembered. Jenai Road comes to a dead end at Keelung Road and there, to your right, you will see the Grand Hyatt Hotel and the striking pink marble facade of the World Trade Centre. If there are any trade shows in progress, you can probably slip in as a 'visiting overseas buyer' and look at the vast array of goods being exported from Taiwan. Just beyond the Trade Centre is the new towering Taipei 101 skyscraper. If you go north on Keelung Road and return toward the city centre on Chunghsiao Road, you will pass by the Ding Hao night market. Scores of boutiques, pubs, fast-food restaurants, jewellery, and bookstores line this road.

Tai Da Area

Tai Da is the popular abbreviation for Taiwan University, the most prestigious on the island. The cream of Taiwan's

The National Taiwan Democracy Memorial Hall (former Chiang Kai Shek Memorial Hall) is one of the most famous landmarks in the city of Taipei.

students rise to the top via the school testing systems and end up here studying law, medicine, science, etc. Adjacent to Tai Da is the Taiwan Normal University, which prepares students to be teachers. With this concentration of young affluent academics, the area was destined to become a hub of culture in the city.

Here you can find some modestly priced international restaurants and shopping bargains. Along Ho Ping East Road fronting the university are some quaint teahouses serving Chinese tea and snacks. Along Roosevelt Road are bookstores. One block away from and parallel to Roosevelt Road is Ding Chow Street. Here you will find attractively priced international restaurants serving Thai, Burmese, Indonesian and Vietnamese food. In the towns around Taipei, you will also find many interesting sights on half-day and one-day excursions.

Guan Du and Guan Yin Mountain

The town of Guan Du lies at the foot of Guan Yin Mountain, about 30 minutes west of Taipei. The sun sets over the mountain, which is seen from Taipei as the reclining facial profile of the Goddess of Mercy. The Guan Du Temple holds a lantern exhibition and competition during the Lantern

Festival. There is a path to hike up the mountain and on its slopes and top you will find thousands of traditional graves. There is heavy traffic up and down the mountain on Tomb Sweeping Day.

Yangming Mountain Park, Seven Stars Mountain and Jinshan Beach

North of the city is the pleasant drive up Yangmingshan. You will pass by the villas and houses of rich Taiwanese and expatriates working for foreign enterprises. You will also pass the University of Culture. From this area, you can take a detour to Seven Stars Mountain. There is a pleasant hiking path here, identified in several guidebooks for foreigners. Drive to the Yangming National Park and take a break. There are trails and a running stream with small waterfalls and makes a pleasant picnic area. When in full blossom in the spring, it gets quite crowded.

Continue driving up the mountain to Macao. The winding road will take you along some breathtaking scenery, making you quickly forget that only 45 minutes ago you left behind a polluted and crowded city. Terraced tea and vegetable plantations appear by the side of the road as you drive to a pass in the mountains. Beyond this point you will start descending along the winding road and, on a clear day, will be able to see the golden beaches of Taiwan's north coast. The road will pass the location of one of our favourite rustic hot springs bathhouses in Macao. You can still park along the road next to the bridge and hike several minutes to see the sulphurous yellow, steaming crevasses from which the boiling water surfaces.

From Macao, you can continue down the mountain to the Jinshan Beach recreation area, and from there to Keelung. You can return to Taipei along the highway, or you can retrace your tracks back to Taipei, perhaps taking the turnoff at Yangming Park that will lead you down the mountain to Peitou. Peitou was a famous R&R center for Japanese and, later, American military personnel, but its reputation as a den of iniquity is all but past. For a romantic evening with your own sweetheart, book a room at the quiet Whispering Pines Inn. It was built by the Japanese in Japanese-style with *tatamis*, *shojis* and hot spring baths in each room.

National Palace Museum

A day excursion in itself, and definitely not to be missed, is the National Palace Museum, located a half-hour north of the city. It houses some 600,000 artefacts, catalogued at the Forbidden City in Beijing, which were removed and guarded by Chiang Kai Shek's minions during a perilous 15-year journey through China and finally to Taiwan. There they were stored in underground bunkers until a modern museum could be erected. Now the National Palace Museum is the single most important repository of Chinese fine art in the world. Porcelain, jade, scrolls and bronze, all of the finest quality, are on display year round.

Jinshan and Fulung Beaches

About one and a half hour's drive from Taipei are two beaches, Jinshan and Fulung. If you like to bake in the sun and take in some moderate body surf, this is the place for you. From the beaches, one can continue along the coast and then into the mountains to the former Japanese retreat called Jiufen. Here Allied prisoner of war slave labor was forced to mine for gold. The town nestled high above the Pacific ocean is now home to museums, coffee shops, bistros, inns and tourist stands.

Maokung

At the southern edge of Taipei, mountains rise that are home to some of Taiwan's tea growing industry. A new cable car gondola system has recently been inaugurated that can be accessed from the MRT Muzha Line, Taipei Zoo station to carry you into the mountains to visit tea plantations and tea houses. Note that as of the time of this writing, the French built gondola was still experiencing numerous glitches that are expected to be ironed out.

Central and East Taiwan

A weekend excursion can be made by car or bus along the northeast coast of Keelung, past the famous Yeliu Stone

The quiet beauty of the scenery in the mountaineous regions contrast with the hustle and bustle of Taipei city.

Formations. Here, where the land meets the sea, strange and attractive rock formations remain, carved over thousands of years by the wind and water. Incidentally, the naturally carved 'Empress's Head' bust was stolen by vandals, who later remorsefully returned it. It has now been cemented back into place.

Continue down past Suao to the turn-off for the interior of the island. Here you can drive through the beautiful Taroko Gorge. Steep cliffs rise up from a cold rushing mountain stream. You can stop at a temple situated nearby, enjoy the sights, and even get your picture taken with an aboriginal maiden. The government has recently punched a 13-km long tunnel highway under Hsueh Shan, one of Central Taiwan's highest mountains, joining south-east Taipei with Hualien. What used to be a three hour journey can now be traversed in 45 minutes.

After this, proceed to Tien Hsiang, a very quiet spot during the weekdays that is not too touristy. There are two places to stay: the Grand Formosa Tien Hsiang Lodge and Youth Activity Centre hostel. Here, deep in this green gorge, with the stars bright in a crystal-clear sky, you can spend a very quiet, relaxing evening. At dawn, walk or drive about three quarters of a mile further west along the main road. Look carefully for a path that goes down from the road to the rushing stream. You will cross a suspension bridge and continue down a rocky path to the water's edge. If you get here early, you will find yourself alone in the splendour of the natural outdoor Wenshan hot spring that mixes with an ice-cold mountain stream. On the way back to the town, don't miss the 'tunnel walk' into the national park with wonderful streams and a breathtaking view of Baiyang waterfall.

If you have the time, continue west from Tien Hsiang to Lishan. This is a quaint orchard town. The scenery from the height of the narrow winding road is not for the queasy or the unsure driver. From here, drive north to the North Cross Island Highway, taking it west to pass Shihmen Reservoir and back to Taipei on the North-south Highway.

If you are an avid hiker, Taiwan has some of the best trails in North Asia. There are various clubs and associations that

The tiny old theatre in the mountain retreat of Jiufen immortalised in Hou Hsiao-hsien's film *City of Sadness*.

導演 侯孝賢

can put you on the right track. Taiwan is also a manufacturer of tents, boots, and all manner of hiking gear, so you can get what you need when you arrive. Several specialist shops are located at the northwest corner of the intersection of Chungshan North Road and Chunghsiao West Road very near the main Taipei Railway Station. Also on the east coast are opportunities to go white-water rafting. Check with tour guides for details.

Tainan

Tainan is the oldest city in Taiwan. It is also where Koxinga is buried. Here you can visit some of Taiwan's finest temples and sample great snacks Tainan is known for at the Hsiaopei Night Market and the Chinatown marketplace.

Kenting

If some cold winter morning you have a hankering for sun and sand, take a trip to Kenting. The journey is either a five-hour drive from Taipei, or can be made by plane and bus. This area, at the southernmost tip of the island, has an internationally managed resort, an underwater park, hiking trails, and beaches.

GETTING OUT OF TAIWAN

Taiwan has lots to see and do and one can spend years exhausting the sites and tastes it has to offer. However, you might find yourself hankering for some other vistas. Taiwan is well located as a jumping off point to visit other countries in the region. Japan and Korea, with their snowy winters, skiing and diverse cuisines and cultures are both two hours north. The Philippines, with its tropical attractions and cheap beer, is 90 minutes south. Hong Kong, the gateway to China, is also 90 minutes southwest. Further afield, you can travel to Singapore, Kuala Lumpur or Bangkok, all four hours distant. Use Taiwan as your aircraft carrier in the Pacific and launch off to run sorties to other interesting places.

LANGUAGE

'That characters have been shaped with aesthetic considerations in mind is an underlying theme in Chinese cultural life. One shudders to write a character that looks unbalanced. The same sensibility, perhaps with somewhat less intensity, existed in the West and has recently resurfaced. If I were a historian of pop culture, I could go on about calligraphy as a manifestation of cultural discipline.'
—A Zee, *Swallowing Clouds: A Playful Journey Through Chinese Culture, Language, and Cuisine*

AMONG THE BIGGEST DECISIONS a resident in Taiwan has to face is whether or not to attempt to learn to speak, read, or write Chinese. It is, of course, possible to live as an expatriate professional or resident in Taiwan for many years without developing any proficiency beyond the most rudimentary. We know many men and women who have done so. They are, however, tethered to the American Club or other foreign support activities and organisations, as well as their chauffeurs and maids, or to pantomime and vigorous histrionics when trying to explain something to a local in English. To them, the single most difficult barrier to their enjoyment of Taiwan is communication. "Even the telephone operator does not speak English," they would complain.

The decision to learn the language should not be taken lightly, but it will reap rewards for you in terms of your cultural understanding, the depth of friendships you can develop and the ease with which you can move through otherwise complex and frustrating situations. Whichever you decide, the basic knowledge of the language's relation to the people, explained below, is a must.

The Kuomintang would have one believe that the population of Taiwan is linguistically monolithic, a population of Mandarin speakers. This is not the case. How could it be on an island that was colonised by Hokkien provincials, ceded to the Japanese in the Treaty

A Chinese opera performance at the Taipei Eye. The organisation promotes traditional arts and aims to raise cultural awareness and appreciation in the country.

A busy street in Taipei. Colourful signboards advertise various shops and services and traffic is usually heavy throughout the day.

A small alley in Jiufen. The charming town is popular with locals and tourists alike and has scenic views of the mountains, quaint streets and traditional teahouses.

The interior (opposite) and exterior of Taipei 101, presently the world's tallest completed skyscraper. An icon of Taiwan, the building contains 101 floors with five basement floors, and features hundreds of trendy stores, restaurants, clubs and other attractions.

The National Taiwan Democracy Memorial Hall (formerly called the Chiang Kai Shek Memorial Hall) in Taipei. The structure is framed on the north and south by the National Theater and National Concert Hall and is surrounded by serene ponds and parks.

of Shimonoseki in 1895, and only returned to Chinese rule in 1945? Language, though, became an important tool in the battle to indoctrinate the local population after 1945. It was forbidden under martial law to teach Hokkien in schools and Hokkien-language television programming was severely limited. The ruling party felt it imperative to linguistically tie Taiwan to Mainland China.

The flip side of this was an emphasis on *fantizi* (traditionally written characters) versus the simplified *jiantizi* (character syllabary) developed by the Communist educators in Mainland China. The use of simplified characters was treated as just another part of the rape of Chinese culture under Communist rule and teachers, students, publishers, and advertisers were, until very recently, forbidden to use them. Somewhere along the way, though, a concession was made. Officials allowed the use of the simplified form of certain characters, such as *tai* (as in Taiwan) with its five strokes rather than the *fanti* form with its 14 strokes.

The distinction between written and spoken languages here is culturally important. The Chinese civilisation has lasted continuously for 4,000 years. Aside from being a great source of cultural pride (the ancient civilisations of Rome, Greece, Turkey, Persia and Egypt have long fallen), what links all Chinese together through this long history is the written language. Each province has its own dialect, and within a province there can be major variations, rendering spoken communication impossible. But, by and large, the written language transcends all the provinces of the Han Chinese.

To understand this better, think of European Romance languages and history. French, Italian and Spanish all derive from Latin. All utilise the same alphabet to spell their words, but in neither the spoken nor the written language can one be sure of what is being communicated by someone in the other language, unless one knows that language. One can guess at meanings because of similar roots, but that is all. The spoken dialects of Chinese have just as much variation in pronunciation as the Romance languages, but the written language is a common denominator. We will discuss the written language in more detail below, but first a review of what you will be hearing.

MANDARIN

Mandarin is known in Taiwan as *guo yu* (national language), signalling the political significance the Kuomintang attached to linguistic unity in China. I was told in Beijing that the word 'Mandarin' comes from *Mandaren* (Great Manchu) because during the Manchu Qing Dynasty this language was the *guan hua*, the language of the government officials who were known to the English-speaking world as 'Mandarins'. As spoken in Taiwan, it is no longer pure Beijing *hua* (patois) with its heavy rolling 'r' addends, but a softened, middle-of-the-road language. Vocabulary notwithstanding, pronunciations vary little from the *putong hua* (common language) taught in Mainland China now and adopted by Singapore as one of its national languages. Because it can be used in these countries and many other places where Chinese people have settled, Mandarin is a valuable asset.

Tones

Mandarin is a tonal language. This means that each word has a pronunciation which carries a tone. Changing the tone changes the meaning. There are four tones and a clear (unstressed) tone:

#1 tone	(yi sheng)	‾	High and even tone
#2 tone	(er sheng)	´	Rising tone
#3 tone	(san sheng)	ˇ	Dipping tone
#4 tone	(si sheng)	`	Falling tone
	(ching sheng)	°	Clear tone

A favourite example used to demonstrate tones is the sentence, *Ma-ma ma ma ma?* (Is mama scolding the horse?)

Grammar

Mandarin grammar is relatively simple. To turn a statement into a question, add *ma* to the end. To put it in the past tense, add *le* after the verb or at the end of the sentence. To put it in the future tense, add *yao* or *hui* (want, will, or can) before the verb. To negate it, add *bu* (present) or *mei* (past) before the verb. For example:

Ni qu xiang gang.	You go to Hong Kong.
Ni qu xiang gang ma?	Are you going (now) to Hong Kong?
Ni qu le xiang gang.	You went to Hong Kong.
Ni yao qu xiang gang.	You will go to Hong Kong.
Ni bu qu xiang gang.	You are not going to Hong Kong.
Ni mei qu xiang gang.	You did not go to Hong Kong.

This is, of course, grossly over-simplified and tuition in Chinese is best left to a language book and tutor.

Forming Phrases

Read the Chinese Romanisations and the translations in the following sentences, then look up the words in the glossary at the back of the book. Understand how the sentences are constructed. Practise constructing your own sentences. As noted before, Chinese grammar is the easiest part of the task at hand.

■ *Wo cong meiguo lai. Wo zhu zai da fandian.*
I came from America. I live in a hotel.

■ *Chen xian sheng shi Taiwan ren. Ta hui shuo ying yu.*
Mr Chen is Taiwanese. He can speak English.

■ *Jin tian wo xiang chi zhongguo fan, wo bu yao chi xi can. Hao bu hao?*
Today, I am thinking of eating Chinese food, I do not want Western food. Ok?

■ *Mingtian ta yao zuo jichengche dao ji chang qu. Ta yao yong duo shao qian?*

Tomorrow, he wants to ride (sit) in a taxi to go to the airport. How much money will he need (use)?

- *Wo zhu de dafandian gui. Yi tian wu qian kuai qian. Qing gaosu wo you mei you pianyi de?*
  The hotel I live in is expensive. One day (costs) NT$ 5,000. Please tell me, are there (have or not have) cheaper (ones)?

- *Zuo qi che dao taizhong yao san ge xiao shi. Ni yao qu ma?*
  It takes three hours to drive to Taichung. Do you want to go?

- *Weishenma bu yao mai zhuozi? Tai gui ma? Duo shao qian?*
  Why don't (you) want to buy the table? Is it too expensive? How much money?

- *Xiexie ni gaosu wo zenma zou dao canting qu.*
  Thank you for telling me how to get (walk) to the restaurant.

- *Qingwen, yiyuan zai nali?*
  Please, where is a hospital?

- *Wo gang dao Taiwan.*
  I just arrived in Taiwan.

- *Yi zhang che piao dao Taibei che zhan.*
  One bus ticket to Taipei Station.

- *Wo yao dao da shi guan qu.*
  I want to go to the embassy.

- *Wo yao yi ge han bao.*
  I want one hamburger.

- *Wo yao mai yi ge dian nao.*
  I want to buy a computer.

TAIWANESE

Taiwanese is the mother tongue spoken outside of school by the majority of the population, who also maintain fluency in

Mandarin and use it interchangeably. It is known in Taiwan by several names:

Mandarin	Meaning	Taiwanese Pronunciation
Tai yu	Taiwan language	*Taigu*
Fujian Hua	Spoken Fujian	*Hokkien Wei*
Minnan Hua	Spoken south of the Min River	*Minnan Wei*

As can be understood from the above, Taiwanese was a dialect brought to Taiwan by immigrants who left the area south of the Min River in the province of Fujian. This distinguishes it from Fujou or *Syamen hua* which are spoken in other areas of the province of Fujian.

It is a tonally rich and complex tongue that rises and falls, lending itself to the passionate oratory of the street hawker or opposition politician. One factor that makes its study daunting is its six changeable tones. Mandarin's four tones only change in closely circumscribed ways. In Taiwanese, a tone may change whether it is at the beginning, the middle, or the end of a sentence. It makes the memorisation of tones all the more difficult. To make matters more complicated, Taiwanese as spoken in Taipei, Tainan and Kaohsiung has variations, though communication between these dialect groups is not difficult.

Several Mandarin/Taiwanese comparisons will let you see how different they are:

Mandarin:	*Ni hao ma? Wo shi meiguo ren.*
Taiwanese:	*Li ho bwo? Ngoa shi Bigok lang.*
English:	How are you? I am an American.

WHAT TO LEARN?

What is one to learn: Mandarin or Taiwanese? The question has become more difficult to answer with the resurgence of Taiwanese, as opposed to Chinese, identity. Until 1997, people would say to Chris "*Ni de guo yu jiang de hen hao*" or "You speak the national language very well." Now they say

"You speak that Beijing dialect very well." Personal identity is compartmentalised with the languages. The ability to converse in Taiwanese will endear you to the Taiwanese population, but will leave Mandarin speakers confused or resentful. Fluency in Mandarin, however, will impress all (even if they consider Taiwanese the better language), can be used throughout China and will generally be easier to learn; texts, tapes, tutors and schools for Mandarin are more readily available than for Taiwanese. Thus, it is probably best to learn Mandarin first and then pick up Taiwanese as and when your friends teach you. Nevertheless it is important to know these two languages exist side by side.

WAYS TO LEARN

Short intensive courses exist for rapidly teaching a foreigner the basics. This is highly recommended if you want to hit the ground running. Keep up the momentum, though. Enrol in a tutorial of several hours per week and use your Mandarin at all available opportunities.

There are four basic ways to learn the language, with or without a teacher:

- By ear, in which case you try to imitate what you hear and do not commit to writing the sounds.
- Using Romanised text.
- Using text with the Chinese phonetic alphabet.
- Using text with Chinese characters only.

The first option is inefficient and will result in many mispro-nounced words, unless you are truly gifted. Option four is for masochists or people with an unbelievably large amount of free time on their hands. That leaves options two and three.

When Chris had been in Taiwan for some time and frequently had long conversations in Chinese with the locals, they would praise his fluency. Wanting to use appropriate self deprecation to deny these compliments, he decided one day to use a common expression meaning "You are excessive in our praise." or *guojiang*. Unfortunately, he used the wrong tones and said *guojiang* or "Fruit Jam!", thus proving that the praise was, indeed, excessive.

Romanisation

There are many famous and several obscure methods of Romanising the Chinese language (i.e. writing the Chinese sounds in the Roman alphabet). But is there a standard, you ask? Sorry. In Taiwan you will see Chinese Romanised in many ways. The Mainland Chinese have instituted the Hanyu Pinyin standard, which has as many deficiencies as any system around and is not accepted by the educators in Taiwan whose system is hardly used at all outside Taiwan.

When pronouncing Romanised text, beware of the linguistic baggage your own mother tongue carries: accents, pronunciation standards, etc. There is no way a Frenchman, Mexican, Bostonian and Singaporean will pronounce the Romanised character *xue* in the same way, yet there is only one correct sound. In this text, we have used the Hanyu Pinyin system. Although developed by the Mainland Communist Chinese educators and previously banned on Taiwan, its use has begun making inroads here, especially in Kuomintang controlled areas like Taipei, on the MRT and street signage. Also, Pinyin is vastly more common in Mandarin textbooks today.

The Phonetic Alphabet

Besides Romanisation, one can learn using the Mandarin phonetic symbols. This is an 'alphabet' of 37 symbols which, when combined, can represent all the sounds in Mandarin. Taiwanese kindergarteners and primary schoolchildren learn this way. In addition, the *Guoyu Ri Bao*, a local daily newspaper, shows the symbols next to all the characters in the text of the paper. By learning the way children do, from fundamental phonetic building blocks, you are much more likely to be able to pronounce correctly. Unfortunately, it is only at the *Guo yu Ri Bau* language classes where you will definitely use these symbols. Check with the individual school where you enrol to see if they use them, but note that the Mandarin phonetic symbols are not seen outside of Taiwan.

A comparison of the phonetic symbols of the different Romanisation systems is given below. As you can see, the difference in spelling suggests a vastly different pronunciation for what should be the same sounds. For more information and the names of streets in various systems, see http://www.romanizations.com.

Yale	Pinyin	Wade-Giles	Kwoyeu Chinese
bwo	bo	po	bor
pwo	po	p'o	po
mwo	mo	mo	mo
fwo	fo	fo	for
de	de	te	dih
te	te	t'e	teh
ne	ne	ne	ne
le	le	le	le
ge	ge	ke	geh
ke	ke	k'e	keh
he	he	he	her
ji	ji	chi	jyi
chi	qi	ch'i	chi
syi	xi	hsi	shyi
jr	zhi	chih	jyy
chr	chi	ch'ih	chyy
shr	shi	shih	shyr
r	ri	jih	ryh
dz	zi	tzu	tzy
ts	c	ts'	tsy
sz	s	sz, ss	sy
a	a	a	a
o	o	o	o

e	e	e	e
e	e	e	e
ai	ai	ai	ai
ei	ei	ei	ei
au	ao	ao	au
ou	ou	ou	ou
an	an	an	an
en	en	en	en
ang	ang	ang	ang
eng	eng	eng	eng
er	r	erh	el
yi	i	i	i
u	u	u	u
yu	u	ui	u

Follow the Bouncing Ball

Once the basic language is picked up, one of the best and quickest ways Chris has found to increase vocabulary and fluency is to learn popular songs. You will hear them playing on the radio and eventually you will catch one that appeals to you. Go out and buy the CD, which invariably includes the lyrics, sit down with your dictionary, look up all the new words, understand and learn the song. It is like solving a mystery. Here is a melody you like and you can hear the emotion of the singer, but you have no idea what they're singing about. As you translate, the story unfolds. The best thing is that once the song is learned, you can sing it to yourself and review the vocabulary that way; it's much easier to remember. You can draw vocabulary, sophisticated and fresh, from the song to use in conversation. Knowing local pop songs will also help to break the ice at a karaoke session!

Letting Your Mouse Teach You

Personal computers and software present another learning opportunity for you. Mandarin and Taiwanese software programs that teach both the written and spoken language are on the market. A computer equipped with a CD-Rom and speakers are all that you need to run the programs. Some of the programs can also grade and correct your spoken repetition of phrases, but you will need a microphone ported into your computer. Note that Microsoft has Chinese versions of Windows 98 and Office 2000; if you buy your computer in Taiwan you might want to request that standard English versions be installed instead for everyday use.

In addition to teaching programs, you can find Chinese word-processing programs that are constantly improving. Two popular ones are Twinbridge Chinese Partner and Chinese Star. These come with dictionaries, translation tools (of spotty reliability), and multiple font types. Both programs can handle simplified and traditional text and work in the English version of Windows XP and Office environments. If your computer is based on a Windows XP platform, you can Asian language tools by opening the Control Panel and selecting Regional Languages. With the above systems you can choose from a selection of text input methods. Most likely you will want to use the *hanyupinyin* input method, in which you type the Romanised version of the word and then select the character you want. Alternatives are to use the Chinese phonetic alphabet or character construct methods in which your keyboard must have the symbols on the keys.

The Internet is alive and well in Taiwan. Most sites are in Chinese. There are online dictionaries that can help you look up characters. In order to translate from Chinese into English, however, you will first have to learn how to enter Chinese text through the keyboard as mentioned above. You should be aware that there are two main coding systems used to capture, transmit, store, and visualise Chinese on the screen. The Big-5 system is a Taiwanese construct and is widely used there. It focuses on the traditional characters. The GB system developed by the Mainland Chinese works on the simplified form of Chinese characters. The Microsoft Asian Languages installation mentioned above will automatically project the contents of the web page in Chinese if you have activated the programs.

Poetry

China has a long and wonderful tradition of poetry. The poetry of the Tang Dynasty (AD 618–907) is a major part of elementary school language studies and pupils must learn to recite the most famous verses. Many of the most revered poems are short and are easily accessible to the foreign student of Mandarin. They will at once give you a deeper understanding of Chinese culture and the universal kinship of man.

Idioms

The Chinese have a long history of pithy expressions. The original writings of Lau Tzu, Confucius, and others were all very spare and obscure. This is why translations vary so widely in quality and content. The translator is trying to express in English, for example, what was said with only four or five characters and finds he needs a dozen or more words to do it justice. From the classics and historical stories come many phrases—four-character expressions called *cheng yu*. There are literally tens of thousands of these which Chinese sprinkle into their conversation from time to time. They defy definition with an equal number of English words. Some examples:

- *Sawiweng shi ma* (old Sai looses his horse) derives from the story of a man who, beset with hardship and misfortune, claims equanimity to his friends who lament his difficulties. In the end his judgement is shown to be correct. The saying is used to express a lack of concern when things do not go right.

- *Zi xiang mao dun* (mutually facing shield and spear) derives from the story of a hawker who is laughed out of town when he tries to simultaneously sell a spear that can penetrate anything and a shield that is impenetrable. This is used to point out basic contradictions in an argument.

Idioms are good to learn from a cultural point of view, can give you a beginner's taste for the traditional language, and can help you to understand other people's conversation. However, they should be used with caution unless one is very sure of the context. They are easily abused. It would be like an American scattering his conversation with Shakespearean quotations on a visit to England.

Jokes

If the television and movie comedies are any indication, the Taiwanese enjoy puerile, slapstick humor—flatulence and food fights. Taiwan has a long history of stand-up comedy and comic dialogues, but, unlike other cultures with other languages, there does not seem to be a widespread cult of joke-telling among the Chinese. Normally, if friends gather together, they might tell humorous tales about themselves, with some exaggeration thrown in to pump up the laughs. They usually would not recite a repertoire of jokes as Westerners do. Self-deprecating humour is well-accepted. Popular comedians tend to be exaggerations themselves; porky, skinny, memorable in a crazy way.

If you wish to tell jokes, you must be careful. English language jokes will fall flat unless your audience is fluent in the language. If you translate foreign humour into Chinese, it will only travel well providing the jokes are not dependent on word play for their meaning and the words create a mental picture that provides the humour. Jokes in which a physical action bolsters the mental image are good.

For example, a Chinese joke that translates well goes like this: 'Three teetotallers walk past a wine house. One man says, "I can't tolerate alcohol. One glass of beer, my face turns red, and I stumble about until I pass out." The next man says, "That's nothing. If I even smell a glass of beer, I turn red and want to pass out, drunk." Then the third man pipes up, "You think you two have a problem. If I even look at someone who has smelled beer, I get drunk!" '

With the presidency of Lee Teng-hui, it seems the government relaxed and the Taiwanese loosened their collar as political humour and skits with characters imitating the president and other members of government became acceptable. Books are sold about Chinese humour, but we have not heard many jokes told. The Taiwanese prefer to laugh at themselves.

On the other hand, an example of a Western joke that translates well is this one:

'A farmer is ploughing the fields with his ox, when suddenly the ox stops pulling, sits down, turns round to the farmer, and says, "It's too goddamn hot. I won't pull another foot." The farmer is stunned and begins a conversation with the animal. His neighbour is walking with his dog down the road and sees the ox taking its leisure. He decides to take a closer look. When he asks the farmer what gives, the ox replies, "It's too goddamn hot. I won't pull another foot." The neighbour is so frightened he picks up his dog and makes a run for it. When he tires out, he settles under the shade of a tree and ponders aloud what he has witnessed, "Gracious, that's the first time I have ever seen a talking ox!". "Me too!" the dog replies.'

Among mixed, gentle company, jokes with a sexual overtone should be avoided, though the hostesses at drinking establishments can probably tell five saucy stories to your every one and would feign enjoy hearing yours. Among members of the same gender, judge for yourself whether the mood and place are right for such humour.

Swearing

The Taiwanese do swear and the most frequent epithet you will hear is *ta ma de*! which literally means 'his mother's'. His mother's what? We are left to suppose. Some rough people will begin or end practically every sentence with this.

Insults tend to be of the dehumanising variety, such as calling a person a dog. The Taiwanese will not understand the intention of most four-letter words in English, but it does not mean you should use them or translate them with impunity. Your angry intentions may well be understood on a visceral level and you might find you have a fight on your hands. Taiwanese are emotional and the wrong people in the wrong place can have a short fuse.

Body Language

The Chinese have a reputation for being inscrutable, but this does not really stem from body language. Many of the body language cues that would tip you off in a Western encounter will be valid in Taiwan: arms folded across the chest ('I do not agree'), yawning ('you are a bore'), stomach rumbling ('let's eat').

What you will find difficult is that much is left unsaid. When two Taiwanese enter into a conversation, they usually have a strong understanding of their own inter-relationship and the rules of that relationship. So, to speak of certain things would be considered rudely abrupt or superfluous. However, you as a Westerner will enter the conversation not only ignorant of the rules, but also of your relationship with them. You might be treating the person condescendingly when they perceive their position as superior to yours, or vice versa.

The American penchant to treat everyone equally can be misconstrued here. A third person who sees you treat their junior the same way as you treated them will not understand your cultural background and may begin twisting in their minds why you have acted that way. You will also frequently come out of conversations without a clear idea of what has been agreed upon in the other person's mind. Learn to graciously act in the superior role when it is appropriate.

Because there is a multitude of possible scenarios, we cannot here go into specific detail about how to act. We suggest you read Chapter Four very carefully to learn more about the unwritten rules in relating to the Taiwanese. In general, remember that it is relative standing that dictates what is proper for a person to say and how she or he treats the other person.

Depending on the culture you come from, you may find Taiwanese personal distance uncomfortable. The Taiwanese do not mind sitting close to someone and if you are a friend (man to man, or woman to woman) they might occasionally touch your hand or take your arm. Do not be alarmed; this is not necessarily homosexual advance, just a gesture from a person who is comfortable enough with you to get that close. It means that you are making progress. Among students or old folk, you will frequently notice members of the same sex walking arm in arm, or sometimes holding hands. This is not abnormal; the contact is gentle and subtle. However, they do not like loud, back-slapping, bear-hugging, cheek-kissing contact of the sort at which some Americans and Europeans excel. Similarly, physical contact with strangers of the opposite sex is limited to handshakes. At what point this person is no longer a stranger and you can feel free to touch them varies according to the individual.

Like other cultures, the Taiwanese sometimes use hand gestures as a form of communication. It is useful to briefly go over these, so that you can understand more about unwritten communication and minimise embarrassing mistakes.

- To encourage a person to move toward you, extend the arm out, palm down, and wave your fingers toward yourself.

- To point to yourself, use your index finger and point at your nose.

- When someone touches their index finger to their cheek and scratches it up and down (especially when saying *diu lian*) they are indicating that a person has 'lost face'.

- To hold the fist up and draw the index finger two or three times, like pulling a trigger, means that someone or something is dead or finished.

- Taiwanese do not use or understand the 'middle finger'. If you angrily shake your fist at someone, though, you will get the deserved response.

- Showing numbers on fingers varies from the West. One through five are initiated with the thumb, but the Chinese have developed special signs for six, eight and ten. Six: hold your fist up, palm up, with the thumb and pinky extended. Eight: hold your fist down, palm down, with the thumb and pinky extended (looks like the character for eight). Ten: create a cross with your left and right index fingers (looks like the character for ten).

THE WRITTEN WORD

Over 50,000 in number, written characters are the hardest part of mastering Chinese. The characters evolved from deep in China's past, from drawings of elements of life essential to the Chinese. Over thousands of years, these rough drawings were stylised, simplified, modified and codified to become the written word of today. Even now, Chinese characters remain pictographs and often show the elements from which they are derived.

Characters are usually made up of two components: the radical and the phonetic complement. One should first become familiar with all the radicals (numbering 214) and their original meanings. Radicals will frequently give a clue to the meaning, or at least the category of the word.

Phonetic complements are written above, below, or beside the radical and help give a clue to the pronunciation.

Stroke Order

Remembering the words is not enough. To claim knowledge of the written language, one must be able to remember the proper stroke order in writing characters. A Westerner fresh off the boat can find any number of ways to complete the image of the character, but there is, alas, only one correct way, and your Chinese friends will not let you forget it if they see you err. There are many practice books prepared for first graders that take a 'paint by numbers' approach and guide you through the proper order. If you want to learn to write, start here. After learning several hundred characters, the stroke order of others will come naturally.

Calligraphy

Still, you have not reached the pinnacle of achievement. To do so, you must now take brush in hand and learn traditional calligraphy. This is an art, a way of life, and a form of personal expression. In other words it can be esoteric and subjective in the extreme, consuming a brief moment of your time or your entire life. It is considered to be meditative, and superior calligraphy is the highest expression of a cultured person's demeanour.

NAMES

Chinese names can be confusing to the Westerner as they are written in the reverse order of English names. The surname or *xing* (family name) appears first, while the *ming* (given name) comes last. For this reason, it is inappropriate to ask questions like, "What is your last name?" or "What is your Christian name?" Better to ask, "What is your surname/given name?"

There are several hundred surnames in Chinese. Some of the most popular are: Lee (aka Li), Chen (aka Tan), Lin (aka Lim), Ma, Wang, Hwang (aka Huang), Guo (aka Kuo), Tsai (aka T'sai) and Su. However, when Romanised on a name card, it is difficult to know whether the person has changed the *xing*/*ming* order to accommodate Westerners, or left it in the original order. Sometimes punctuation can give a clue. Consider, for example, the name Lee Guo Tsai. Each of these words is a potential surname. Is he Mr. Lee or Mr. Tsai? 'Lee Guo-tsai' or 'Lee, Guo Tsai' tells you his surname is Lee. Many Taiwanese will forego Romanising their given names and simply put 'G T Lee' for example, thereby making things a lot easier for you.

However, some Taiwanese business people have added a Western given name to their cards. While most of these are simple off-the-shelf names, like Robert or Simon, others are more obscure, like Jubilee, Beauty or Banjo. Get into the habit of underlining the surname of business contacts on their name cards when you meet them. To make matters more confusing, there do exist several Chinese surnames which are two characters. They are rare but you should be aware of them. *Si Tu* is an example. More common, but still unusual, are single-character given names.

Names are important to the Taiwanese. They denote one's family lineage and can refer to one's status within that family.

For instance, the title *xian sheng* (Mr) literally means 'first born' and shows the importance placed within the family on the number-one son. Similarly, *tai tai* means 'wife' or 'Mrs', but literally translated means 'ultimate, ultimate'— the number-one wife, as opposed to the lesser-standing concubines and mistresses of tradition. *Xiao jie*, on the other hand, means 'Miss' or, literally, 'little big sister'.

Much time is spent in naming children according to their date of birth, zodiac sign, and the propitious number of strokes to be included in the characters that make up the whole name. The Taiwanese want the name to be as lucky and auspicious as possible. Note also that, in many families, the first character of the given name (or middle name) indicates the generation of the person within the family tree.

In other words, all members born in that generation of that family line will have the same character in their names. For example, Wu Ling-li's sisters are Ling-yu, Ling-mei and Ling-lan.

Armed with this knowledge, several productive and endearing minutes can be spent with Taiwanese friends, fully understanding the significance of their names.

How to Address the Taiwanese

How you address your Taiwanese friends and contacts will, of course, depend on their relation to you (business or personal), and whether you are speaking English or Mandarin. Let's assume you are learning to speak the language. If this is your first business contact with a particular person, it is best to address him or her with their surname followed by the title on the name card. For instance, you should call *Lee Chang Jang*, 'Factory Manager Lee', or *Chen Zong*, 'General Manager Chen', if these are their job designations. This gives proper attention to their title (of which they should be proud) and helps you to avoid the problem of how to address a businesswoman of whose marital status you are unsure.

If you are speaking English, it is best to stick with Mr, Mrs, Madame or Miss, plus the person's surname. When you become better friends, he or she may ask you to use their adopted English name. Even among close Taiwanese friends, it is not common to use the given name. Nicknames are more common. Adding the term *lau* (old) to the surname of elders is quite common, e.g. *Lau Lee* or *Lau Chen*. However, a person will tell you when you can address them as such. Assume nothing!

Adopting a Chinese Name

In Japan, Westerners' names are usually only transliterated into *kana* (Japanese characters) on name cards so local people can read them. Westerners do not take a Japanese name. To do so makes the Japanese uneasy. Not so in Taiwan and China. Foreigners often choose Chinese names, but if you want one it must be chosen carefully: you will have it for a long time, it will leave an impression (good or bad), and it may even say something rude about you if you are not careful.

There are two basic ways of taking a name, and help from a local is advised in either case. First you can transliterate the sound of your surname into close-sounding Chinese characters. For example, Smith is normally transliterated using the three characters, *si mi zi*. Many surnames already have equivalents and your teacher or friend can help you find yours. If you want a new name in Chinese, then consider variations of the many names you will come across on a day-to-day basis. To spare confusion, the surname should perhaps approximate the sound of your original surname, while more whimsy can be used on your given name. Some examples are:

Western Name	Chinese	Meaning
Kirke Hart	He Ke	*He* overcomes
Mark Rabin	Lei Peng	Lightning Peng (mythical bird)
Chris Bates	Bai Syau Ying	White Dawn Eagle

We did have a friend, Mr Gautier, whose name best transliterated into *guo tie*, meaning 'fried dumplings', so care must be exercised!

Red Ink

You have got your Chinese name and maybe even have a sample of your own calligraphy to seal. Now you need a 'chop'. The chop, or *jang*, is a personalised seal and is considered an indispensable accoutrement. Among the Taiwanese, Japanese and Chinese, it constitutes their signature. It is registered with the government and used on cheques, contracts, and other legal documents. Its historical importance is reflected in the massive size and ornateness of the emperors' seals on display in museums. It is guarded absolutely and much concern and dread is felt if it is lost. Advertisements must be run in the newspapers and one holds one's breath until it is properly de-registered or recovered.

As a foreigner, unless you manage a company or sit on a board of directors, you will probably not have a chop registered as your own. It does not stop you from owning one, though. They can be made in almost any neighbourhood and common materials for a cheap one are wood or plastic. Larger, fancier ones are carved from stone and are frequently embellished with images of animals, perhaps your Chinese zodiac sign. Vermillion ink pads come with the chop, which has a notch or dot to indicate the proper orientation of the characters. Place the document or article to be chopped on a flat, preferably slightly cushioned surface (a desk mat is perfect), prime the chop in the red paste, then apply it to the document with even downward force. Rock it ever so slightly and remove it straight upwards. You have now made your mark as a Chinese scholar!

BUSINESS—THE MEANING OF LIFE

'The business society in Taiwan is not orderly. If placed on a scale with the German's 'Order must prevail' approach on one end and the Thai's 'It can't be helped' approach on the other, Taiwan would be decidedly towards the Thai end of the spectrum. Taiwanese business people often maintain that anything not specifically outlawed is encouraged.'
—Kevin Chambers, *Succeed in Business: Taiwan*

TAIWAN HAS BECOME AN ECONOMIC POWERHOUSE, a geographically small, but flexible and adaptive player in the world manufacturing scene. It is, as mentioned in the first chapter, one of the most successful of the so-called 'Four Little Tigers of Asia', the other three being South Korea, Hong Kong, and Singapore. But Taiwan has not had trouble with the student protests and strikes that have plagued Korea. It is larger in population and land mass than Hong Kong and Singapore, giving it a larger pool of educated labour and room to spread out. In 2002, it recorded a trade surplus of US$ 131 billion (US$ 5,458 for every man, woman, and child on the island) and went on to become one of the richest nations in the world when measured by foreign-exchange reserves of US$ 180 billion. It also earned increased scrutiny from its trading partners, who were caught on the negative side of that trade imbalance.

So how could a diplomatically isolated, tiny island nation of over 20 million people generate enough momentum to be one of the top ten trading nations in the world? First prepare the ground works with beneficial education, land reform, and investment policies. Add the fertiliser of foreign aid, foreign investment and technology transfer. Even with all this, your seed has to be strong and hardy. This is where the beliefs and cultural traditions of Taiwan have served it well. The shame-based culture, with its strongest source of influence being closest to the individual (i.e. his or her family), generates immediate feedback, a strong will to succeed, and an ability to sacrifice present comfort for future return to the family.

The Mandarin term for business, *shengyi*, literally translated means 'the meaning of life'. For most Taiwanese, then, the ultimate rewards of existence do not lie in heaven or enlightenment, but in the accumulation of wealth for the family. Indeed, we can view business as the fourth aspect of Taiwan's cultural tradition, equal in importance to Buddhism, Confucianism, and Taoism. If you understand that the people you are employing and associating with treat business this seriously, you will be a step further along the road toward successfully dealing with them.

Conversation with a Local Entrepreneur

"How is business?" I asked.

"Not good lah!" he chimed, his nicotine and betel-stained teeth forming a bloody grin. With the crash of the stock market, people were buying fewer of the car stereos sold by his small speciality shop located among a dozen other small speciality shops selling exactly the same thing. Business (*shengyi*) to Chinese is literally the meaning of life. Life was not too good, but his smile and nature were as easy as ever.'

—from *Unwanted Vocabulary* by Chris Bates

You might interpret this to mean that the Taiwanese businessman is a 'family man' in the Western sense. You might even invite him to your house to show him how you get along with your children and provide for their needs (i.e. to show that you share a common goal with respect to your families). Know, though, that the Taiwanese businessman is very likely looking at your 12-year-old and wondering why he or she is listening to music, riding a bike or playing video games instead of studying. The Taiwanese businessman does not acquire wealth to make his family necessarily more comfortable (though this is frequently a side effect). Rather, he does so to make them more productive, to provide his children with the environment and tools which will enable them, in turn, to create wealth that may be shared with him and his wife in their twilight years.

Let us review the post-war history of business in Taiwan, then look more closely at a typical Taiwanese business and how you should approach dealing with them.

THE ECONOMY OF TAIWAN

The island's basic infrastructure was mainly developed during the Japanese colonisation. The population was sufficiently educated (albeit in Japanese) and, with Taiwan's retrocession at the end of World War II, the foundation was laid for one of Asia's postwar 'miracles'. After some initial fumbling, the Kuomintang got their act together and, in the 1950s, promoted agricultural extension services, crop research, and land reform, which put ownership of regulated sizes of farm plots back in the hands of the farmers. At that time, the bulk of Taiwan's work force was agricultural. The government established many *gong jia ji guan* or 'public corporations', such as Taiwan Power, China Petroleum, China Steel, China Airlines, and RSEA (a construction company employing retired servicemen). These provided several boosts to the economy, namely, employment at a time when a massive influx of immigrants had arrived from Mainland China; stable and controlled commodity pricing; and a source of business for hundreds of small suppliers of tools, commodities, raw materials and services to these large companies.

The economy slowly began to shift away from its agricultural base. Today, manufacturing and services share roughly equal levels of employment at 41 and 42 per cent respectively, while agriculture has dropped to 17 per cent. Textiles, clothing, electronics, processed foods, chemicals, steel, ships and plastics became principal products.

In the 1960s and 1970s, manufacturing was either backed by foreign investment or took the form of contract manufacturing in support of foreign manufacturers. Another growth industry at the time was pirate production, counterfeiting and 'copy cat' manufacturing of lower-quality goods for a limited local or regional market. China and Taiwan have no history of intellectual property protection. Indeed, if we look at China's arts and crafts, the tradition is to learn through rote and precise imitation of past masters, leading to mastery of tradition rather than mastery of expression. It has been argued that part of China's historical lack of success in capitalising on the discoveries of its scientists and inventors was the absence of any way of protecting intellectual property. There was no incentive to invent beyond personal necessity.

In the 1980s, several important political and economic channels began to converge. Mainland China began to be seen as a credible (and cheaper) manufacturing alternative to the 'Four Tigers'. Western nations, and especially the United States, put pressure on Taiwan to correct its trade imbalance. The Cold War drew to a close and the United States began to actively withdraw its support for the one-party regimes it had backed during the long struggle with Communism.

The confluence of these macro-trends resulted in massive change for Taiwan. With the appreciation of the Taiwan dollar from NT\$ 40 to NT\$ 25 against US\$ 1, coupled with the ever more attractive choice of Mainland China for business, foreign manufacturers fled the island. Chris recalls in the mid-1980s that every time he changed clothes in the locker room of the American Club he would overhear businessmen discussing plans to pull their plants out of Taiwan.

Taiwanese industry had to rapidly shift gears. Manufacturers have done this in two ways. The less imaginative have pulled their plants out of Taiwan and followed the foreign manufacturers to Thailand, Malaysia and China (which became an option with political liberalisation). They are chasing cheap labour and the ability to continue producing mediocre to good quality products and assemblies on a contract manufacturing basis for other companies that own the designs and brands. More daring Taiwanese companies, however, are investing in creating a brand image with unique high quality product lines of their own and are trying to create their own branded sales channels. Companies like Acer, Tera and UB are in this category. They feel that Taiwanese industry's only long-term chance for survival is to follow the example of major corporations in the industrialised world and develop, promote, and maintain proprietary corporate identities.

With this new local imperative, the cry has gone out to protect intellectual property. Now that Taiwanese corporations are producing intellectual property to protect, they want the backup of the legal system. Legislation was enacted in the late 1980s to step up investigation into counterfeiting activities and increase penalties for it. Although copy Rolex watches are still readily available, the pirate market is less of a free-for-all than it used to be.

What we have not seen, though, is a shift to the massive corporation, comparable to the Korean or Japanese development models. The government enterprises still operate and are now slowly being privatised. But only several large-scale Taiwanese corporations exist; Formosa

Small- and Medium-sized Entreprises

Advantages

- The smaller companies are more flexible and can change corporate direction 'on a dime'.
- They maintain low overheads and attempt to remain competitive at all costs because they are the life blood of the owners.
- Tight control of overheads and margins allows them to remain competitive as a supplier of OEM sub-assemblies.

Disadvantages

- They have limited research, marketing, and strategic planning resources.
- They maintain an over-dependency on the owner for decision-making.
- They do not develop the 'critical mass' necessary to be more than a component supplier.

Plastic and Evergreen Shipping come to mind. Even these companies, as big as they are today, were started by individual entrepreneurs. The rest of the economy is fueled by the entrepreneurial engine; there exist literally tens of thousands of small- and medium-sized businesses. They manufacture, provide services, export, import, and trade. They have created a network of 'niche' players and copy cat artists.

LAND OF THE ENTREPRENEUR

It is a cultural imperative that drives the Chinese to be their own bosses. We believe it stems from the family focus of their vision of Confucianism. "Why should I dedicate my knowledge, skills, and resources to a company when my family can best benefit from them more directly?" they would argue. After sufficient knowledge has been acquired in a core business, they leave to start up on their own, frequently with seed capital from in-laws. Another possible reason for this tendency is that, in a society that is highly regulated by the family, a personal enterprise becomes an expression of and outlet for one's individuality. If one works for a company and one's family, one is only attached to external visions of the self. Setting up one's own company allows the creation of a unique vision of oneself, over which one can exert maximum control.

Of course, not all Taiwanese break off to set up on their own, otherwise no publicly listed corporation could survive! But it is a significant cultural trait. More successful small- and medium-sized enterprises try to prevent the exodus of their top managers with 'golden handcuffs' and more and more high tech firms have set up, some using Silicon Valley style stock options to retain key staff.

ALL IN THE FAMILY

The predominance of small- and medium-sized firms leads to another phenomenon: nepotism. The word is usually used negatively in the West, but in Taiwan it is considered natural and necessary. "Who else can I trust?" is the question in the businessman's mind. "Certainly not someone from outside my family. And why should I let another family benefit anyway?" You will frequently find companies wherein the wife is the accounts or finance manager and the younger brother is the export sales manager, his MBA studies abroad having been financed by the older brother.

This scenario also facilitates more shady activities, such as maintaining two sets of books to reduce taxation. If you are investigating the credit-worthiness of a company that has reason to cooperate with you (such as a distributor or supplier), ask for a set of their accounts. Then have a credit bureau supply you with another set. Compare them and feel free to ask unpointed questions about discrepancies.

If you are running a company, it is best to discourage or even ban the hiring of relatives. This is a preventive measure which reduces the possibility that they will work together to put their family interests before company interests. If you don't take this precaution, you may see the effects of nepotism manifesting themselves in areas like hiring, contract approval, accounts anomalies, missing inventory and disappearing customers. It also precludes several related people from acquiring enough information about your business to quit together and readily set up as a successful competitor. For one employee to successfully do this alone, he or she would probably have risen through the ranks to acquire the perspective of several middle managers. By the time your higher employees do this, you should have been able to identify him or her as a 'comer' and cement a long-term relationship with stock or bonus incentives.

Do not feel that this is harsh or discriminatory toward the Taiwanese family value system. Such an opinion is typical of the 'straight, gullible, naive' approach with which the Chinese stereotype Westerners. One company I worked with had several members from three families in the management, but there was a standing rule against staff marrying or even dating. If you wanted to date, one of you had to go. Another company established by four unrelated partners had a standing rule covering all personnel that no relatives could be employed. Tell your staff that you will not employ your nephew from Arkansas or Minsk and they will not employ their wife, brother, sister, cousin, etc.

AN APPOINTMENT WITH A TYPICAL TAIWANESE COMPANY

As with all things in life, there is never an absolute 'typical'. However, there are experiences and perceptions which, when repeated over and over again, give one a feel for the typical in aggregate. We mentioned above that Taiwan's economy has bred a vast sea of small- and medium-sized enterprises which support each other, support foreign buyers, and support the larger Taiwanese companies.

These enterprises are normally started by one man (occasionally a woman or husband-and-wife team) who has garnered some practical experience from a former employer and sets out on his own, in some way, to repeat the success he has observed. They start out modestly with little capital and long hard hours of work. But they succeed and slowly build the business up. Among these enterprises, it is rare to see a corporate identity or office ambiance. Only the visionary companies, or those looking at selling out, have one. For sure, you may visit much larger and modern corporations with conditions that are most opulent and 'Western', but if you visit any of their suppliers, you will then see the typical company, which we will now visit.

The Pick-up

You have made an appointment to see Mr. Fliver Chen, President of Wholesome Goodies Ltd. Fearing that you cannot find his office in its out-of-the-way place, he personally comes to your hotel to pick you up. Despite the fact he has had to drive in 70 minutes of downtown traffic, he arrives only 10 minutes late. The hotel receptionist points you out to him, he comes over with a big smile on his face, and then firmly shakes your hand, introducing himself in English and extending a name card to you. You take his card in both hands, examine it carefully and thank him for giving it to you, extending one of your own to him in return.

He is dressed in a European-style, short-sleeved shirt with an open collar, slacks, and scuffed leather shoes (it's impossible to keep shoes clean between the dust, debris and damp in Taiwan). He is carrying a *shoji* (cellular phone) and a large bunch of keys. He beckons you to come out to his waiting car. He has given you face by coming personally to fetch you and you thank him for this undeserved attention.

You sit in the front seat of his BMW 525 and the air-conditioning quickly cuts through your shirt, making you chill. He has an imported CD player on which he is playing Western classical music. As the car pulls out into the traffic, he asks you if this is your first trip to Taiwan, what you think of the traffic, the food, etc.

During the hour-long start-and-stop drive to his office, the conversation is mostly social. He wants to get to know you. So, you should use the opportunity to get to know him. Feel free to ask of him any question he has asked of you: sports, travel, family, how he came to know you or your company, your schedule.

Finally, he pulls through a red metal gate in a high gray concrete wall. A painted brass company plaque is affixed to the wall, proclaiming the home of 'Wholesome Goodies'. There is not much maneuvering room in the parking area but he takes a space reserved for his car near the front door.

The Building

You enter the building through a sliding glass door. Inside, on the ground level, are eight desks, carefully arranged to fit in an area of about 800 square feet. The floor is made of a composite of concrete and stone chips, and is polished and gray. Several fans with blue blades, not recently cleaned, are mounted to the walls. They swing back and forth, distributing a breeze through the office. Against the walls around the room are filing cabinets, catalog shelves, a fax machine, a copy machine, an aquarium with one large sleek fish and a bottled-water dispenser. Seated at four of the desks are office girls. They have computers on their desks and look busy. Two of the other desks are empty and two are occupied by younger men wearing ties who are reading the morning newspapers.

Mr. Chen leads you upstairs to his office. The second level was carpeted long ago and trails now show where the heaviest traffic flows. You are left in a small meeting room and the window air-conditioner is turned on. Mr. Chen excuses himself. You are sitting on a low sofa with a coffee table in front of you. You are probably uncomfortable, finding your knees up against your chest.

As the room cools down you look around. There is a colorful calendar from a Japanese supplier on one wall. On the wall facing you, hanging high near the ceiling, is a black carved wooden plaque with gold-leaf Chinese characters on it. It is an expression of good fortune, given to the company on its founding day many years ago. On the coffee table is a marble ashtray, cigarette lighter and humidor set, placed atop a lace doily. Under the coffee table are industrial magazines and catalogs.

A secretary appears and asks whether you would like tea or coffee. You tell her your choice and she disappears again. Mr. Chen shortly returns and apologises for having had to make several calls. The secretary presents your drink and retreats, leaving you and the boss to talk.

The Meeting

Depending on the nature of your business and the nature of his business, the meeting can take many different directions at this point. Very probably he will introduce you to his lieutenants and you will have a detailed discussion about the prospects of your respective companies doing business.

If he has a factory and it is located in the same place as the office, he will probably be happy to let you tour it. There will inevitably be difficulties in language, but a smile and some patience will give all parties the time to find a way of expressing the point in a different way.

During the meeting, the accountant brings in a small stack of papers for Mr. Chen to 'chop'. He excuses himself, looks over each one carefully, but not excessively, then chops each one in the appropriate place with his seal and red ink. It is very possible that Mrs. Chen also works in the company, very possibly as the finance or accounts manager.

Mr. Chen is clearly 'the boss'. The company revolves around him. He listens to his lieutenants' input and your thoughts, but the decision is his to make. Indeed, to insist in a challenging way that he must accept your point of view would be disastrous. Better to wait for a quiet moment alone after a few drinks to express your respect for the strength of his convictions, but that you feel it is in his company's best interest to follow your suggestions.

Lunch and Siesta

The discussions have gone well and it is way past noon. Mr. Chen says they have planned a lunch for you. He invites his right-hand man to attend and you all head downstairs. The lights are out and you notice a macabre sight: formless bodies slouched at each desk. One of the secretaries pulls her coat from her head and you now know this is the *xiuxi* or *wushui* (siesta period after lunch). The office staff have put their coats over their heads and are resting on the desks. At 1:30 p.m. the lights will come back on and the office will reanimate.

You have told Mr. Chen that you love Chinese food, so lunch is at a pleasant air-conditioned eatery, not far away. Beer is served, but it is evident that the Taiwanese want to save the heavy drinking for the evening. Several cold appetisers are quickly brought to the table including peanuts, *doufu* threads with shredded carrots and celery and marinated clams fragrant with soy sauce, garlic and chilli. *Weisheng kuai zi* (sanitary wooden chopsticks) are used, which everyone ceremoniously snaps apart like wishbones. Mr. Chen is a modern fellow and asks the waitress to bring chopsticks and spoons solely for serving purposes.

Several hot courses of seafood, meat and vegetables are brought to the table, accompanied by white steamed rice. A soup is also delivered. A dessert of fresh fruit follows.

Mr. Chen's lieutenant is asked to drive you back to your hotel. Before parting, Mr. Chen asks whether you are free that evening. You respond that you are and would like to invite him out. He insists that you be his guest and a time is set to pick you up. Smiles and thanks follow, and you return to your hotel.

NETWORKING TAIWANESE-STYLE

How would you have made contact with Mr. Chen? You arrived in Taiwan and knew no one. How do you set up?

It is very important that you get to know people as soon as possible. The buzzword from the United States is 'networking' and Taiwan is certainly a highly networked society. The family is the first channel of networking. So, if you don't have family in Taiwan, then you will have to develop contacts.

The importance of generating and cultivating contacts cannot be over-stressed. In Taiwan, this is called *guan xi* and means 'relations'. Of course, you must maintain 'good relations' with everyone, from your hired help onward. But this is not the real Taiwanese meaning. Good *guan xi* is developed with people normally at your level or above in the social and business hierarchy; in other words, with those people who can instruct or obstruct, decide or desist, nod or shake. Good *guan xi* opens doors, smooths out troubles, leads to further *guan xi*, ad infinitum. It is a web that grows. Just as a spider tends to its web and keeps it in good repair and working order, so too your network must not be neglected. Think of it as networking, with the cultural imperatives layered on, and you will find it an easier task.

The type of contacts you will need to develop will vary depending on your purpose in coming to Taiwan. You can begin to generate contacts by visiting organisations like your country's Chamber of Commerce or Business Association. Some businessmen will be able to make beneficial contacts through the China External Trade Development Council (CETRA) and other ROC trade organisations. There are a variety of specific industrial associations, the Taiwan

Spectacles Manufacturers Association, for example. However, this type of association will probably not have fluent English speakers, so you must be prepared to organise help in that area. In addition, your friends, associates of sister companies, or even your corporate attorney or auditor may also provide a useful lead that provides another lead that moves you in the right direction.

As you construct your web of contacts, maintain it. Sending thank-you notes to people who introduced you to people, follow-up calls, perhaps an invitation to dinner or golf would justify their confidence in helping you express your sincere gratitude; and earn *ren qing wei* points. If any of your contacts calls you back, do not dismiss them or not return the call. Yes, they probably want something, but it may be help you can provide, or a contact you can offer, which will one day be returned. The web strengthens.

As illustrated in our visit to a Taiwanese company, certain behavior will make the Taiwanese more comfortable with you. Dress as formally as dictated by your business. If you are overdressed, you can slowly loosen up, so it is better to err on the side of conservatism.

Name Cards
The exchange of name cards is a simple ritual that must not be neglected. Like the Japanese, the Taiwanese value name cards. They are the physical reminder of one's *guan xi*. The exchange of cards is not a new thing in China; it was certainly used in the last century, if not earlier. The use of a written description of one's position or status, usually prepared by a government official to bestow status or power, is millennia-old. A person might give you their card to take when visiting another person. It conveys their *guan xi*.

Treat the name card of the person you meet with the deference you give the person. Look at it closely, study it, understand their title and name, and comment on their company's corporate identity if it is nice or new. Do not make the same mistake as the culturally clumsy American vice president of Chris' acquaintance who offended the Chinese customers he met by collecting a stack of name cards like scrap paper and then dealing out his name cards across the table back to the guests like a brusque Las Vegas croupier. Also, do not run out of cards. In a busy week of networking or sales it is easy to go through 100 cards. Also consider getting a Chinese name.

Be agreeable and inquisitive. Be concerned about the person you are meeting and their company. Be frank, open, relaxed, unhurried, and well-rounded. At the same time, remember that until a relation is well-established, you will not want to be too liberal in 'tipping your hand'. On the other hand, do not be overly secretive either. Sounds like a fine line to draw, doesn't it? Try to avoid giving answers like, "I am sorry, I cannot tell you. It's confidential information." You are telling the person in a direct and perhaps face losing way that you do not trust them or their company. The Taiwanese would say the same thing much more indirectly, for instance, "The information is not ready yet. Can I get you a copy when it's finished?" The person spoken to may or may not expect to get the information later.

What Do They Expect From You?

So, what is a Taiwanese businessperson looking for in their relationship with a foreigner? Whether you are buying or selling, we feel that what they seek can be summarised in order of importance as follows:

- **Maximisation of Profits**

    The Taiwanese businessperson will naturally try to maximise their profits in their relations with you. If you are selling, they will squeeze for price, or terms, or consignment, or all three. Explain how they can profit from your current sales package and what you will do to see that the program is a success. Do as much background checking as possible to verify or discount their claims that a price break is needed for them to be able to profit. Then make your proposal to your management, or make the decision yourself, whichever is appropriate. If you are buying from them, be prepared to be promised the moon and receive the late delivery of something less!

■ **Dealings on the Right Level**
The Taiwanese are very conscious of hierarchy. Based on their own cultural perspective, a person ranked too low will be seen as ineffectual or a stepping stone, rather than a conduit to working with your office. Not knowing you, they will give you the benefit of the doubt at first. If you are not empowered to make decisions and do not establish good *guan xi* with your business ties, they will go around you. Of course, they can tolerate the occasional, "I'll have to check with headquarters," but not consistently.

■ **Long-term Relations**
The Taiwanese business partner would much rather have the opportunity of establishing a long-term relationship with you, rather than a one-off. It saves them having to understand yet another raft-load of foreigners if they change supplier or customer; it allows them to exercise *guan xi* to the fullest; and it smooths out their long-term cash-flow projections.

■ **Friendship**
Though it may take several years, your business contact will hope to eventually make friends with you. The Taiwanese are friendly, relaxed folk. The friendship will mature after many shared experiences and hardships.

Bribery, Corruption, Grease and Gifts

Yes, *hong bao* do still exist. So does bribery. And, no, it is not absolutely necessary. In fact, the book *Doing Business in Taiwan* (see Bibliography) indicates that, in resolving questions of legality, a resort to bribery and *guan xi* may be disastrous. If your case is strong, the law will prevail. Other sources also indicate that Western companies which operate within the law and which successfully resist opportunities to bribe and corrupt, are able to get the business on the merit of their offer. We agree and disagree.

Let us play a little 'line-drawing' game here. Where does a gift become a bribe? Although not a legal opinion, a bribe is a substantial inducement given (usually after the event) to guarantee the outcome of an event. A gift, on the other hand, is a token of esteem used to cement friendly relations and express sincerity. It is usually given before the outcome of the event is known and with no guarantee as to the outcome being expressed.

Taiwanese are emotional people. They have a finely tuned social awareness. If they do not like you or your company for some emotional reason, they see no reason to favour your offers. They should feel that you and your company are the right ones to deal with. Giving a gift the wrong way, to the wrong person, or indeed giving the wrong gift, can be more disastrous than not giving one at all. Do not treat gifts as bribes or inducements. Get to know the person with whom you want to establish good relations and understand their needs and fears (they have some vision for their department, factory, company). Then treat the gift as something given freely, without coercion, between friends.

If you do not get the business, do not collar the fellow and ask pointedly why you did not get the contract. Instead, invite him out again, ask in what ways your company's offer can be improved in the future, and whether there are any other jobs you can approach him for. Strengthen the network. Who knows? He may even tell you that all is not lost and he is willing to reopen the bidding.

MANAGING TAIWANESE STAFF

You have read Chapter Four and have begun to understand what the Taiwanese think of you. As you are a foreign manager, they will have certain conceptions about how you will work with them and operate the company. Many Taiwanese express relief when working for Western companies because structured chances for advancement exist, doors are open, and the pay is marginally better. You do not have to stomp in like your conception of a paternalistic, autocratic, Taiwanese, family-owned business manager to make them feel comfortable.

However, sympathy and understanding of the dynamics of Taiwanese interpersonal relations are important. First, understand what you represent to them. You are the 'boss', the *lao ban*, or if you are a woman, the 'bossette', *lao ban niang*. You are expected to retain an air of control and respectability. Do not show panic or discomfort. Show displeasure only when you can express it privately and in such a way as not to make the person lose face. The Western penchant for the snide, satirical comment, or backhanded compliment is not appreciated. When they understand, it is resented, otherwise it is generally not understood. Remember the Western management maxim 'Criticise in Private, Praise in Public', but choose your words simply and without ambiguity.

Getting Your Staff Involved

A frequent difficulty expressed by Western managers in Taiwan is getting their staff to 'open up'. Remember again that Taiwan has a shamed-based culture. People are motivated by trying to avoid being shamed. If you call a staff meeting and find yourself giving a monologue, you need to draw out or begin to tap your managers' reserves of creativity and individuality. They do not want to criticise others in public for fear of reprisals and do not want to stick their necks out with new risky ideas either.

Opening them up can be done in several ways. If the company is large and the problem great, you can hire a management consultant to help facilitate the blossoming of your staff. On the other hand, if your office is small, you can initiate change yourself. Start with private meetings. Ask about the person's past (college, team sports, career) and aspirations. What do they like about the company? Explain that you are not Taiwanese, but you feel you understand that they are concerned about not taking a risk by extending opinions. You understand.

At the same time, you come from a different culture, one which may reward risk-takers, even when they fail, because having learned a valuable lesson they will do much better the next time. Perhaps you could offer an example from your own history. You also come from a culture where individuals succeed in teams. Explain that the rules of success in your company are based on participation, cooperation, and risk-taking. Ask the person to think about this.

At the next staff meeting, remind everyone of your conversation and then perhaps bring up something good that has come up during the week that was done by the managers working as a team. Thank them for that. Then bring up something done by an individual that showed merit and point out why it is of mention. Then bring up a topic that you feel needs to be urgently addressed, perhaps one that is on your desk, not theirs. Ask for their input on the proper solution. Do not criticise any of the proposals, but rather express how and in what way it has shed light on some aspect of the problem that was not evident before. In other words, even wrong answers have merit. Because it is a problem on your desk, a decision need not be made on the spot—no judgment required.

It will take time and many meetings to open up your staff. It is most important, though, to create an environment where they feel safe to do so. Remember, however, that you are ultimately in command and are expected to provide the example of leadership.

Gossip

Gossipmongering is a frequent problem in Taiwanese companies and creates and perpetuates ill-will between staff. The bad thing is that your Mandarin may not pass muster yet and the gossip could be about you! It is very important that you have a local person on your staff whom you feel you can trust more fully, someone who can be your eyes and ears in the organisation. This might be your personnel or accounts manager. If you have a really large organisation, choose more than one person for this job. Take your staff out to socialise and loosen up. Dinner, drinking, or golf with a customer are good choices. Share some good times and some adventure with them. This in itself may slow the rumor mill about you and get you valuable insights into the human resource at your command.

Intermediaries

One time-honored Taiwanese tradition you can effectively employ is the use of an intermediary. If an employee is having a problem or under-performing, you might use the 'eyes and ears' mentioned above to communicate with the party in question. This saves that person losing face in front of you when explaining their problem.

Ren Qing Wei

Ren qing wei is also very important. Feelings and emotions are the power of human and corporate relationships in Taiwan, not duty or obligation. All the more so in times of high employment, when staff can walk across the street for a slightly higher-paying job because they do not like the feeling they have around you. Do you inspire confidence, loyalty, and direction? Can they feel that you understand them and their motivations, both personal and cultural? When they come to work with a white ragged armband pinned around their sleeve, do you ask them to remove it before going out to see an important customer, or do you inquire as to who died and express condolences?

Corruption

Be on your guard against dishonesty, corruption, or thieving within the ranks. This is not to say that Taiwanese are overly dishonest, corrupt, or thieving. It takes place in every culture, in every country. But you are a stranger here. You do not understand the language. You do not know what the hell is going on around you, even under your very nose. Install proper corporate procedures for accounting, personnel, and management. Use as much as you can from your headquarters manual. Then, when you are comfortable that you are in control of your business, feel free to 'tweak' the system to make it fit your Taiwanese staff just right. Loosen up just enough. Middle Management Do's and Don'ts

Most of the above tips are written for the manager who is 'the boss' with many Taiwanese working for him or her. However, increasingly more foreigners work in Taiwan for Taiwanese and these are tips for you.

- Excellent English and Western management or marketing skills are probably what they hired you for, but the better you get at Mandarin, the more real value you will have. Constantly strive to improve your Mandarin and don't get frustrated when you realise that it is a never ending battle.

- Be willing to integrate with local people and customs. Taiwanese feel *ren qing wei*. If you act cold or insincere, they will feel it, talk about it and stone wall you.

- Taiwanese will appreciate your skills at presentation and organising if this is your strong suit. Taiwanese are often shy to get up in front of a crowd to talk. If you can present in Mandarin as well, so much the better.

- Showing you are not afraid of working hard, pulling in long hours or on the weekend without complaint, if it does not distinguish you from your Taiwanese peers (because they will work hard) at least will not mark you as a foreign slacker.

- Spend time with your peers and subordinates off hours, relaxing with a beer or singing karaoke to build your web of *guan xi* and bonding.

- Do research on your industry in English to try to learn business intelligence your boss may not have picked up on yet. He or she will be happy and impressed with your initiative.

Always make your boss look good. This is as true in Taiwan as it is in America.

BUSINESS SAFEGUARDS

Let's say you want to procure half a million pieces of a unique patented alarm clock radio designed by your company. You may wish to install certain safeguards. There are lots of middlemen in Taiwan, so ask if the person you are talking to is a middleman. If he is not, ask where his factory is and if you can tour it. Try to get straight to the manufacturer. The person you are dealing with may only make the plastic moulded shell and have the printed circuit board made outside. In that case, you may want to also insist on a meeting with the PCB manufacturer at his factory.

When you have set on a supplier, you will need to try to protect yourself from a design copyright or patent perspective. Pirating is not the free-for-all it once was, so take the measures the law affords you. The patent registration procedure is covered fully in English in the book *Doing Business in Taiwan* (*Refer to* Further Reading *on page 285*).

You will have a contract that covers technical specifications, returns, terms, delivery dates, etc. It is legal and valid and is necessary for due diligence, but, ultimately, choosing the right supplier is a matter of choosing the right supplier Roping the wrong guy into the right contract will bring you nothing but misery.

Finally, unless you have facilities or headquarters personnel who can perform the inspection of the goods at several stages of manufacture, then you should hire one of the many specialised service firms (many run by Westerners) which can provide inspection services.

BUSINESS SOCIALISING AND ENTERTAINMENT

Now for the fun part: wining, dining, hitting little white balls around large green fields and loosening your tie with some of Asia's most practiced 'good ol' boys'. The Taiwanese like to entertain and be entertained. They like loud restaurants, saucy stories, and they admire a person who can hold their liquor. Unfortunately, none of this is as economical as it once was. In fact, it is downright expensive. Make sure that your company has budgeted sufficiently for entertainment. Depending on the company size, even several per cent of gross revenue might not be too much.

Daytime entertainment is restricted to lunches and golf. If you are a golfer, take advantage of the fact and do some business on the greens. It would not be appropriate to actually discuss business during the game, but the saunas, coffee shops, or dinner that come afterward offer many opportunities. The important thing is that you have a shared experience to help cement your business relationship.

Evening offers even more entertainment opportunities. A typical full-blown evening might comprise a grand dinner with beer or Chinese wine, retiring to a karaoke lounge to drink more, sing some songs, and converse with a hostess or two, followed by a midnight snack. This might be at *Di Hua Jie* where Snake Alley and Lungshan Temple are located, or it might be at a coffee shop or night market.

Taiwanese enjoy drinking games. These are all boisterous and insanely fun competitions… if you are a drinker! The simplest game is the famous 'paper, scissors, rock' game. Slightly more complicated is another game of hand signs, whereby the participants quickly and simultaneously show a random number of fingers on one hand, while both shout out the number they guess the sum of the two hands will form. If they are both wrong, the sequence is repeated, but if one of them is correct the loser has to take a shot. Aficionados will play this game with lightning speed, that is, until the effect of the alcohol takes its toll! Other experts will also say code words (like the city name 'Ilan' rather than the number *yi*, 'one'), making the game even funnier. The most complicated version we have seen involves the use of two hands for each participant. Keep in mind that repetitions are frequent and, to the uninitiated, it all sounds like a harried auctioneer calling out numbers. Through the haze of alcohol, the waving hands and voices blur. You will invariably lose more and more as the evening progresses.

The 'Face' of Entertaining

Whether you are being entertained or are entertaining, do not forget the importance of face. If being entertained, make sure the host knows you are enjoying yourself. To act otherwise would not only mark you as an ingrate, but make him lose face as well. Allow yourself to trust your host completely, even enough to let the two of you drink yourselves to the point of slap-happy oblivion (although not vomiting hysteria) if you are both so inclined. If you allow him to feel as though he has introduced you to an exotic experience, it will certainly draw the two of you closer.

When entertaining, remember face. If you invite the guests to a Chinese dinner, either let them order what they like, or have one of your local employees do so. If inviting them out for Western food, keep in mind that they may not be familiar with the kinds of food offered on the menu, or with special dining utensils, such as escargot clips or a place setting of three knives and forks. This could be embarrassing to them. In such a situation, initiate an explanation of the cuisine to them.

Don't patronise them with a set of instructions for boors, but give instead an emotional rendering of why you like this food, why you want to introduce them to it, and what it's all about. Don't opt for heavy-going Western foods which are usually considered an 'acquired taste' (Blue Stilton cheese, for instance). And be prepared to order for yourself something you think they would like, as they may feel compelled to order the same as you. If you recommend certain dishes to them, you should order one of them yourself.

Monkey Business

Taiwan is not the 'male paradise' it was once considered to be by businessmen seeking bedroom amenities while on the road. However, the Japanese and Taiwanese men still look for female company here. As the 'Taipei A-Z Guide' in the back of *Taipei Living* comments, 'There are many different types of barber shop in Taipei. Those listed below cut hair only.' Indeed before Chen Shui-bian's Taipei mayoralty, Jilin Road had hundreds of barber shops, employing as many as 20,000 women. Simply put, the women did cut hair and give manicures, but the private rooms and reclining chairs were put to more extensive use. As Taipei has been cleaned up, these recreational activities have moved around the city, keeping ahead of enforcement, or gone to the suburbs and down island.

Hostesses are found in many karaoke and hostess lounges. Be aware that you are charged per girl for the amount of time they chat with you. Of course, you pay for their drinks as well, so bills run up quickly. Unless you or your guest really enjoy this sort of company, it may be better to opt for entertainment in one of the several 'pubs' which are advertised. These tend to be more like a Western bar or pub, and comprise lots of laughing, darts and beer.

For the Businesswoman

It is quite possible for women to succeed in business in Taiwan. The current head of Taiwan High Speed Railway is, in fact, a woman. For a foreign woman, all the lessons already discussed in this book still apply, but there are also a few more tips.

As we have said, entertainment is an important part of making contacts, developing *guan xi*, showing *ren qing wei*, and getting business. Obviously, Taiwanese (and probably expatriate) men would be uneasy at your presence with them at a 'barber shop'. But you can successfully entertain. Golfing would be a great alternative, especially if you are a good player and can give them a run for their money. Dinners are innocuous and if you are a good drinker they will be impressed. However, the extent to which you want to become 'one of the guys' will probably not be misconstrued in a romantic way if you draw clear boundaries.

Karaoke bars (with or without hostesses) will relieve you from the possibility of having to dance with one of your guests, an entertainment that would be inappropriate. If it is a hostess bar, do not be embarrassed or think that they equate you, as a working woman, with 'working women' in the traditional sense. Indeed, they treat hostesses themselves as entertainers, not prostitutes. The banter with these women is sometimes saucy, with double entendres and innuendo, but it is rarely raunchy. It is not very common to see men leaving the bar with a hostess either.

A final word: if you are a general manager, take note that your calm resolve, ability to think through problems, and provision of acculturated leadership will be under constant scrutiny by your staff, even when entertaining.

Have a good time in Taiwan. Live long and prosper!

'For diplomats and businesses around the world that
wish the whole PRC-versus-Taiwan matter would just
'go away', it does not look too promising. Many polls
show that most Taiwanese residents favour the
status quo of undeclared independence.'
—Kevin Chambers, *Succeed in Business: Taiwan*

Official Name
Taiwan, Republic of China

Capital and Administrative Centre
Taipei

Flag
Red with a dark blue rectangle in the upper hoist-side corner bearing a white sun with 12 triangular rays

Time
Greenwich Mean Time plus 8 hours (GMT + 0800)

Land
Eastern Asia, islands bordering the East China Sea, Philippine Sea, South China Sea, and Taiwan Strait, north of the Philippines, off the south-eastern coast of China

Area
total: 35,980 sq km (13,892 sq miles)
tand: 32,260 sq km (12,455.7 sq miles)
water: 3,720 sq km (1,436.3 sq miles)

Highest Point
Yu Shan

Major Rivers

Jhuoshuei River, Gaoping River, Danshuei River, Dajia River, Wu River and Zengwun River

Climate

Tropical; marine; rainy season during south-west monsoon (June to August); cloudiness is persistent and extensive all year

Natural Resources

Small deposits of coal, natural gas, limestone, marble and asbestos

Population

22,858,872 (2007 est.)

Ethnic Groups

Taiwanese (including Hakka), Mainland Chinese and aborigine

Major Religions

A mixture of Buddhist, Confucian and Taoist, Animism as well as Christianity

Languages and Dialects

Mandarin Chinese (official), Taiwanese and Hakka dialects

National Anthem

San Min Chu I ('The Rights of the People')

Government

Multiparty democratic regime headed by popularly-elected president and unicameral legislature

Administrative Regions

Includes central island of Taiwan plus numerous smaller islands near central island and off coast of China's Fujian Province; Taiwan is divided into 18 counties (*hsien*, singular and plural), five municipalities (*shih*, singular and plural), and two special municipalities (*chuan-shih*, singular and plural). Counties are Chang-hua, Chia-i, Hsin-chu, Hua-lien, I-lan, Kao-hsiung county, Kin-men, Lien-chiang, Miao-li, Nan-t'ou, P'eng-hu, P'ing-tung, T'ai-chung, T'ai-nan, T'ai-pei county, T'ai-tung, T'ao-yuan, and Yun-lin. Municipalities are Chia-i, Chi-lung, Hsin-chu, T'ai-chung and T'ai-nan. Special municipalities are Kao-hsiung city and T'ai-pei city

Currency
New Taiwan dollar (TWD or NT$)

Gross Domestic Product (GDP)
US$ 528.6 billion (2003 est.)

Agricultural Products
Rice, corn, vegetables, fruit, tea, pigs, poultry, beef, milk and fish

Industries
Electronics, petroleum refining, chemicals, textiles, iron and steel, machinery, cement and food processing

Exports
Computer products and electrical equipment, metals, textiles, plastics and rubber products and chemicals

Imports
Machinery and electrical equipment, minerals and precision instruments

Ports and Harbours
Chi-lung (Keelung), Hua-lien, Kao-hsiung, Su-ao and T'ai-chung

Airports
Total of 40 (2003 est.), 37 of which have paved runways. The major international airports are Chiang Kai Shek Memorial International Airport in Taoyuan and Kaohsiung International Airport at the south-western tip of the main island

Railways
With a total of 2,544 km of tracks, operated by the Taiwan Railway Administration

FAMOUS PEOPLE
Chen Shui Bian
Known as A-Bian to his supporters, he is the current president of Taiwan. Born in Tainan, he became an opposition party mayor of Taipei in the 1990's and was Taiwan's first non-Kuomintang president. During campaigning for his second presidential election run, he, along with running mate Annette Lu, were shot and wounded in an assassination attempt. The murky circumstances around this episode and the subsequent clamp-down on election day led opposition party members to call for an investigation. Chen is variously ignored or vilified by mainland Chinese politicians because of his pro-Taiwan independence stance.

Chiang Kai Shek
The Kuomintang general who fought warlords, Japanese and communists, finally losing China to the latter and retreated to Taiwan with his army. He died in Taiwan after ruling as president and presiding over Taiwan's economic transformation.

Ang Lee
Film director famous for such movies as *Crouching Tiger, Hidden Dragon*; *Eat Drink Man Woman*, *The Wedding Banquet*, *The Hulk* and *Sense and Sensibility*. Born in Pingtung, Taiwan, Lee is considered one of the most notable contemporary filmmakers in the world.

Hu Gua
A popular television compere.

Chang Hui Mei (A-Mei)
A Taiwanese aborigine pop-star who has also become popular in mainland China. In the year 2000, the Coca-Cola company, who enlisted her to promote Sprite in China, had to withdraw its ad campaign after A-Mei sang at Taiwan President Chen

Shui-bian's inauguration. She is now an icon of the Taiwan tourist industry, inviting foreign visitors to enjoy Formosa.

Jerry Yang
Co-founder of Internet giant Yahoo!, born in Taipei, Taiwan. Moved to San Jose California when he was ten years old and later earned degrees in electrical engineering from Stanford University before teaming up with David Filo to create the Yahoo! Internet portal.

F4
A Taiwan boy band.

Jolin Tsai
A famous female teen idol singer.

Richie Ren
A Taiwanese singer turned actor who now makes action movies in Hong Kong.

Nickie Jin (aka Takeshi Kaneshiro)
The ruggedly handsome son of a Japanese father and Taiwanese mother, he has starred in Chinese films like *House of Flying Daggers* as well as Japanese films.

Shu Qi
A former soft porn local film star who has gained critical acclaim in films like *Millenium Mambo* and risen to international stardom in movies like *The Transporter*.

Wu Bai
A pioneer of Taiwanese dialect rock music.

Jay Chou
Currently the most famous Taiwanese pop composer/singer.

Nicky Wu
Former member of the boy band *Syau Hu Dui* (Little Tiger Band) who went on to star in films.

Lin Huai-min
Founder of the world famous Taiwanese modern ballet troupe Cloud Gate Dance Ensemble.

Hsingyun Fashih
Ven. Master Hsingyun, famed Buddhist teacher and head of the Foguangshan Temple in Kaohsiung. The organisation does a lot of charity work all over Taiwan.

Zhu Ming
World famous wood sculptor, best known for his carvings depicting Taichi postures.

Lee Ao
A famous Taiwanese radical author and critic of the government, he is now a TV talk show host and legislator.

Hsieh Chang-ting
The seldom heard of Premier of Taiwan and chairman of the DDP was the former mayor of Kaohsiung and a pioneer proponent of democratisation and independence for Taiwan.

Sisy Chen
A first rate debater who has become a TV talkshow hostess and political commentator.

Lee Denghui
The first Taiwanese-born president. He was vice president under Chiang Chingkuo (Chiang Kai-shek's son) and took over as president after he died. He was subsequently re-elected. In his retirement, he has become an advocate of Taiwan independence.

Lien Chan
Former chairman of the Kuomintang and failed presidential candidate. He is the grandson of a famous Taiwanese historian, Lien Heng. He was the first Kuomintang official since the fall of China in 1949 to meet publicly with China

Communist Party officials during a landmark 2005 visit to China. His departure from Taiwan for this trip was marked by violent clashes between his party supporters and pro-independence supporters at the international airport in Taoyuan precipitating the resignation of several high level officials.

Ma Ying Jeou

The current Kuomintang Party Chairman and former Taipei mayor is slated to run for president in 2008.

Wang Yongching

The founder of giant Formosa Plastic, he is a famed local entrepreneur.

Xu Wenlong

The founder of Chimei Group, the world's largest manufacturer of ABS plastic resin, and a former supporter of Taiwan independence and Chen Shuibian, he has recently resigned as a presidential advisor and is accused by locals of having 'gone red' because of his huge investments in China.

Tsai Kang Yong

Famous television talk show host who publicly admits his gay lifestyle.

Annette Lu

The current vice president of Taiwan under Chen Shuibian, this fiesty Harvard law graduate is outspokenly pro-independence.

Yuan T Lee

Winner of the Nobel Prize in chemistry in 1986, Lee is Taiwan's sole Nobel laureate.

Wen-Ho Lee

Chinese-American computer scientist born in Nantou, Taiwan, who was charged with spying (specifically, stealing U.S. nuclear arsenal secrets) while he was employed at Los

Alamos National Laboratory in the United States of America. Lee was later acquitted of the charge although he pleaded guilty to improperly downloading classified data.

PLACES OF INTEREST
- Jade Mountain
- Taroko Gorge
- Kending
- Alishan Mountain Railway
- Sun Moon Lake

CULTURE QUIZ

So, you have read the book, but are you ready to try out your knowledge before subjecting the locals to your cultural faux pas? Just to see how much you have learned from each chapter, have a go at the true/false quiz below. Some of the answers may surprise you. Also watch out for the red herrings that have been thrown in to keep you on your toes. You may want to re-read the relevant sections referred to in the answers, depending on your score!

QUESTIONS

1. Taiwan is a part of China.

2. Because Taiwan is a tropical island, the weather is great all year round.

3. You can wait and get your visa at the airport when you arrive in Taiwan.

4. Because of the traffic problem in Taipei, it is advisable to only ride the 'wild chicken' taxis as these get you to your destination quicker.

5. Many expatriates in Taipei settle in the area around Tienmu or Yangmingshan.

6. ICRT is a local English language radio station that is very helpful to foreigners.

7. Real estate agents in Taiwan only get a commission from you, so they are on your side during the negotiation.

8. Bargaining is still an accepted practice in many stores.

9. A jin is a unit of weight.

10. Because Taiwan exports so many clothes to the West, fashions of all sizes are readily available.

11. In Taiwan, driving is a nightmare but parking is a dream.

12. It is easy to get along just speaking English in Taiwan.

13. It is possible for a foreigner to learn to speak Chinese.

14. Learning popular songs is a good way of improving your spoken Chinese.

15	A person's chop (seal) is just a relic of the past used for signing letters in the traditional way.
16	Confucianism, Buddhism, and Taoism have had the most profound philosophical effect on the everyday life of the Taiwanese.
17	Because Taiwan was a colony of Japan, the Taiwanese are very similar culturally to the Japanese.
18	The Taiwanese have nothing but respect for foreigners, whom they see as shrewd negotiators.
19	Face is still very important in relating to the Taiwanese.
20	Chinese culture is shame-based.
21	*Ren qing wei* is a special, exotic, erotic, aphrodisiac dinner menu, only served on special occasions.
22	When giving gifts to the Taiwanese, it's the thought that counts, rather than the type, size, or brand name.
23	Taiwanese appreciate it if you express concern for their health and offer medical advice.
24	Vast sums of money are spent on weddings.
25	*Re nao* is the Chinese word for 'dog meat'.
26	Confucian etiquette demands that a check for a dinner be split between diners.
27	Banquet etiquette demands that you serve your partner with your chopsticks.
28	The Taiwanese like gambling.
29	*Shengyi* translates literally as 'the meaning of life' but is a general term for 'business'.
30	The Taiwanese prefer drawn out, relatively emotional answers to their questions, rather than a short, perfunctory 'yes' or 'no'.
31	Clocks are considered good gifts because they symbolise that your friendship will last for a long time.
32	The importance of education to Chinese people has a history that goes back several thousand years.

33	If a Taiwanese friend has an illness, they will appreciate it if you openly express your concern for their health and tell of other people you know who had the same illness.
34	Confucian modesty dictates that funerals should be simple, quiet, and frugal affairs.
35	For a quiet night out, a fancy European-style restaurant is still the best bet in Taipei.
36	At the end of a restaurant meal with Taiwanese, if it is your turn to pay, it is important that you do not let them pick up the tab, regardless of who offered the dinner invitation.
37	During a formal Chinese banquet, it is customary to leave some of the last dish (usually rice or noodles) remaining in your bowl to signify that you have eaten your fill.
38	'Yellow cows' are ticket scalpers.
39	Warner Village is a Christian missionary enclave deep in the mountains.
40	The Dragon Boat Race is perhaps the only sporting event in the world inspired by a drowning bureaucrat.
41	During the Ghost Month, particularly cautious Taiwanese will be very careful in their undertakings and not get married or start a new business.
42	In the area around Taiwan's premier university, Tai Da, you can find many bargains and modestly priced international restaurants.
43	Because Taiwanese family members work well together, your company should be encouraged to hire relatives of employees.
44	After eating lunch, office workers will pull their coats over their heads and take a siesta.
45	Guan xi should be thought of as 'networking', but with Taiwanese cultural imperatives layered on.

46	The exchange of name cards should be done with formality to give face to the person who is presenting their card to you.
47	Because your Taiwanese counterpart may have invited you out for some very exotic food, you should reciprocate by taking them to a very exotic Western restaurant.
48	The Taiwanese drink tap water, but you should not.
49	Typhoons and earthquakes are potential emergencies that should be prepared for.
50	Because the economy is so strong and unemployment zero, there is very little crime in Taiwan.

Answers

1	Trick question. Taiwan's political situation is exceptional. It has been a 'renegade province' of China since the Kuomintang fled the Mainland in 1949 and set up an island retreat. See Chapter Two.
2	False. Read more in Chapters One and Five.
3	False. Make sure you leave enough time to have a valid passport and visa prepared before you arrive in Taiwan. See Chapter Five.
4	False. Read more in Chapter Five.
5	True. Read more in Chapter Five.
6	This used to be true, however, ICRT has new management that is emphasising more local language programming. The expatriate community has circulated a petition demanding that it resume broadcasting to its original constituents.
7	False. They get commissions from both sides. Read more in Chapter Five.
8	True and false. Fewer stores accept bargaining than in the past, but it is still acceptable in some stores and situations. Read more in Chapter Five.
9	True. See Chapter Five.

10	False. See Chapter Five.
11	False. Driving is a nightmare and you are dreaming if you think you can readily find a parking space in Taipei. Read Chapter Five.
12	False. You should try to learn at least the basics to make your life in Taiwan easier. See Chapter Eight.
13	True. And you should really try to do so. Read more in Chapter Eight.
14	True. See Chapter Eight.
15	False. The seal is a necessary article for business and identification even today. See Chapter Eight.
16	True. Read more in Chapter Two.
17	True and false. Taiwan was a colony of Japan and retains close links. Many older Taiwanese can still speak Japanese, but the Taiwanese are very definitely culturally distinct from the Japanese.
18	False. Read more in Chapter Four.
19	True. Read more in Chapter Three.
20	True. Read more in Chapter Three.
21	False. Read more in Chapter Three.
22	False. Taiwanese prefer branded products that confer prestige. See Chapter Three.
23	False. Read more in Chapter Four.
24	True. Read more in Chapter Four.
25	False. Read more in Chapter Six.
26	False. Read more in Chapter Six.
27	False. Use the 'public use' chopsticks. Read more in Chapter Six.
28	True. See Chapter Seven.
29	True. Read more in Chapter Nine.
30	True. See Chapter Three.
31	False. See Chapter Three.
32	True. See Chapter Three.
33	False. See Chapter Three.

34	False. The opposite applies. See Chapter Four.
35	True. See Chapter Six.
36	False. Your turn to pay comes when they accept a dinner invitation from you. If they invited you, you are expected to fight for the check but lose in the end and thank the host profusely. See Chapter Six.
37	True. See Chapter Six.
38	True. See Chapter Seven.
39	False. It is a movie cineplex. See Chapter Seven.
40	True. See Chapter Seven.
41	True. See Chapter Seven.
42	True. See Chapter Seven.
43	False. They do work well together, but with the language and other problems, you do not want a family group setting themselves up to rival you. Read more in Chapter Nine.
44	True. See Chapter Nine.
45	True. Read more about this important subject in Chapter Nine.
46	True. See Chapters Eight and Nine.
47	True and false. It is perfectly proper to attempt to reciprocate, but try to be sensitive to the Taiwanese palate and help them order something they will probably enjoy. Read more in Chapter Six.
48	False. The Taiwanese generally do not drink water straight from the tap. They boil it first. Follow this custom or get bottled water. See Chapter Five.
49	True. See Chapter Five.
50	False. There is less violent crime than in many Western countries but, despite its economic strength, Taiwan still has plenty of theft, gangsters, and racketeering. Read more in Chapter Five.

DO'S AND DON'TS

DO'S

- Compliment English when it is spoken to you.
- Try to learn the language. The most modest efforts will endear you to the locals.
- Try to understand the standing of the persons you are dealing with and show respect at all times.
- Try to reciprocate when your Taiwanese friends take you out for a meal or a drink.
- Try to pay the bill on outings with your Taiwanese friends and if it has not been established who should pay.
- Give gifts when appropriate to cement ties.
- Negotiate on the price of 'big ticket' items like computers, home rental, and tailored clothes. The more expensive the item is, the tougher the negotiation.
- Exercise prudence in the conduct of your company business. If you are new to Taiwan and do not have language skills, much of the relevant information and cues crucial to decisions you make may be obscured.

DON'TS

- Correct your Taiwanese counterpart's English unless you have been asked to do so.
- Say you have no interest at all in learning Chinese.
- Believe the compliments people pay you for these are frequently exaggerated to give you face.
- Ignore the check and forget to thank your host.
- Assume that because your Taiwanese friends have refused your invitation to an event they do not want to go. Ask them again.
- Wrap gifts in white unless for a funeral, and avoid making presents of watches or clocks.
- Feel compelled to bargain at every transaction since not everybody is trying to rip you off.
- Buy from the first vendor you go to for expensive, non-negotiable items such as airline tickets.
- Delegate responsibility to employees before instilling your corporate culture and management practice.

GLOSSARY

People

Wo	I
Ni	You
Ta	Him/Her
Women	We/Us
Nimen	You
Tamen	They/Them
Xian sheng	Mr
Tai tai	Mrs
Xiao jie	Miss
Ren	Person
De	Possessive Particle

Courtesies

Qing	Please
Xie xie	Thank you
Dui bu qi	Excuse me
Ni hau ma?	How are you?
Qing wen?	May I ask?
Zao an	Good morning
Wan an	Good evening
Zai jian	Good bye

Basic Verbs

Qu	To go
Yao	To want
Lai	To come
Zou	To walk
Chi	To eat

Kan	To read/see
Zuo	To sit
Mai	To buy
Xie	To write
Shuo	To say
Ting	To hear
Xiang	To think
Kai	To open
Guan	To close
Ju	To live (in)
Shi	To be
Hui	To be able
Hao	To be good
Yong	To use
You	To have
Gao su	To tell
Zhi dao	To know
Ma?	Question
Le	Past tense
Bu/Mei	Verb negator

Directional

Dau	To/Towards
Xia	Down
Shang	Up
Li mian	Inside
Wai mian	Outside
Cong	From
Zai	At
Zhe ge	This
Nei ge	That
Zhe li	Here
Na li	There

Places

Ji chang	Airport
Da fan dian	Hotel
Xue xiao	School
Can ting	Restaurant
Yi yuan	Hospital
Jia	Home
Dian ying yuan/Xi yuan	Cinema
Ce suo	Toilet
Jiu ba	Bar
Ao zhou	Australia
Mei guo	America
Yin ni	Indonesia
Shou piao qu	Ticket window
Di xia tie/Jie yun	Subway/Underground
Ru kou/Chu kou	Entrance/Exit
Bai huo gong si	Department store
Jing cha ju	Police Station

Things

Qi che	Autommobile
Fei ji	Airplane
Ji cheng che	Taxi
Dian hua	Telephone
Dian shi	Television
Men	Door
Xing li xiang	Suitcase
Yi zi	Chair
Shu	Book
Yao shi	Key
Kuai zi	Chopsticks
Wan	Bowl

Bei zi	Glass
Ke kou ke le	Coca-cola
Pi jiu	Beer
zhuo zi	Table
Bai fan	Steamed rice
Shui	Water
Guo yu	Mandarin
Ying yu	English
Zhong guo fan	Chinese food
Xi can	Western food
Cai shi chang	Vegetable market

Numbers

Yi	One
Er	Two
San	Three
Si	Four
Wu	Five
Liu	Six
Chi	Seven
Ba	Eight
Jiu	Nine
Shi	Ten
Shi liu	Sixteen
Er shi	Twenty
Bai	Hundred
San bai	Three hundred
Qian	Thousand
Qi qian	Seven thousand
Qian	Money
Kuai qian	Dollar
Gui	Expensive
Pian yi	Cheap

Note the progression of Chinese numbers: hundred (*yi bai*), thousand (*yi chyan*), ten thousand (*yi wan*), ten ten thousands (*shr wan*), a hundred ten thousands (*bai wan*), one thousand ten thousands (*chyan wan*), one hundred million (*yi yi*). A car may be priced at NT$620,000 or *Syin Taibi lyou shr er wan* (62 ten thousands).

Question Words

Shen ma?	What?
Wei shen ma?	Why?
Zen ma?	How?
Shen ma shi hou?	When?
Duo Shao?	How much?
Na li?	Where?

Useful Words and Phrases

Wo shi meigwo ren/jianada ren/ouzhou ren.	I am American/Canadian/European.
Ni hui/bu hui jiang ying yu/ guo yu ma?	Do you/do you not speak English/Mandarin?
Qing jiang man yi dian.	Please speak slowly.
Qing dzai shuo yi bian.	Please repeat.
Wo yao: xia che zhao ling qian mai dan kan bing	I want to: get off the bus/train/car make change pay the bill see a doctor

RESOURCE GUIDE

EMERGENCY AND GENERAL NUMBERS

- **Fire and medical assistance,** tel: 119
- **Police,** tel: 110
  English-speaking police,
  - tel: (02) 2555-4275/2556-6007 (Head Office)
  - tel: (02) 2881-3853 (Tienmu)
  - tel: (02) 2511-1395 (Chung San)
- **English directory assistance,** tel: 106
- **Overseas operator,** tel: 100
- **Tourist information hotline,** tel: (02) 2717-3737
- **Government Information Office,** tel: (02) 2322-8888; website: http://www.gio.gov.tw.
- http://iff.npa.gob.gov.tw/fore-eng/en_index.htm
  An excellent site for general information for foreigners from the government.
- Visa extension and alien resident certificates, tel: (02) 2381-7494. The latest information from the government on visas is available in English at the following website: http://iff.npa.gob.gov.tw/fore-eng/en_index.htm
- **Visa renewals and resident visas,** tel: (02) 2343-2888
- **CLS International Airport Tourist Sevice Centre,** tel: (03) 383-4631
- **Motor Vehicle Department Information** is available in English at http://www.tcmvd.gov.tw/d2k/english_ drivingpermit. htm
- **Sungshan Domestic Airport Travel Information Service,** tel: (02) 349-1580
- **Kaohsiung International Airport Tourist Service Centre,** tel:(07) 805-7888
- **Alcoholics Anonymous,** tel:(02) 2836-6994
- **National Network of Foreign Spouses,** website: http:// www.tainan.com
- **YWCA,** tel: (02) 2331-3848

HOSPITALS
Hospitals in Taipei

- **Adventist Hospital**, 42 Pateh Road Sec 2
  Tel: (02) 2771-8151
- **Air Force General**, 131 Chienkang Road
  Tel: (02) 2764-2151
- **Cathay General**, 280 Sec 4 Jenai Road
  Tel: (02) 2708-2121
- **Central Clinic**, 77 Sec 4 Chunghsiao East Road
  Tel: (02) 2751-2121
- **Mackay Memorial Hospital**, 92 Jungshan North Road
  Tel: (02) 2543-3535
- **Chang Gung Memorial Hospital**, 199 Dunhua North Road
  Tel: (02) 2713-5211
- **Cheng Hsin Medical Centre**, 45 Chenghsin Street, Shi Pai
  Tel: (02) 2826-4400
- **Dr Kao's Family Practice Centre**, 11-9 Lane 69 Tienmou
  East Road
  Tel: (02) 2874-4545
- **Sun Yat Sen Hospital**, 125 Lihder Road, Pei Tou
  Tel: (02) 2897-0011
- **Yang-ming Hospital**, 105 Yusheng Street, Shih Lin
  Tel: (02) 2835-3456
- **National Taiwan University Hospital**, 1 Changteh Street
  Tel: (02) 2312-3456
- **Shin Kong Memorial**, 95 Wenchang Road, Shih Lin
  Tel: (02) 2833-2211

Hospitals in Taoyuan

- **Changkeng Hospital,** 5 Fushung Road, Kwei Shan
  Tel: (03) 328-1200
- **Ijien General Hospital,** 30 Lane 321 Yangshing North
  Road, Yangmei
  Tel: (03) 485-5566
- **Mingsheng General Hospital,** 106 Sec 3 Shengming 3 Road
  Tel: (03) 337-9340
- **Hsin Kuomin General Hospital,** 152 Fushing Road,
  Chungli City
  Tel: (03) 422-5180

- **Provincial Taoyuan Hospital,** 1492 Chungshan Road
  Tel: (03) 369-9721
- **Yangming General Hospital,** 56 Sec 2 Yuanping Road,
  Pingjenn City
  Tel: (03) 492-9929

Hospitals in Kaohsiung
- **Chung Ho Memorial,** 100 Shinchuan 1 Road
  Tel: (07) 3121101
- **Kaohsiung Veterans General Hospital,** 386 Tachung 1 Road
  Tel: (07) 342-2121
- **Municipal Min Sheng,** 134 Kaihsuan 2 Road
  Tel: (07) 751-1133
- **Navy General,** 553 Chunhsiao Road
  Tel: (07) 581-7121
- **Yuan's Memorial,** 162 Chengkang 1 Road
  Tel: (07) 335-1121
- **Kai-Suan Psychiatric,** 2 Fucheng Street
  Tel: (07) 751-3171
- **Kaohsiung Medical College Hospital,** 100 Shrchiuan 1 Road
  Tel: (07) 312-1101
- **Women and Children's General,** 976 Chenghua 1 Road
  Tel: (07) 312-2565

Hospitals in Taichung
- **Taichung Veterans General Hospital,** 160 Junggang
  Road Sec 3
  Tel: (04) 359-2525
- **China Medical College Hospital,** 95 Siueshr Road
  Tel: (04) 205-2121

Hospitals in Hsinchu
- **Hsin Chung Hsing Hospital,** 43 Hsingan Road
  Tel: (03) 521-3163
- **Hui Min Hospital,** 298 Sec 2 Chunghua Road
  Tel: (03) 525-3177
- **Hung En Hospital,** 147 Sec 2 Chinkuo Road
  Tel: (03) 533-5172

- **Hsinchu Hospital,** 25 Lane 442 Sec 1 Chinkuo Road
  Tel: (03) 532-6151
- **Nan Men Synthetic Hospital,** 20 Linsen Road
  Tel: (03) 526-1122

Hospitals in Hualien

- **Tzu-chi Buddhist General Hospital,** 707 Jungyang Road Sec 3
  Tel: (03) 856-1825

ACCOMMODATION
Hotels in Taipei

- **The Ambassador Hotel,** tel: (02) 2551-1111
- **Far Eastern Plaza Hotel,** tel: (02) 2378-8888
- **Fortuna Hotel,** tel: (02) 2563-1111
- **Grand Hotel,** tel: (02) 2886-8888
- **Grand Hyatt Taipei,** tel: (02) 2720-1234
- **Hilton Taipei,** tel: (02) 2311-5151
- **Lai Lai Sheraton Hotel,** tel: (02) 232-1551
- **Hotel Royal Taipei,** tel: (02) 2542-3266
- **Feeling Motel,** tel: (02) 2873-5511
- **Golden China,** tel: (02) 2521-5151
- **Brother Hotel,** tel: (02) 2712-3456
- **Grand Formosa Regent,** tel: (02) 2523-8000
- **Imperial Inter-Continental,** tel: (02) 2596-5111
- **Howard Plaza Hotel,** tel: (02) 2700-2323
- **Les Suites Taipei,** tel: (02) 8773-3799
- **Long Life,** tel: (02) 2396-9321
- **Rainbow,** tel: (02) 2311-9193
- **Regal,** tel: (02) 2713-8600
- **Riverview,** tel: (02)2311-3131
- **Rivera,** tel: (02) 2585-3258
- **Royal Best,** tel: (02) 2729-5533
- **Season's Garden,** tel: (02) 2378-5668
- **Sowa,** tel: (02) 2579-6162

Hotels in Taoyuan

- **Chuto Plaza,** tel: (03) 376-6177
- **Fortune Garden,** tel: (03) 346-5566
- **Hard Zura,** tel: (03) 355-8833

- **Majesty,** tel: (03) 336-6600
- **Monarch Plaza,** tel: (03) 316-9900
- **Taoyuan Holiday,** tel: (03) 325-4021

Service Apartments

- **Agora Garden,** 68 Sung Kao Road, tel (02) 8780-5168
- **ASE Suites,** 3 Fu Chun Street, Hsinchu, tel: (03) 529-6888
- **Season's Garden Executive Suites,** 10 Lane181 Sec 2 An Ho Road, tel: (02) 2378-5668
- **The Core,** Suite 6 11 floor 188 Nanking East Road Sec 5, tel: (02)2747-8800

MANAGING YOUR MONEY
Taxes

- **Taiwan tax administration regulations** and guidelines for foreigners in Taiwan, website: http://www.ntat.gov.tw.

Foreign Banks

- **ABN Amro Bank,** tel: (02) 2503-7888
- **American Express International Bank,** tel: (02) 2715-1581
- **Bangkok Bank,** tel: (02) 2506-2800
- **Banca Commerciale Italiana,** tel: (02) 2718-0750
- **Bank of America,** tel: (02) 2715-4111
- **Citibank,** tel: (02) 2715-5931
- **Deutsche Bank AG,** tel: (02) 3707-8338
- **Bank of Tokyo-Mitsubishi,** tel: (02) 2514-0598
- **Development Bank of Singapore,** tel: (02) 2713-7711
- **Overseas-Chinese Banking,** tel: (02) 2718-8819
- **Standard Bank of South Africa,** tel: (02) 2545-1060
- **Standard Chartered Bank,** tel: (02) 2716-6261
- **Union Bank of Switzerland,** tel: (02) 2718-6999

Securities Investment

- **Citicorp Securities,** 2F 55 Sec 4 Minsheng Road
  Tel: (02) 2545-3777
  Website: http://www.citibank.com.tw
- **Master Link,** 16F 171 Sunder Road
  Tel: (02) 2345-6188
  Website: http://www.mlsi.com.tw

- **National Investment,** 7F 6 Minchaun East Road
  Tel: (02) 2504-1000
  Website: http://www.nitc.com.tw
- **Taiwan International,** 32F 99 Sec 2 Tunhwa South Road
  Tel: (02) 2325-9000
  Website: http://www.tisc.com.tw
- **Standard Chartered,** 7F 168 Tunhwa Road
  Tel: (02) 2547-9873
  Website: http://www.standardchartered.com.tw
- **Aetna Securities,** 4F 210 Sec 1 Keelung Road
  Tel: (02) 8780-4980
  Website: http://www.asim.com.tw
- **Baring Service,** Room 8802 129 Sec 3 Minsheng East Road
  Tel: (02) 2717-6866
  Website: http://www.baring-asset.com

ENTERTAINMENT AND LEISURE
Cinemas

- http://www.taipeiforyou.com.
  Showtimes are available in the English China Post and Taiwan News. Adult tickets cost NT$ 250. A discount is available if you present a student I.D.
- **Capital,** 219 Ching An East Road
  Tel: (02) 2741-5991
- **Chung Hsiao,** 201 Chunghsiao East Road Sec 4
  Tel: (02) 2721-4555
- **Great Century,** 325 Roosevelt Road Sec 3
  Tel: (02) 2362-9629
- **Hoover,** 89 Wuchang Street Sec 2
  Tel: (02) 2331-5067
- **Kuang Hua,** 289 Chung Cheng Road
  Tel: (02) 2881-2446
- **Lux,** 83 Wuchang Street Sec 2
  Tel: (02) 2311-8628
- **Majestic,** 166 Hanchung Street
  Tel: (02) 2331-2770
- **New Oscar,** 115 Omei Street
  Tel: (02) 2361-1691

- **New World,** 116 Hanchung Street
  Tel: (02) 2331-2752
- **Oriental Pearl,** 14 Nanking West Road
  Tel: (02) 2511-2486
- **Oscar,** 251 Chang An East Road Sec 2
  Tel: (02) 2711-8298
- **President,** 59 Chung Hua Road
  Tel: (02) 23885576
- **Shin Shin,** 246 Linsen North Road
  Tel: (02) 2537-1889
- **Sun,** 87 Wuchang Street Sec 2
  Tel: (02) 2331-5256
- **Ting Hao,** 1 Lane 126 Fuhsing South Road
  Tel: (02) 2711-9305
- **Tung Kuang No,** 431 Linsen North Road
  Tel: (02) 2541-9300
- **Universal,** 200 Nanking East Road Sec 5
  Tel: (02) 2746-7201
- **Warner Village,** 18 Sung Shou Road
  Tel: (02) 878-5566

Libraries

These libraries may have some restrictions on usage.

- **American Resource Centre,** tel: (02) 2305-2382
- **Hsin Yi Foundation Preschool Education Resource Centre,** tel: (02) 2396-5303
- **Institute of Modern History Library Academia Sinica,** tel: (02) 2782-2916
- **Institute of Ethnology Library Academia Sinica,** tel: (02) 2652-3376
- **National Central Library,** tel: (02) 2311-0155
- **National Institute of Educational Resources and Research,** tel: (02) 2361-5021
- **Ricci Institute for Chinese Studies,** tel: (02) 2368-9968

Cultural Centres

- **American Cultural Centre,** 54 Nanhai Road, Taipei, tel: (02) 2322-7981

- **Chinese Cultural and Movie Centre,** 34 Chichan South Road, Sec 2, Taipei, tel: (02) 2322-9010
- **Institute of Cultural Affairs ,** 3F 12 Lane 5, Tien Mou West Road, tel: (02) 2871-3150; website: http://www.icaworld.org.

Associations and Clubs

- **American Club in China,** tel: (02) 2885-8260
- **Australian and New Zealand Social Group,** tel: (02) 2872-4664/ 2862-6051
- **British Social Club,** tel: (02) 2874-3512/9947
- **Canadian Society in Taiwan,** tel: (02) 2514-9477
- **Taipei City Club,** tel: (02) 2713-9955
- **Independents Abroad Taiwan,** tel: (02) 2833-8221
- **Taipei Christian Women's Club,** tel: (02) 2751-8755
- **Taipei International Women's Club,** tel: (02) 2788-7415
- **Taipei Youth Program Association,** tel: (02) 2873-1815
- **Adventure Kayak Club,** tel: (02) 2913-9752
- **Taipei Boat Club,** tel: (02) 2620-5159 (English)
- **Taipei Boat Club,** tel: (02) 2452-4200 (Chinese)

Museums

Opening hours are not consistent and you should call in advance. Also, many museums describe their pieces in Chinese.

- **Butterfly Museum,** 71 Sec 1 Chinan Road, tel: (02) 2321-8679
- **Chiang Kai-Shek Memorial Hall,** 21 Chungshan South Road, Taipei, tel: (02) 2343-1100
- **Grand Crystal Museum,** 16 Lane 515 Sec 4 Chungyang North Road, Peitou, tel: (02) 2895-8861
- **Kaohsiung Museum of History,** 272 Chungcheng 4 Road Yan-Cheng District, Kaohsiung, tel: (07) 531-2560
- **Land Reform Museum,** 10F 1 Tunhwa South Road Sec 1, Taipei, tel: (02) 2579-2458
- **National Palace Museum,** 221 Chinese Road Sec 2 Taipei, tel: (02) 2881-2021
- **Taipei Fine Arts Museum,** 181 Chungshan North Road Sec 3, Taipei, tel: (02) 2595-7656
- **Taiwan Folk Art Museum,** 32 Yuya Road, Peitou, tel: (02) 2891-2318

- **National Taiwan Art Education Centre,** 47 Nanhai Road, Taipei, tel: (02) 23110574
- **Postal Museum,** 45 Sec 2 Chungking South Road, tel: (02) 23945185
- **Taipei Children's Museum of Transportation,** 2 Tingchou Road Sec 3, Taipei, tel: (02) 23654248,

Art Galleries

- **Artasia Fine Asian Antiques and Art Consultancy,** 312 Tunhwa South Road Sec 1, Taipei, tel: (02) 2703-7562
- **Gallery Firenze,** 4F D Building 222 Chunghsiao East Road Sec 4, Taipei, tel: (02) 2781-8080
- **Photo Space,** 130 Tunhwa South Road Sec 1 Taipei, tel: (02) 2773-7434
- **Pogiart Mart,** 8F 222 Chunghsiao East Road Sec 4, Taipei, tel: (02) 2772-2535
- **Pottery Lovers,** 14/1 Chanchung Road, Taipei, tel: (02) 2563-3970
- **Lee Shih-Chiao Fine Arts Museum,** 3F A Building 218-7 Chunghsiao East Road Sec 4, Taipei, tel: (02) 2781-3979
- **Metaphysical Art Gallery,** 5F 218-2 Chung Hsiao East Road Sec 4, Taipei, tel: (02) 2751-9974

TRANSPORT AND COMMUNICATIONS

- **Tourism Bureau, Ministry of Transportation & Communications** Website: http://www.tbroc.gov.tw.
- **Taipei Tourism and Transportation Guide** Website: http://www.dot.taipei.gov.tw.
- **Taipei Rapid Transit Authority** Website: http://www.trtc.com.tw
- **Rent.A.Car,** Tel: (02) 2822-1000 [Taipei], (07) 802-0800 [Kaohsiung], (04) 425-7000 ([aichung]
- **VIP Car Rental Co.,** Tel: (02) 2713-1111
- **WHOSE Travel.com** is a Taichung based travel agent with an online, English language travel website. It can be used to book economy travel in the region. Website: http://www/whosetravel.com

CITY AND COUNTRY CODES

- **USA** (AT & T)   008-010-2880
- **Australia**   008-061-0061
- **Canada**   008-061-0061
- **Germany**   008-049-0049
- **Hong Kong**   008-085-2111
- **Italy**   008-039-0039
- **Japan** (KDD)   008-81-0051
- **Korea**   008-082-0082
- **Malaysia**   006-60-0060
- **Philippines**   008-63-0063
- **Singapore**   008-065-6565
- **United Kingdom**   008-044-0044

LANGUAGE TRAINING CENTRES

The language centres listed below are attached to universities. There are also many private schools offering tuition in Mandarin and Taiwanese to students.

- **Mandarin Learning Centre, Chinese Cultural University,** B1 231 Chien-kuo South Road Sec 2, Taipei
  Tel: (02) 22700-5858 ext 28/29
  Website: http://www.cec.pccu.edu.tw
- **Chinese Language Centre, Fengchia University,** 100 Wenhwa Rd Seatwen, Taichung
  Tel: (04) 252-2250, ext 2155/2156/2157
  Website: http://www.fcu.edu.tw
- **Language Centre, Fujen University**
  Tel: (02) 2903-1111 ext 2414
  Website: http://www.svdcc.fju.edu.tw
- **Chinese Language Centre, National Chengchi University**, 64 Sec 2 Chinan Road Wenshan, Taipei
  Tel: (02) 2938-7102
  Website: http://140.119.190.90.
- **Chinese Language Centre, College of Liberal Arts, National Cheng Kung University**
  Tel: (02) 2788-7415, ext 52040
  Website: http://www.ncku.edu.tw.
- **Chinese Language Education Centre, Providence University,** 200 Chung-Chi Road 433 Shalu, Taichung Hsien

Tel: (04) 632-8001 ext 2009
Website: http://www.pu.edu.tw.
- **Chinese Language Centre, Tunghai University,** Campus Box 862, Tunghai University, Taichung
Tel: (04) 359-0259

NEWSPAPERS
- **Taiwan Headlines**
Website: http://www.taiwanheadlines.gov.tw.
- **China Economic News Service**
Website: http://www.cens.com.
- **China Post** offers the online edition of one of Taiwan's English-language daily newspapers.
Website: http://chinapost.com.tw
- **Taipei Times** offers the online edition of another of Taiwan's dailies.
Website: http://www.taipeitimes.com

RELIGIOUS INSTITUTIONS
Christian Churches
- **AGAPE International Christian Assembly** (charismatic service), 6F 3 Bei Pin West Road, Taipei Railway Station East 2 Gate, tel: (02) 2598-1009
- **Calvary International Baptist Church,** 21 Sec 2 Yang De Da Dau, tel: (02) 2831-3458
- **Church of Christ,** 3F 257 Sec 3 Tingchow Road/63 Tienyu Street, Tien Mou, tel: (02) 2368-6314/2871-4742
- **Church of the Good Shepherd,** 509 Chungcheng Road, tel: (02) 2873-8104
- **City Revival Church,** B1 210 Sec 4 Chunghsiao East Road, tel: (02) 8773-6861
- **East Gate Presbyterian Church,** 76 Sec 2 Jenai Road, tel: (02) 2351-3589
- **Grace Baptist Church,** tel: (02) 2362-5321

Catholic Churches
- **Corpus Christi Catholic,** 2 Hwakang Road Yang Ming Shan, tel: (02) 2861-6185

- **Holy Family Catholic Church,** 50 Sec 2 Hsingcheng South Road, tel: (02) 2321-2444
- **Tien Mu Mother of God Catholic Church,** 171 Sec 7 Chungchan North Road, tel: (02) 2871-5168

Mosques and Synagogues

- **Taipei Grand Mosque,** 62 Sec 2 Hsinsheng South Road, tel: (02) 2392-7364
- **Taipei Jewish Services,** 41 Sec 2 Minchuan East Road/ 7 Jalane 343 Sec 2 Shihpai Road, tel: (02) 2597 1234/ (02) 2874-2763

Others

- **Christian Science Services,** 10 Lane 201, Sec 2 Chang An East Road, tel: (02) 2873-8151
- **Jesus Christ of Latter-Day Saints** (Mormon), 25 Lane Chunhwa Street 256 Aikuo East Road, tel: (02) 2321-1045 (Chinese)/ 2836-7517 (English)
- **Seventh-Day Adventists,** 424 Sec 2 Pateh Road, tel: (02) 2771-8151 ext 2959
- **Bahai Faith,** 3F 149-13 Sec 1 Hsingcheng South Road, tel: (02) 2707-0392/47
- **Bahai Centre,** 3F 43 Lane 160 Sec 1 Tunhwa South Road, tel: (02) 2781-8288

BUSINESS INFORMATION

- **Taipei International Business Centre,** 4F 25 Sec 1 Tunhwa Road
  Tel: (02) 2577-4352
- **Taiwan World Trade Centre,** 5 Hsinyi Road Sec 5, Taipei
  Tel: (02) 2725-1111
- **Anglo-Taiwan Trade Committee,** 9F 99 Jenai Road Sec 2, Taipei
  Tel: (02) 2322-4242
- **Australian Commerce and Industry Office,** Room 2605, 333 Keelung Road Sec 1, Taipei,
  Tel: (02) 2720-2833
- **Austrian Trade Delegation,** 205 Tunhwa North Road
  Tel: (02) 2715-5220

- **Belgian Trade Association,** Suite 901 World Wide House 131 Minslieng East Road Sec 3 Taipei
  Tel: (02) 2715-1215
- **Representative Office of British Columbia, Canada,** 7F 7G03 5 Sec 5 Hsinyi Road
  Tel (02) 2722-0805
- **Canadian Trade Office,** 9F 365 Fuhsing North Road, Taipei
  Tel: (02) 2713-7268
- **British Trade and Culture Office,** 9-10F 99 Sec 2 Jenai Road
  Tel: (02) 2322-4242
- **European Council of Commerce and Trade,** 9F 285 Sec 4 Chunghsiao East Road, Taipei
  Tel: (02) 2740-0236
- **Hong Kong Trade Development Council,** 10F 315 Sungchiang Road, Taipei
  Tel: (02) 2516-6085,
- **German Trade Office,** 9F 4 Minsheng East Road Sec 3, Taipei
  Tel: (02) 2363-5597
- **Malaysian Friendship and Trade Centre,** 8F 102 Tunhua North Road, Taipei
  Tel: (02)27132626,
- **Mexican Trade Services,** Room 2905 333 Sec 1 Keelung Road, Taipei
  Tel: (02) 2757-6526,
- **Moscow-Taipei Economic and Cultural Commission,** 10F 2 Sec 5 Hsinyi Road, Taipei
  Tel: (02) 2878-0311
- **Philippine Trade and Investment Office,** Room 7B 19 5 Sec 5 Hsinyi Road, Taipei
  Tel: (02) 2723-2527
- **Singapore Trade Office,** 9F 855 Jenai Road Sec 4, Taipei
  Tel: (02) 2722-1940
- **Thailand Trade and Economic Office,** 7F, 150 Fuhsing North Road
  Tel: (02) 2712-1882

GENERAL ONLINE RESOURCES
- http://www.englishintaiwan.com/index.htm
  Designed as a resource for foreigners teaching English in

Taiwan. It has many useful pages pertaining to banking, medical, driving, culture shock, getting a teaching job and entertainment

- http://202.39.225.132/jsp/eng/html/search/index.jsp
  Naruwan-Welcome to Taiwan is an excellent site that includes flight schedules, attractions, exhibition calendar, maps, travel tips, news and events, weather, practical living advice, shopping tips and many special interest links in English.

- http://www/hicatw.org.tw/members.htm
  This is a Hsinchu expatriate website with all you need to know about settling into this central Taiwan high-tech manufacturing centre including shops, schools, health, housing and restaurants.

- http://www.executiveplanet.com/business-etiquette/taiwan.html
  A business etiquette guide for visitors to Taiwan.

- http://www.yam.com/en/yam
  The English-language mirror site of Taiwan's most popular portal. Here you can find hundreds of links to various topics. Note that many of the links will be to Mandarin-only sites.

- http://tw.yahoo.com
  Yahoo acquired a popular local site in 2000, but the site is only in Chinese. However, you can enter Taiwan related search terms in English and come up with some useful matches. The site also operates a local online auction.

- http://www.gio.gov.tw
  The website of the Government Information Office has lots of useful information for tourists and visitors, and has mirror sites in several languages.

- http://www,forumosa.com
  It bills itself as a Taiwan-oriented member community. It has many discussion forums on various topics of interest to visitors and expats alike.

- http://www.tealit.com
  The name of the website, 'Teaching English and Living in Taiwan', sums it up.

- http://www.taiwanjoblink.com
  Job postings, information about visas, living in the country, accommodation.

FURTHER READING

GENERAL

Taipei Living. Taipei: The Community Services Centre, 2004.

- The first book you should buy about Taiwan, after this one! It delves very deeply into areas given more cursory treatment here, such as where to buy drapes or how to get your driver's licence. It deals only briefly in cultural preparation which is the main purpose of our work. Order it, preferably before you move.

Insight Guides: Taiwan. Daniel Reid. Hong Kong: APA Publications, 1989.

- An excellent guide book to the island's many nooks and crannies, with a good many cultural insights. Written by a fellow long-term Taiwan resident.

This Month in Taiwan.

- Not a book, but a magazine and free at that! This indispensable magazine can be picked up at any good hotel. It has useful addresses and phone numbers, basic maps, hotel and restaurant lists, advertisements for many services you might need, and the latest news about the doings in the expatriate community.

DOING BUSINESS

Doing Business in Taiwan

- You can now download global accounting firm Deloitte Touche Tomatsu's complete guide to conducting business in Taiwan. It is frequently updated.
  http://www.deloitte.com/dtt/article/0,1002,cid%253D57275,00.html

HISTORY

The Soong Dynasty. Sterling Seagraves. London: Sidgewick and Jackson, 1985.

- This author certainly took off the gloves when he wrote about the three Soong sisters, whose powerful family origins and highly political marriages partly shaped modern China. It also reveals a darker side to the history of the Kuomintang in Mainland China.

Formosa Betrayed. George Kerr. Boston: Houghton Mifflin, 1965.
- A detailed account of U.S. involvement in Taiwan after World War II, along with a frank description of the infamous Er Er Ba Massacre. This book is now available as a free download online at http://www.romanisation. com/books/formosabetrayed/.

TAOISM, BUDDHISM, & CONFUCIANISM
The Tao of Health, Sex, and Longevity: A Modern Practical Guide to the Ancient Way. Daniel Reid. Fireside, 1989.

Guarding the Three Treasures. Daniel Reid. New York: Simon & Schuster, 2001.
- Both these highly readable books deal with the practical application of Taoist medical theory in building your own longevity program.

Also look out for books by Thomas Cleary, a prolific and lucid translator who has focused on ancient masterpieces of Chinese and Japanese thought. R L Wing has also done some good practical translations of Taoist thought.

AN ALTERNATIVE VIEW
- MondoTaiwan website (http://www/angelfire.com/mt/ mondotaiwan/culture.html), has some humorous and accurate detail about some of the uglier sides to Taiwan culture, including betel nut babes and KTV.

The Ugly Chinaman and the Crisis of Chinese Culture. Bo Yang, Ed. J. Cohn and Jing Qing. St. Leonards, New South Wales: Allen and Unwin, 1992.

- A former political prisoner in Taiwan, Bo Yang minutcly details the negative sides of the Chinese persona.

Thick Face, Black Heart. Chin-Ning Chu. Warner Books, 1994.
- This book purports to teach Westerners how to adopt the dark secrets of success used by 'Asian Business Minds'.

Banzai You Bastards. Jack Edwards. Souvenir Press Ltd, 1991.
- A bitter account of the World War II Allied prisoners of war in Taiwan and their harsh treatment and forced labor in the mines of Jiufen written by a survivor of the ordeal. You can also read an online summary contained in a modern book, *Formosan Odyssey*, at http://www.romanization.com/books/formosan_odyssey/kinkaseki.html

If you cannot get these titles in your country, you can find most of them at **Caves Bookstore**, 103 Chungshan North Road, Sec. 2, Taipei, Taiwan. This shop has long been a first stop for people visiting Taiwan.

Eslite Bookstore has over 40 branches across Taiwan, including some 24-hour locations. It is Taiwan's equivalent of Border's bookstore—comfortable, well stocked, and with a coffee shop attached. Sadly, their website and online store are only available in Chinese as of the time of printing, but you can still check it out at http://www.eslite.com.

ABOUT THE AUTHORS

Wu Ling-li was born and bred in an old and traditional part of downtown Taipei. She grew up in an extended family of grandparents, parents, aunts and uncles, and then tested her way up the academic ladder to win herself a place at Providence College, where she studied Business Science.

Chris Bates was bounced around between Atlanta, Georgia and Fairfield, Connecticut for the first 17 years of his life, until he pursued a lifelong dream of training in Asian martial arts. He took a Bachelor of Arts degree in Chinese Studies and spent his senior year at Tunghai University in Taichung, Taiwan.

Through *yuan fen* (the principle that the fates of two people are inextricably entwined), Chris and Ling-li met whilst at college in Taichung in 1977. They were married a year later. Their life together has taken them on several tours of the United States (one year each), one tour of Taiwan (six years), and three tours of Singapore (15 years in total). They have worked for Western companies and have certainly endured their share of culture shock.

Much of their time has been spent at the interface of the expatriate and local communities. Ling-li has befriended many Westerners in her climb to a Masters ranking in American contract bridge, while Chris has befriended many

Chinese and Taiwanese, training in Burmese and Chinese martial arts under some of the finest masters alive.

Chris is presently an award winning executive recruiter sourcing talent for companies in Greater China and Ling-li presently manages her own business, providing market research and management consulting services to both Western and Asian companies. They also have three children.

Chris is the author of *The Wave Man*, a thriller set in Asia and acclaimed for its authenticity. The book is available online at http://www.koryubooks.com/store/wm.html. *CultureShock! Taiwan* is their first collaborative work.

Diana Bates grew up in Taiwan and Singapore and was exposed to both the local and expatriate communities. After taking her degree in Political Science at New York University, she spent several years in the Big Apple working as an editor and writer. She now resides in Taipei.

INDEX

Titles in the CultureShock! series:

Argentina
Australia
Austria
Bahrain
Beijing
Belgium
Bolivia
Borneo
Brazil
Britain
Bulgaria
Cambodia
Canada
Chicago
Chile
China
Costa Rica
Cuba
Czech Republic
Denmark
Ecuador
Egypt
Finland

France
Germany
Hawaii
Hong Kong
Hungary
India
Ireland
Italy
Jakarta
Japan
Korea
Laos
London
Malaysia
Mauritius
Morocco
Munich
Myanmar
Netherlands
New Zealand
Paris
Philippines
Portugal

Russia
San Francisco
Saudi Arabia
Scotland
Shanghai
Singapore
South Africa
Spain
Sri Lanka
Sweden
Switzerland
Syria
Taiwan
Thailand
Tokyo
Turkey
United Arab
   Emirates
USA
Vancouver
Venezuela

For more information about any of these titles, please contact any of our Marshall Cavendish offices around the world (listed on page ii) or visit our website at:

www.marshallcavendish.com/genref